Open The Books and See All The People

Published by Queens Borough Public Library

Illustrations on cover and in Chapter 3
by Sean Murtha.

Illustrations from Black Like Kyra, White Like Me
by Judith Vigna, c1992 by Judith Vigna. Reprinted
by permission of Albert Whitman & Company.

Illustrations from The Kids' Around the World Cookbook
by Deri Robins, c1994 by Deri Robins.
Reprinted by permission of Kingfisher Books.

This publication was made possible by a grant from the
Carnegie Corporation of New York. The statements made
and views expressed are solely the responsibility of the
Queens Borough Public Library.

ISBN 0-9645337-2-3

Printed in the United States of America

Table of Contents

Preface

The publication of *Open the Books and See All the People* is the direct result of Queens Borough Public Library's strategic planning process. One of the goals of that process is to the meet the needs of the two million people in Queens (NYC), among the most ethnically and culturally diverse counties in the U.S. We at Queens Library believe that children are indeed our future. Libraries have a significant role to play in their development and growth.

Its production provided an opportunity for a wide range of staff to contribute professionally to addressing an identified need, that of making library resources available to help children and their caregivers experience and appreciate the breadth of the human condition. I am proud to be able to share their work with the library and educational communities.

It is my hope that this will stimulate a dialogue among all of you, as it did among all of us, about what constitutes "human diversity." Your feedback will be most welcome. Our commitment was to do something in building our collections for youth, not just talk about diversity.

It is also my hope that our colleagues in the publishing industry will see this as a call to arms. We need high quality materials for a variety of age- and reading levels that address complex social issues. Go out on a limb – there truly is a market out here.

Many thanks to the many, many Queens Library staff members who contributed time, professional experience, spirited opinion and support. Many thanks, also, to the Carnegie Corporation of New York who made publication possible.

Gary E. Strong
Library Director, The Queens Borough Public Library
June, 2000

Foreword

Looking toward the 21st Century, the Queens Borough Public Library published it's Mission and Vision statements (see Appendix) as part of an on-going process of strategic planning to keep the Library a dynamic institution, serving the needs of our diverse and growing population.

As part of this process, Queens Library is concentrating its energies on four Strategic Directions:

- Customer Service
- State-of-the-Art Community Libraries
- Books and Reading
- Children and Teens

The main goal of the "Children and Teens" objective is that "Children and Teens in Queens access the educational and informational resources they need to be successful." Under that goal were a number of more specific topics that our strategic decision-making teams felt needed to be addressed to improve our services to young people.

In 1997, a five-person work team was selected to survey our Children's Collections in the Central Library and all 62 Branches to see how well they reflected the committee's charge that "Queens Borough Public Library has materials for children that reflect the full range of human diversity." For their first task, the work team defined diversity, a far more difficult job than it might at first have seemed.

The working definition was as follows:

1. Physical appearance and traits, e.g. height, weight, eyeglasses, hair, physical differences, left-handedness, etc.
2. Gender roles
3. Sexual orientation
4. Physical challenges
5. Mental challenges
6. Learning disabilities
7. Family structure, including extended families, birth order, stepfamilies, etc.
8. Family problems, including alcoholism, various forms of abuse, and others.
9. Chronic illness and death
10. Racial, cultural and ethnic diversity
11. Other languages
12. Religious diversity
13. Historical and geographic settings
14. City and urban life and relocation
15. Education
16. Socio-economic status.

The team realized that this would be a very big project, and decided to ask the Administration to expand their numbers to 16 people plus the facilitator. This allowed four teams to begin to assemble lists of books, web sites, videos, recordings and other materials that were available on the various topics. With input from the Coordinator and Assistant Coordinator of Children's Services, the team also realized they would have to consider this as a multi-year project. As they worked on the initial lists, they also decided that it was a large enough task to concentrate on the book collections alone.

Each year, the work teams tackled approximately one third of the topics. Each four-person work team was assigned one or more areas of the diversity list for researching available titles. These lists were then discussed with the larger team and vetted by the Coordinators. Checklists were prepared in the format QBPL uses for replacement orders and sent to each agency. Holdings were then checked and tabulated. A second copy of the list was then sent back to the agencies for ordering.

In the first cycle, Strategic Direction funds were set aside from the general budget to give each Children's Room money to use on the replacement project. In the second cycle, branches were expected to budget from their own funds (which were generous that year) to allow for the lists. And then the Coordinator of Children's Services was asked a fine new question, "If you could have [almost] unlimited money for the Children's Rooms, what would you do with it?" Feeling a bit like the Elephant's Child (who never knew quite what would set off a round of spanking) she said, "We need a comprehensive overhaul of our Math and Science collections, and we need money to finally finish off the Diversity Project." Feeling very warm and greatly astonished, she was told to make up a budget and submit it by the end of the week! A request for funding to publish this list was added as well. The whole request was then incorporated into a successful grant proposal to the Carnegie Corporation, and the result is now in your hands.

Esther Pollock, Regional Manager, was the original facilitator of this project. After her retirement, Caren Shilling took the helm as both facilitator of the teams and editor of this book. All of the Children's Librarians who have contributed to this document are listed in the Acknowledgements.

The bibliography may be completed, but the goal of providing "materials that reflect the full range of human diversity" continues. The Library's monthly juvenile order lists include a regular section of "Diversity Titles" so that our Children's Book Selection Committee can highlight new books for our agency selectors. Our Children's Librarians, both those who worked on the bibliographic project, and those who order regularly for collections, have increased their awareness of this type of material and the need for all collections to provide it to our customers. Web sites and multi-media have not been ignored, but because of their fluidity, are being addressed in pathfinders and order lists that reflect only current material. These lists are not included in this volume.

Queens' Librarians were using the order lists as a reference tool even before the annotations were added. We hope that other librarians will find this a useful reference guide to books that are widely available, and, at this printing still In-Print. Many wonderful titles that still live on library shelves were eliminated from the list because they are now out-of-stock or out-of-print.

Introduction

The topics covered in this bibliography may be found in the Foreword and again in the Table of Contents. Since titles may appear under more than one category, the full listing and annotation appears only in the first listing. The books are also indexed by title and author.

Entries include author, title, publisher and date of publication with a descriptive annotation. Prices are not included.

All of the books listed were in print as of April 2000. Titles available in both hard cover and paperback are so noted if they appeared under different publishers.

At the end of several sections, the editor has included listings of relevant series that address the subject. Individual titles within the series are not annotated. These series titles were not reviewed in detail, and individual titles may vary in literary quality, accuracy or timeliness.

This bibliography was not intended to be comprehensive, rather, it is a selective list of books considered by the staff of the Queens Borough Public Library to be worthy of inclusion in our collections which address the topics for children from pre-school to age 12.

Rosanne Cerny, Coordinator of Children's Services

Caren Shilling, Editor

Acknowledgements

The Queens Library would like to thank the Online Computer Library Center (OCLC) for allowing us to use some annotations taken from their WorldCat © database.

We would like to thank the Carnegie Corporation of New York for providing a grant to print this publication.

And finally, thanks to all of the following Queens Borough Public Library staff members who contributed to compiling, writing and designing "Open the Doors and See All the People" during the course of this project.

Elsa Bakke

Ju-Yi Chang

Rosanne Cerny

Barb Conkin

Carolyn Fain

Martha Flotten

LaDonna Frankenheim

Paula Goings

Carol Goldman

Lynn Gonen

Judy Gordon

Elizabeth Heino

Diane Jobsky

Mary Lee

Barbara Linehan

Monica Lohe

Lenore Mironchik

Anuradha Nath

Eva Patterson

Esther Pollock

Laura Reed

Mildred Rivera-Said

Susan Scatena

Leah Schanke

Caren Shilling

Mary Smith

Janis Swartz

Irene Symons

Nancy Titolo

Elizabeth Tumino

Sheri Walter

Ellen Zilka

The Public Relations Department

Technical Services Department

And for their leadership and continuing support for this project, Gary E. Strong, Director and Thomas Alford, Deputy Director for Customer Services.

Families

Family Problems • Family Structure

Families

Family Problems – Alcoholism – Picture Books

1. Daly, Niki. MY DAD. McElderry, 1995.
   A father's drinking causes pain and embarrassment to his family, until he begins to attend Alcoholics Anonymous meetings.

2. Tabor, Nancy. BOTTLES BREAK. Charlesbridge, 1999.
   A child describes how it feels when his mother drinks. Includes sources of help for children whose parents are alcoholics.

3. Vigna, Judith. I WISH DADDY DIDN'T DRINK SO MUCH. Whitman, 1988.
   After a disappointing Christmas, Lisa learns ways to deal with her father's alcoholism with the help of her mother and an older friend.

Family Problems – Alcoholism – Fiction

4. Brooks, Bruce. VANISHING. Laura Geringer, c1999.
   Eleven-year-old Alice is unwilling to return to live with her alcoholic mother and her stern stepfather, so she refuses to eat to the point of slowly starving herself, in order to remain in the hospital.

5. Hassler, Jon. JEMMY. Fawcett, 1989.
   Sixteen-year-old Jemmy struggles to fight her way out of poverty, and to discover her identity as an Indian, a woman, and an artist.

6. Hermes, Patricia. CHEAT THE MOON: A NOVEL. Little Brown, c1998.
   With her mother dead and her father an alcoholic who disappears for days at a time, Gabrielle must assume responsibility for her younger brother Will and herself, barely making ends meet and afraid to put her trust in anyone.

7. Ryan, Mary E. THE TROUBLE WITH PERFECT. Simon & Schuster, 1995.
   Thirteen-year-old Kyle, who is hopeless in math, is tempted to cheat on an exam to please his demanding, heavily drinking father.

8. Rylant, Cynthia. A BLUE-EYED DAISY. Simon & Schuster, 1985.
   Relates episodes in the life of eleven-year-old Ellie and her family, who live in a coal mining town in West Virginia.

Family Problems – Alcoholism – Non-Fiction

9. Hall, Lindsey. DEAR KIDS OF ALCOHOLICS. Gurze Bks, 1988.
   A young boy imparts facts about alcoholism by discussing his father's sensitivity to alcohol, his destructive behavior, and his recovery process.

Family Problems – Abuse – Picture Books

10. Paris, Susan. MOMMY AND DADDY ARE FIGHTING. Illus. by Gail Labinski. Seal Press, 1986.
    A young girl tries to come to terms with her parents' quarreling and fighting.

11. Powell, Sandy. DAISY. Illus. by Peter J. Thornton. Carolrhoda, 1991.
    A young girl deals with the emotional and physical problems of being a victim of child abuse.

12. Stanek, Muriel. DON'T HURT ME, MAMA. Illus. by Helen Coganberry. Whitman, 1983.
    A kind and sensitive school nurse sees that a young victim of child abuse and her abusing mother get help.

Family Problems – Abuse – Fiction

13. Coman, Carolyn. WHAT JAMIE SAW. Peter Smith, 1999.
    Having fled to a family friend's hillside trailer after his mother's boyfriend tried to throw his baby sister against a wall, nine-year-old Jamie finds himself living an existence full of uncertainty and fear.

14. Hunt, Irene. LOTTERY ROSE. Berkley Pub. Group, 1986.
    A young victim of child abuse gradually overcomes his fears and suspicions when placed in a home with other boys.

15. Roberts, Willo D. DON'T HURT LAURIE! Atheneum, 1988 (pap).
    Laurie, who is being physically abused by her mother, is afraid to escape and afraid no one will believe her story.

Family Problems – Abuse – Non-Fiction

16. Bernstein, Sharon Chesler. A FAMILY THAT FIGHTS. Whitman, 1991.
    Henry's parents fight often and his father sometimes hits his mother, causing Henry to feel frightened and ashamed.

17. Kehoe, Patricia. SOMETHING HAPPENED AND I'M SCARED TO TELL. Parenting Press, 1987.
    Discusses, in simple terms, sexual and physical abuse, explains why adults may become abusive, and encourages children to report such abuse to a trusted adult.

18. Terkel, Susan Neiburg. FEELING SAFE, FEELING STRONG. Lerner, 1984.
    Fictional vignettes depict acts of child sexual abuse, such as pornography, incest, rape, and obscene phone calls; and information on handling such situations is offered.

Family Problems – Hard Times – Picture Books

19. Ackerman, Karen. BY THE DAWN'S EARLY LIGHT. Illus. by Catherine Stock. Aladdin, 1994 (pap).
    A young girl and her brother stay with their grandmother while their mother works at night.

20. Adler, David A. THE BABE AND I. Harcourt Brace, c1999.
    While helping his family make ends meet during the Depression by selling newspapers, a boy meets Babe Ruth.

21. Bartone, Elisa. PEPPE THE LAMPLIGHTER. Illus. by Ted Lewin. Lothrop, 1993; Mulberry, 1997 (pap).
    Peppe's father is upset when he learns that Peppe has taken a job lighting the gas street lamps in his New York City neighborhood.

22. Cooper, Melrose. GETTIN THROUGH THURSDAY. Lee & Low, c1998.
Since money is tight on Thursdays, the day before his mother's payday, Andre is upset when he realizes that his report card and the promised celebration for making the honor roll will come on a Thursday.

23. DiSalvo-Ryan, Dyanne. UNCLE WILLIE AND THE SOUP KITCHEN. Mulberry, 1997.
A boy spends the day with Uncle Willie in the soup kitchen where he works, preparing and serving food for the hungry.

24. Estes, Kristyn Rehling. MANUELA'S GIFT. Chronicle, c1999.
Manuela wants a new dress for her birthday, but times are hard and she is disappointed when she receives a hand-me-down instead.

25. Mitchell, Margaree King. UNCLE JED'S BARBERSHOP. Illus. by James Ransome. Simon & Schuster, 1993; Aladdin, 1998.
Despite serious obstacles and setbacks, Sarah Jean's Uncle Jed, the only black barber in the county, pursues his dream of saving enough money to open his own barbershop.

26. Mora, Pat. TOMAS AND THE LIBRARY LADY. Knopf, c1997.
While helping his family in their work as migrant laborers far from their home, Tomas finds an entire world to explore in the books at the local public library.

27. Williams, Vera B. A CHAIR FOR MY MOTHER. Greenwillow, 1982.
A child, her waitress mother, and her grandmother, save dimes to buy a comfortable armchair after all of their furniture is lost in a fire.

Family Problems – Hard Times – Easy Reader

28. Turner, Ann Warren. DUST FOR DINNER. Illus. by Robert Barrett. Harper, 1995; Trophy, 1997 (pap).
Jake narrates the story of his family's life in the Oklahoma dust bowl, and the journey from their ravaged farm to California during the Great Depression.

Family Problems – Hard Times - Fiction

29. Hesse, Karen. JUST JUICE. Scholastic, 1998.
Realizing that her father's lack of work has endangered her family, nine-year-old Juice Faulstich decides that she must return to school and learn to read in order to help their chances of surviving and keeping their house.

30. Sonenklar, Carol. MY OWN WORST ENEMY. Holiday, c1999.
As she begins classes at a new middle school, Eve decides to try to fit in so that her father, who has just lost his job, will have less to worry about, but she finds that being true to herself is really the best thing to do.

Family Problems – Hard Times – Nonfiction

31. Hoyt-Goldsmith, Diane. MIGRANT WORKER. Holiday, 1996.
Describes the way of life of Mexican American families and their children, who work as migrant agricultural laborers in Texas.

Family Problems – Homelessness – Picture Books

32. Bunting, Eve. FLY AWAY HOME. Illus. by Ronald Himler. Clarion, 1991.
A homeless boy who lives in an airport with his father, moving from terminal to terminal and trying not to be noticed, is given hope when he sees a trapped bird find freedom.

Family Problems – Homelessness – Fiction

33. Ackerman, Karen. THE LEAVES IN OCTOBER. Yearling, 1993 (pap).
After her mother leaves them, nine-year-old Livvy struggles to understand and forgive as her father loses his job and takes her and her younger brother to live in a shelter for homeless people.

34. Carlson, Natalie Savage. THE FAMILY UNDER THE BRIDGE. Harper, 1958; Trophy, 1989 (pap).
Old Armand, a Parisian hobo, enjoyed his solitary, carefree life until he found three homeless children and their working mother had claimed his shelter under a bridge.

35. Doherty, Berlie. STREET CHILD. Orchard, 1994.
A novel based on the life of Jim Jarvis, a young orphan who escapes the workhouse in London in the 1860's and survives brutal treatment until he is taken in by Dr. Bernardo, founder of a school for the city's "ragged" children.

36. Douglas, Evans. SO WHAT DO YOU DO? Front Street, 1997.
Two sixth graders discover that their beloved third-grade teacher is living on the streets.

37. Fenner, Carol. THE KING OF DRAGONS. McElderry, c1998; Aladdin, 2000 (pap).
Ian and his Vietnam veteran father have been homeless for several years. When they move into the old and unused courthouse, Ian thinks they've found the perfect spot. Then Ian's father fails to come home and Ian must survive on his own.

38. Fox, Paula. MONKEY ISLAND. Orchard, 1991; Yearling, 1991 (pap).
Forced to live on the streets of New York after his mother disappears from their hotel room, eleven-year-old Clay is befriended by two men who help him survive.

39. George, Jean. MISSING 'GATOR OF GUMBO LIMBO. Harper, 1992; Trophy, 1993 (pap).
Sixth-grader Liza, one of five homeless people living in an unspoiled forest in southern Florida, searches for a missing alligator destined for official extermination.

40. Haugaard, Eric. LITTLE FISHES. Peter Smith, 1967.
A tale of the tragedy of war: A twelve-year-old orphaned beggar in occupied Italy searches daily for food and for meaning in the life he witnesses, and develops the compassion and understanding needed to help him survive.

41. Howe, James. DEW DROP DEAD. Atheneum, 1990; Aladdin, 1999 (pap).
While setting up a homeless shelter at the church, Sebastian and his friends solve the mystery of a dead man found in an abandoned inn.

42. Spinelli, Jerry. MANIAC MAGEE. Little Brown, 1990.
After his parents die, Jeffrey Lionel Magee's life becomes legendary, as he accomplishes athletic and other feats which awe his contemporaries.

Family Problems – Homelessness – Nonfiction

43. Chalofsky, Margie. CHANGING PLACES: A KID'S VIEW OF SHELTER LIVING. Gryphon, 1992.
    The voices of eight homeless children, ages six to thirteen, are captured here with stunning illustrations that give you a poignant look at shelter life.

44. HOME: A COLLABORATION OF THIRTY DISTINGUISHED AUTHORS AND ILLUSTRATORS OF CHILDREN'S BOOKS TO AID THE HOMELESS. Harper, 1992.
    Thirty of the world's best-loved children's book authors and illustrators have pooled their considerable talents to create a book filled with stories, poems, and pictures about what makes a house a home.

45. Hubbard, Jim. LIVES TURNED UPSIDE DOWN: HOMELESS CHILDREN. Simon & Schuster, 1996.
    Two girls and two boys, ages nine to twelve, talk about their own personal experiences with homelessness and life in shelters.

46. O'Connor, Karen. HOMELESS CHILDREN. Lucent, 1989.
    Discusses the causes and prevention of homelessness and what is being done to help solve this problem.

47. Wolf, Bernard. HOMELESS. Orchard, 1995.
    Text and photographs tell the story of a homeless family that has been referred to the Henry Street Settlement Urban Family Center on New York City's Lower East Side.

Family Problems – Moving – Picture Books

48. Asch, Frank. GOODBYE HOUSE. Prentice Hall, 1986.
    Just before leaving with his family for the move to their new home, Little Bear says good-bye to his favorite places in and around the old house.

49. Cadnum, Michael. THE LOST AND FOUND HOUSE. Viking, 1997.
    A young boy describes how he and his parents feel when they leave their old house and move to a new house in another town.

50. Carlson, Nancy L. LOUDMOUTH GEORGE AND THE NEW NEIGHBORS. Carolrhoda, 1983; Lerner, 1997 (pap).
    When a family of pigs moves in next door, George, a rabbit, wants nothing to do with them.

51. Golembe, Carla. ANNABELLE'S BIG MOVE. Houghton Mifflin, 1999.
    In two stories, a dog must adjust when her family moves to a new house and she makes new friends on a visit to the beach.

52. Greenfield, Eloise. GRANDMAMA'S JOY. Illus. by Carole Byard. Putnam, 1980; Penguin, 1999 (pap).
    A little girl tries to cheer up her despondent grandmother by reminding her of some very important things.

53. Johnson, Angela. THE LEAVING MORNING. Illus. by David Soman. Orchard, 1992.
    A young African American boy and his sister experience moving day, saying goodbye to shopkeepers, friends, and cousins, watching men load the truck, giving a last glance around their rooms, and driving off to their new home.

54. McGeorge, Constance W. BOOMER'S BIG DAY. Illus. by Mary Whyte. Chronicle, 1994.
Moving day proves confusing for Boomer, a golden retriever, until he at last explores his new home and finds his own favorite and familiar things.

55. Sharmat, Marjorie Weinman. GILA MONSTERS MEET YOU AT THE AIRPORT. Illus. by Byron Barton. Simon & Schuster, 1980; Aladdin, 1980 (pap).
A New York City boy's preconceived ideas of life in the West make him very apprehensive about the family's move there.

56. Viorst, Judith. ALEXANDER, WHO'S NOT (DO YOU HEAR ME? I MEAN IT!) GOING TO MOVE. Illus. by Rogin Price Glasser. Atheneum. 1995; Aladdin, 1998 (pap).
Angry Alexander refuses to move away if it means having to leave his favorite friends and special places.

57. Waber, Bernard. GINA. Houghton, 1995.
When Gina moves to a new apartment building, she discovers there are plenty of boys, but no girls her own age to play with.

Family Problems – Moving – Easy and Intermediate

58. Altman, Suzanne. MY TOP SECRET!! WORST DAYS DIARY: NAME MAUREEN ("MO"). Gareth Stevens, 1996; Bantam, 1995 (pap).
Mighty Mo reveals in her diary some of the most embarrassing moments during her first year at a new school.

59. Carbone, Elisa Lynn. STARTING SCHOOL WITH AN ENEMY. Knopf, c1998.
Worried about finding friends when she moves from Maine to Maryland, ten-year-old Sarah gets off to a bad start by making an enemy of a boy.

60. Johnson, Angela. MANIAC MONKEYS ON MAGNOLIA STREET. Illus. by John Ward. Knopf, 1999.
Ten-year-old Charlie adjusts to her move to a new neighborhood when she befriends Billy, with whom she hunts maniac monkeys, braves Mr. Pinkbelly's attack cat, and digs for fossils and treasure.

61. Ray, Karen. THE T. F. LETTERS. DK Pub., c1998.
Seven-year-old Alex starts to lose her baby teeth, begins a correspondence with the Tooth Fairy, and tries to accept the fact that her family is moving to a distant state.

62. Rylant, Cynthia. HENRY AND MUDGE AND ANNIE'S GOOD MOVE. Simon & Schuster, c1998; Aladdin, 2000 (pap).
Henry's cousin, Annie, is moving in right next door. Henry is happy but Annie is worried about leaving her old friends.

Family Problems – Moving – Fiction

63. Danziger, Paula. P.S. LONGER LETTER LATER. Scholastic, c1998.
Twelve-year-old best friends Elizabeth and Tara-Starr continue their friendship through letter-writing after Tara-Starr's family moves to another state.

64. Delton, Judy. KITTY FROM THE START. Houghton Mifflin, 1987.
Kitty moves to a new neighborhood and eventually makes a successful transition into her new third grade.

65. Freeman, Martha. THE YEAR MY PARENTS RUINED MY LIFE. Holiday, c1997; Bantam, c1997.
Twelve-year-old Kate has her entire world turned upside-down when she has to move from California to snowy Pennsylvania, where she tries to adjust to a new climate, a new school, and new friends.

66. Giff, Patricia R. MATTHEW JACKSON MEETS THE WALL. Dell, 1991 (pap).
Matthew's family move from New York to Ohio is difficult enough as they leave behind good friends, but the disappearance of their cat, and a neighbor boy so tough he's called the "Wall", add to Matthew's anxieties.

67. Hopper, Nancy J. CASSANDRA – LIVE AT CARNEGIE HALL! Dial, c1998.
Moving with her parents and younger sister from Connecticut to her father's studio in Carnegie Hall during World War II is difficult for thirteen-year-old Cassandra.

68. Koss, Amy Goldman. THE ASHWATER EXPERIMENT. Dial, c1999.
Twelve-year-old Hillary, who has traveled across the country all her life with her parents who sell crafts, finds herself facing a stay of nine whole months in Ashwater, California.

69. Lord, Bette Bao. IN THE YEAR OF THE BOAR AND JACKIE ROBINSON. Trophy, 1984 (pap).
In 1947, a Chinese child comes to Brooklyn where she becomes Americanized at school, in her apartment building, and by her love for baseball.

70. Lowry, Lois. ANASTASIA AGAIN. Houghton, 1981; Yearling, 1985 (pap).
Twelve-year-old Anastasia is horrified at her family's decision to move from their city apartment to a house in the suburbs.

71. Namioka, Lensey. YANG THE YOUNGEST AND HIS TERRIBLE EAR. Dell, 1994.
Recently arrived in Seattle from China, musically untalented Yingtao is faced with giving a violin performance to attract new students for his father.

72. Paton-Walsh, Jill. GAFFER SAMSON'S LUCK. Farrar Straus, 1984 (pap).
James' adjustment to a new school and life in the Fens is further complicated by the request of an elderly neighbor to find his lucky piece.

73. Sonenklar, Carol. MY OWN WORST ENEMY. *SEE 50.*

74. Spinelli, Eileen. LIZZIE LOGAN WEARS PURPLE SUNGLASSES. Simon & Schuster, 1995, Aladdin, 1998 (pap).
When her family moves to a new neighborhood, Heather meets ten-year-old Lizzie, whose brash and bossy ways make Heather wonder if they can ever be friends.

75. Wallace, Bill. ALOHA SUMMER. Holiday, c1997.
In 1925 fourteen-year-old John, an Oklahoma farm boy, has to accept many changes in his life when his father takes a job on a pineapple plantation in Hawaii and the family moves there.

Family Problems – Divorce – Picture Books

76. Girard, Linda W. AT DADDY'S ON SATURDAYS. Illus. by Judith Friedman. Whitman, 1987.
Although her parents' divorce causes her to feel anger, concern, and sadness, Katie discovers that she can keep a loving relationship with her father even though he lives apart from her.

77. Spelman, Cornelia. MAMA AND DADDY BEAR'S DIVORCE. Whitman, 1998.
The littlest bear in the family, Dinah is scared and sad when her parents get divorced and Daddy moves to another house, but over time she becomes used to the new arrangement, which still allows her to be with Daddy.

Family Problems – Divorce – Intermediate

78. Bunting, Eve. SOME FROG! Illus. by Scott Medlock. Harcourt Brace, c1998.
Billy is disappointed when his father doesn't show up to help him catch a frog for the frog-jumping competition at school, but the one he and his mother catch wins the championship and Billy begins to accept his father's absence.

Family Problems – Divorce – Fiction

79. Blume, Judy. IT'S NOT THE END OF THE WORLD. Simon & Schuster, 1982; Dell, 1986 (pap).
When her parents divorce, a sixth-grader struggles to understand the reasons why sometimes people are unable to live together.

80. Cleary, Beverly. DEAR MR. HENSHAW. Morrow, 1983.
In his letters to his favorite author, ten-year-old Leigh reveals his problems in coping with his parents' divorce, being the new boy in school, and generally finding his own place in the world.

81. Cleary, Beverly. STRIDER. Morrow, 1991; Avon, 1992 (pap).
In a series of diary entries, Leigh tells how he comes to terms with his parents' divorce, acquires joint custody of an abandoned dog, and joins the track team at school.

82. Cruise, Robin. THE TOP-SECRET JOURNAL OF FIONA CLAIRE JARDIN. Harcourt Brace, c1998.
At the suggestion of her therapist, ten-year-old Fiona begins to keep a journal in which she records her fears, feelings, and gradual adjustment in the year after her parents' divorce.

83. Giff, Patricia. RAT TEETH. Dell, 1985.
Fifth-grader Cliffie feels that nothing has been right in his life since his parents got their divorce and his front teeth began growing out over his lower lip.

84. Hurwitz, Johanna. DEDE TAKES CHARGE. Morrow, 1984.
A year after her father has left home for good, fifth-grader DeDe helps her mother cope with the realities of life after divorce.

85. Johnson, Angela. SONGS OF FAITH. Orchard, c1998; Knopf, 1999 (pap).
Living in a small town in Ohio in 1975 and desperately missing her divorced father, thirteen-year-old Doreen comes to terms with disturbing changes in her family life.

86. Kehret. Peg. SEARCHING FOR CANDLESTICK PARK. Dutton, c1997; Puffin, 1999 (pap).
Determined to find his father and relive their good times, twelve-year-old Spencer takes his cat, slips away from home in Seattle, and sets out for San Francisco's Candlestick Park.

87. Paulsen, Gary. HATCHET. Aladdin, 1996 (pap).
After a plane crash, thirteen-year-old Brian spends fifty-four days in the wilderness, learning to survive with only the aid of a hatchet, and learning also to survive his parents' divorce.

88. Siebold, Jan. ROPE BURN. Whitman, 1998.
While working on a writing assignment at his new school, Richard learns the meaning of various proverbs and how to express his feelings about his parents' divorce.

89. Voigt, Cynthia. A SOLITARY BLUE. Simon & Schuster, 1983.
Jeff's mother, who deserted the family years before, reenters his life and widens the gap between Jeff and his father, a gap that only truth, love, and friendship can heal.

Family Problems – Divorce – Nonfiction

90. Brown, Laurene Krasny. DINOSAURS DIVORCE. Atlantic Monthly Press, 1986; Joy Street Books, 1986 (pap).
Dinosaur characters introduce aspects of divorce such as its causes and effects, living with a single parent, spending time in two separate households, and adjusting to a stepparent.

91. Cole, Julia. MY PARENTS' DIVORCE. Copper Beech, 1998.
Discusses why divorce happens, how to cope with it, and how to deal with difficult feelings as well as friends whose parents are divorced.

92. Krementz, Jill. HOW IT FEELS WHEN PARENTS DIVORCE. Knopf, 1984.
Nineteen children from ages seven to seventeen, from diverse backgrounds, share their deepest feelings about divorce. By listening to them, all children of divorced parents can find valuable ways to help themselves through the grim times.

93. Prokop, Michael. DIVORCE HAPPENS TO THE NICEST PEOPLE: A SELF-HELP BOOK FOR KIDS (3-15) AND ADULTS. Allegra, 1996.
Discussion, questions and a brief story examine many of the common concerns and feelings that frequently accompany divorce.

94. Stern, Zoe. DIVORCE IS NOT THE END OF THE WORLD: ZOE AND EVAN'S COPING GUIDE FOR KIDS. Tricycle Press, c1997.
A teenage brother and sister whose parents are divorced discuss topics relating to this situation, respond to letters from other children, and offer tips based on their experience. Includes insights from their mother.

Family Problems – Family in Prison – Fiction

95. Calvert, Patricia. GLENNIS, BEFORE AND AFTER. Atheneum, 1996; Avon, 1999 (pap).
While her father serves his term in a detention center, twelve-year-old Glennis learns that not all prisons are made out of stone, and spiders aren't the only ones who can weave webs.

96. Hickman, Martha W. WHEN ANDY'S FATHER WENT TO PRISON. Illus. by Larry Raymond. Whitman, 1990.
When Andy's father is sent to prison for robbery and the family moves to be near him, Andy is afraid of what the kids at his new school will think.

97. Testa, Maria. NINE CANDLES. Illus. by Amanda Schaffer. Carolrhoda, 1996.
After visiting his mother in prison on his seventh birthday, Raymond wishes it were his ninth birthday, when mama has promised to be home with his dad and him.

Family Problems – Death – Picture Books

98. Clifton, Lucille. EVERETT ANDERSON'S GOODBYE. Illus. by Ann Grifalconi. Holt, 1983.
    Everett has a difficult time coming to terms with his grief after his father dies.

99. De Paola, Tomie. NANA UPSTAIRS AND NANA DOWNSTAIRS. Putnam, 1973; Puffin, 1973 (pap).
    A small boy enjoys his relationship with his grandmother and great-grandmother, but he learns to face their inevitable death.

100. Miles, Miska. ANNIE AND THE OLD ONE. Illus. by Peter Parnall. Little Brown, 1971.
    A Navajo girl unravels a day's weaving on a rug whose completion, she believes, will mean the death of her grandmother.

101. Old, Wendie. STACY HAD A LITTLE SISTER. Illus. by Judith Friedman. Whitman, 1995.
    Stacy has mixed feelings about her new sister Ashley, but when the baby dies of Sudden Infant Death Syndrome, Stacy is sad and misses her.

102. Vigna, Judith. SAYING GOODBYE TO DADDY. Whitman, 1991.
    Frightened, lonely and angry after the death of her father in a car accident, Clare is helped through the grieving process by her mother and grandfather.

103. Yolen, Jane. GRANDAD BILL'S SONG. Putnam, 1998 (pap).
    A boy asks others how they felt when his grandfather died, and then shares his own feelings.

Family Problems – Death – Fiction

104. Boyd, Candy D. CIRCLE OF GOLD. Scholastic, 1994 (pap).
    Fearing that her family is falling apart after the death of her father, Mattie vows to do whatever she can to renew her mother's spirit and hopes that the purchase of a beautiful, but expensive, gold pin will help.

105. Coerr, Eleanor. SADAKO AND THE THOUSAND PAPER CRANES. Putnam, 1977; Puffin, 1999 (pap).
    Hospitalized with the dreaded atom bomb disease, leukemia, a child in Hiroshima races against time to fold one thousand paper cranes, to verify the legend that by so doing a sick person will become healthy.

106. DeClements, Berthe. THE FOURTH GRADE WIZARDS. Puffin, 1990 (pap).
    After her mother dies, Marianne becomes a daydreamer and begins to fall behind in her schoolwork.

107. Dragonwagon, Crescent. WINTER HOLDING SPRING. Macmillan, 1990.
    In discussing her mother's death with her father, eleven-year-old Sarah comes to see that in endings there are new beginnings and in winter there is the promise of spring.

108. Greenfield, Eloise. SISTER. Harper, 1974.
    After her father dies, a young African American girl watches as her sister withdraws from her and their mother.

109. Lowry, Lois. AUTUMN STREET. Houghton Mifflin, 1980; Dell, 1982 (pap).
    When her father goes to fight in World War II, Elizabeth goes with her mother and sister to her grandfather's house, where she learns to face up to the always puzzling and often cruel realities of the adult world.

110. Lowry, Lois. A SUMMER TO DIE. Houghton Mifflin, 1977; Bantam, 1993 (pap).
Thirteen-year-old Meg envies her sister's beauty and popularity; her feelings don't make it any easier for her to cope with Molly's strange illness and eventual death.

111. Martin, Patricia. MEMORY JUG. Hyperion, 1998.
Since the death of her father in a fire, Mack believes that getting close to people will only lead to pain.

112. Paterson, Katherine. FLIP-FLOP GIRL. Dutton, 1994; Puffin, 1996 (pap).
Uprooted following the death of their father, nine-year old Vinnie and her five-year-old brother cope in different ways with the help of Lupe, the flip-flop girl.

113. Rylant, Cynthia. MISSING MAY. Orchard, 1992; Dell, 1992 (pap).
After the death of the beloved aunt who has raised her, twelve-year-old Summer and her uncle Ob leave their West Virginia trailer in search of the strength to go on living.

114. Wilson, Nancy Hope. FLAPJACK WALTZES. Farrar Straus, 1998.
Not only did Natalie lose her teenage brother, but in their grief her parents seem to have become emotionally removed from her.

Family Problems – Sibling Rivalry – Picture Books

115. Blume, Judy. THE PAIN AND THE GREAT ONE. Illus. by Irene Trivas. Bradbury, 1984; Dell 1984 (pap).
A six-year-old and his eight year-old sister see each other as troublemakers.

116. Bernstein, Margery. MY BROTHER, THE PEST. Millbrook, c1999.
A girl has a terrible time getting along with her little brother, who is a pest, but she comes to appreciate him when she needs a playmate to keep her company.

117. Carlson, Nancy L. HARRIET AND WALT. Carolrhoda, 1982.
Harriet decides that her little brother Walt isn't as big a pest as she once thought he was.

118. Havill, Juanita. JAMAICA TAG-ALONG. Illus. by Anne Sibley O'Brien. Houghton, 1989.
When her older brother refused to let her tag along with him, Jamaica goes off by herself and allows a younger child to play with her.

119. Hoban, Russell. A BABY SISTER FOR FRANCES. Illus. by Lillian Hoban. Harper, 1968.
Jealous of her sister's birthday, Frances becomes mean and selfish, until the birthday spirit moves her to reluctantly give a gift.

120. Keats, Ezra Jack. PETER'S CHAIR. Viking, 1998; Puffin, 1998 (pap).
When Peter discovers his blue furniture is being painted pink for a new baby sister, he rescues the last unpainted item and runs away.

121. Viorst, Judith. I'LL FIX ANTHONY. Illus. by Arnold Lobel. Harper, 1969; Aladdin, 1983 (pap).
A little brother thinks of the ways he will someday get revenge on his older brother.

122. Yorinks, Arthur. OH, BROTHER. Illus. by Richard Igielski. Farrar Straus & Giroux, 1989.
An offbeat story of twin boys who are separated from their parents in a shipwreck. They become skilled tailors in America, are knighted by the Queen of England, and are unexpectedly reunited with their parents.

Family Problems – Sibling Rivalry – Easy Readers

123. Bonsall, Crosby. THE DAY I HAD TO PLAY WITH MY SISTER. Harper, 1972.
A young boy finds trying to teach his little sister to play hide-and-seek very frustrating.

124. Minarik, Else Holmelund. NO FIGHTING, NO BITING! Illus. by Maurice Sendak. Harper, 1958.
Sometimes Rosa and Willy behave like the two little alligators in the stories cousin Joan tells them.

125. Van Leeuwen, Jane. AMANDA PIG AND HER BIG BROTHER OLIVER. Illus. by Ann Schweninger. Dial, 1982.
Five stories in the lives of Oliver and Amanda, about telling secrets, playing alone, and more.

Family Problems – Sibling Rivalry – Fiction

126. Blume, Judy. THE ONE IN THE MIDDLE IS THE GREEN KANGAROO. Illus. by Amy Aitken. Bradbury, 1981; Dell, 1991 (pap).
Lately second grader Freddy Dissel has that left-out kind of feeling, squeezed between an older brother and a younger sister. But now for the first time it's Freddie's turn to show everyone how special he is and, most of all, prove it to himself!

127. Blume, Judy. TALES OF A FOURTH GRADE NOTHING. Dutton, 1972; Dell, 1972 (pap).
Living with his little brother, Fudge, makes Peter Hatcher feel like a fourth grade nothing. Whether he's throwing a temper tantrum in a shoe store, smearing mashed potatoes on the walls at Hamburger Heaven, or scribbling all over Peter's homework, Fudge is never far from trouble.

128. Cleary, Beverly. BEEZUS AND RAMONA. Morrow, 1955; Avon, 1990 (pap).
Beezus' biggest problem is her four-year-old sister Ramona. Even though Beezus knows sisters are supposed to love each other, with a sister like Ramona it seems impossible.

129. Hurwitz, Johanna. ELISA IN THE MIDDLE. Morrow, 1995; Puffin, 1998 (pap).
Five-year-old Elisa has an older brother and a new baby brother, but her grandmother says the middle is the best, just like the filling in a sandwich.

130. Paterson, Katherine. JACOB HAVE I LOVED. Harper, 1990.
Feeling deprived all her life of schooling, friends, mother and even her name by her twin sister, Louise finally begins to find her identity.

131. Sachs, Marilyn. THIRTEEN GOING ON SEVEN. Dutton, 1993.
When her twin sister begins to assert her individuality and her grandmother suddenly dies, thirteen-year-old Dezzey finds some comfort in her relationship with her grandfather and a new friend.

132. Steig, William. THE TOY BROTHER. Harper, 1996.
An apprentice alchemist finds that his despised kid brother is the only one who can help him after he concocts a potion that transforms him into the size of a peanut, in a story about sibling rivalry set in medieval times.

Family Problems – Sibling Rivalry – Nonfiction

133. Landau, Elaine. SIBLING RIVALRY: BROTHERS AND SISTERS AT ODDS. Millbrook, 1994.
    Explores sibling rivalry through interviews and firsthand accounts, examining its causes, manifestations, and cures.

Family Structure - General – Picture Books

134. Cooper, M. I GOT A FAMILY. Illus. by Gail Gottlieb. Holt, 1993.
    In rhyming verses, a young girl describes how the members of her family make her feel loved.

Family Structure – General – Fiction

135. Kroll, Virginia. BEGINNINGS: HOW FAMILIES CAME TO BE. Illus. by Stacey Schuett. Whitman, 1994.
    Parents and children discuss how their families came to be, covering birth families, adoptive families, two parent-families, and single-parent families.

136. Skutch, Robert. WHO'S IN A FAMILY? Illus. by Laura Nienhaus. Tricycle Press, 1995.
    This equal opportunity, open-minded picture book has no preconceptions about what makes a family a family. There's even equal time given to some of children's favorite animal families.

137. Tax, Meredith. FAMILIES. Feminist Press, 1996 (pap).
    Six-year-old Angie tells everything she knows about many different kinds of families.

Family Structure – General – Nonfiction

138. Clay, Rebecca . TIES THAT BIND: FAMILY AND COMMUNITY. Blackbirch Press, 1996.
    Describes the various functions performed by the family throughout the world, regardless of the differences in how families are formed. Profiles family types in the Americas, Africa, Europe, the Middle East, Asia, Australia and the South Pacific.

139. Fletcher, Ralph J. RELATIVELY SPEAKING: POEMS ABOUT FAMILY. Orchard, c1999.
    A collection of poems that describe the experiences and relationships in a close-knit family.

140. Jenness, Aylette. FAMILIES: A CELEBRATION OF DIVERSITY, COMMITMENT AND LOVE. Houghton, 1990 (pap).
    Photographs and text depict the lives of 17 families from around the country, some with step-relationships, divorce, gay parents, foster siblings, and other diverse components.

141. Leedy, Loreen. WHO'S WHO IN MY FAMILY. Holiday, 1995.
    Young readers will learn about family trees and genealogy in a brightly illustrated look at students who share their ancestry with one another and learn how every family is special in its own way.

Family Structure – Single Parent – Picture Books

142. Bartone, Elise. PEPPE THE LAMPLIGHTER. *SEE 21.*

143. Binch, Caroline. SINCE DAD LEFT. Millbrook, 1998.
Sid must learn to deal with his parents' separation and the lifestyle his father has chosen.

144. Bunting, Eve. FLY AWAY HOME. *SEE 32.*

145. Simon, Norma. I WISH I HAD MY FATHER. Illus. by Arieh Zeldich. Whitman, 1983.
A Father's Day is tough for a boy whose father left him years ago and never communicates with him.

146. Stanek, Muriel. ALL ALONE AFTER SCHOOL. Illus. by Ruth Rosner. Whitman, 1985.
When his mother must take a job and can't afford a babysitter, a young boy gradually develops confidence about staying home alone after school.

147. Stanek, Muriel. I SPEAK ENGLISH FOR MY MOM. Illus. by Judith Friedman. Whitman, 1989.
Lupe, a young Mexican American, must translate for her mother who speaks only Spanish, until Mrs. Gomez decides to learn English in order to get a better job.

Family Structure – Single Parent – Easy Reader

148. Brenner, Barbara. WAGON WHEELS. Illus. by Don Bolognese. Harper, 1984; Trophy, 1993 (pap).
Shortly after the Civil War, a black family travels to Kansas to take advantage of the free land offered through the Homestead Act.

Family Structure – Single Parent - Fiction

149. Delton, Judy. ANGEL'S MOTHER'S BOYFRIEND. Houghton, 1987.
Ten-year-old Angel finds plenty to worry about when she learns that her mother's new boyfriend is a clown.

150. MacLachlan, Patricia. SARAH, PLAIN AND TALL. Harper, 1985; Trophy, 1987 (pap).
When their father invites a mail-order bride to come live with them in their prairie home, Caleb and Anna are captivated by their new mother and hope she will stay.

151. Mead, Alice. SOLDIER MOM. Viking, 1997.
Eleven-year-old Jasmyn gets a different perspective on life when her mother is sent to Saudi Arabia at the beginning of the Persian Gulf War, leaving her and her baby half brother behind in Maine in the care of her mother's boyfriend.

152. Paterson, Katherine. PARK'S QUEST. Puffin, 1989 (pap).
Eleven-year-old Park makes some startling discoveries when he travels to his grandfather's farm in Virginia to learn about his father, who died in the Vietnam War.

Family Structure – Single Parent – Non-Fiction

153. Lindsay, Jeanne W. DO I HAVE A DADDY? Illus. by Cheryl Boeller. Morning Glory Press, 1991.
A single mother explains to her son that his daddy left soon after he was born.

Family Structure – Nuclear Family – Picture Books

154. Bunting, Eve. DAY BEFORE CHRISTMAS. Illus. by Beth Peck. Clarion, 1992.
Four years after the death of her mother, seven-year-old Allie goes with her grandfather to a performance of "the Nutcracker," and hears about the special day he had with her mother when he took her to her first "Nutcracker."

155. Cannon, Annie. THE BAT IN THE BOOT. Orchard, 1996.
A family finds a baby bat in their mud-room and takes care of him until his mother comes back for him.

156. Carlstrom, Nancy White. BETTER NOT GET WET, JESSE BEAR. Illus. by Bruce Degen. Simon & Schuster, 1988; Aladdin, 1997 (pap).
Jesse Bear is admonished not to get wet under a variety of tantalizing circumstances, until finally he receives permission to get wet in his own wading pool.

157. Cooney, Barbara. HATTIE AND THE WILD WAVES. Viking, 1990.
A young girl from Brooklyn enjoys her summer at the beach where she can paint and listen to the wild waves.

158. Hoban, Russell. BEDTIME FOR FRANCES. Illus. by Garth Williams. Harper, 1960; Trophy, 1996 (pap).
Frances has trouble going to sleep because of frightening sounds and objects that may be out to get her.

159. Hutchins, Pat. IT'S *MY* BIRTHDAY. Greenwillow, c1999.
Billy is reluctant to share his birthday presents with the other little monsters, but then something happens to make him change his mind.

160. Lawson, Robert. THEY WERE STRONG AND GOOD. Viking, 1940.
Relates the story of the author's grandparents and parents, who, although they were not famous, are notable for having helped build the United States with many other everyday people.

161. Sharmat, Mitchell. GREGORY, THE TERRIBLE EATER. Illus. by Jose Aruego and Ariane Dewey. Four Winds, 1980; Scholastic, 1980 (pap).
A very picky eater, Gregory the goat refuses to eat the usual goat diet staples of shoes and tin cans in favor of fruits, vegetables, eggs, and orange juice.

162. Zolotow, Charlotte. WILLIAM'S DOLL. Illus. by William Pene DuBois. Harper, 1972; Trophy 1972 (pap).
William's grandmother is the only member of the family who understands why he wants a doll as well as a basketball and an electric train.

Family Structure – Nuclear Family - Fiction

163. Hill, Elizabeth S. EVAN'S CORNER. Puffin, 1993 (pap).
Needing a place to call his own, Evan is thrilled when his mother points out that their crowded apartment has eight corners, one for each family member.

164. Namioka, Lensey. YANG THE THIRD AND HER IMPOSSIBLE FAMILY. Little, 1995; Yearling, 1996 (pap).
Third daughter Mary Yang makes an unexpected new friend while trying to hide a kitten from her family.

165. Petersen, P.J. SOME DAYS, OTHER DAYS. Atheneum, 1994.
Jimmy is reluctant to get out of bed, because some days at home and at school are good days, but some are bad days.

Family Structure – Nuclear Family – Nonfiction

166. Hoberman, Mary A. FATHERS, MOTHERS, SISTERS, BROTHERS; A COLLECTION OF FAMILY POEMS. Illus. by Marilyn Hafner. Puffin, 1993 (pap).
Humorous poems celebrate every kind of family member, including aunts and uncles, step-brothers and sisters, cousins, and even cats!

167. Stein, Sara Bonnett. THAT NEW BABY; AN OPEN FAMILY BOOK FOR PARENTS AND CHILDREN TOGETHER. Illus. by Dick Frank. Walker, 1984.
Helps prepare children for the experience of having a new baby in the family and suggests ways parents can facilitate the adjustment.

Family Structure – Extended Family – Picture Books

168. Buckley, Helen E. GRANDFATHER AND I. Illus. by Jan Ormerod. Lothrop, 1994.
A child considers how Grandfather is the perfect person to spend time with, because he is never in a hurry.

169. Buckley, Helen E. GRANDMOTHER AND I. Illus. by Paul Galdone. Lothrop, 1994.
A child considers how Grandmother's lap is just right for those times when lightning is coming in the window, or the cat is missing.

170. Flournoy, Valerie. THE PATCHWORK QUILT. Illus. by Jerry Pinkney. Dial, 1985.
Using scraps cut from the family's old clothing, Tanya helps her grandmother and mother make a beautiful quilt that tells the story of her family's life.

171. Sisulu, Elinor. THE DAY GOGO WENT TO VOTE: SOUTH AFRICA APRIL 1994. Little, 1996 (pap).
Thembi and her beloved great-grandmother, who has not left the house for many years, go together to vote on the momentous day when black South Africans are allowed to vote for the first time.

172. Torres, Leyla. LILIANA'S GRANDMOTHERS. Farrar Straus & Giroux, 1998.
One of Liliana's grandmothers lives in New England and the other in tropical Colombia. Liliana loves to visit them both and do different things with them: quilting and crossword puzzles with Mima, gardening and dancing with Mama Gabina.

Family Structure – Extended Family - Fiction

173. Matthews, Mary. MAGID FASTS FOR RAMADAN. Illus. by E. B. Lewis. Clarion, 1996.
Magid, an eight-year-old Muslim boy in Cairo, is determined to celebrate Ramadan by fasting, despite the opposition of family members who feel he is not yet old enough.

174. Newman, Leslie. REMEMBER THAT. Clarion, 1996.
Though Grandmother is aging, she still has important lessons to teach about life as she asks her granddaughter to "remember that".

175. Taylor, Mildred. ROLL OF THUNDER, HEAR MY CRY. Dial, 1976; Puffin, 1997 (pap).
A Black family, living in the South during the 1930's, is faced with prejudice and discrimination, which is not understood by the children.

Family Structure – Adoption – Picture Books

176. Caines, Jeannette. ABBY. Illus. by Steven Kellogg. HarperCollins, 1973; Trophy, 1973 (pap).
Abby is an adopted child loved by her parents and her older brother, Kevin.

177. Curtis, Jamie Lee. TELL ME AGAIN ABOUT THE NIGHT I WAS BORN. Illus. by Laura Cornell. Harper, 1996.
A young girl asks her parents to tell her again the cherished family story of her birth and adoption.

178. Girard, Linda. ADOPTION IS FOR ALWAYS. Illus. by Judith Friedman. Whitman, 1986.
Celia's mother, father, and teacher help her to understand that she will always belong to her adoptive parents.

179. Girard, Linda. WE ADOPTED YOU, BENJAMIN KOO. Illus. by Linda Shute. Whitman, 1989.
Nine-year-old Benjamin Koo, adopted from Korea as an infant, describes what it's like to grow up adopted from another country.

180. Koehler, Phoebe. THE DAY WE MET YOU. Bradbury, 1990; Aladdin, 1997 (pap).
Mom and Dad recount the exciting day when they adopted their baby.

181. Pellegrini, Nina. FAMILIES ARE DIFFERENT. Illus. by Nina Pellegrini. Holiday, 1991.
An adopted Korean girl discovers that her classmates have different types of families.

Family Structure – Adoption – Fiction

182. London, Jonathan. A KOALA FOR KATIE. Illus. by Cynthia Jaber. Whitman, 1993.
On a trip to the zoo, Katie gets a special present that helps her realize how much her adoptive parents love her.

183. Mora, Pat. PABLO'S TREE. Illus. by Cecily Lang. Simon & Schuster, 1994.
Each year on his birthday, a young Mexican American boy looks forward to seeing how his grandfather has decorated the tree he planted on the day the boy was adopted.

184. Myers, Walter Dean. ME, MOP AND THE MOONDANCE KID. Dell, 1991 (pap).
Although adoption has taken them out of the New Jersey institution where they grew up, eleven-year-old T.J. and his younger brother Moondance remain involved with their friend Mop's relentless attempts to become adopted herself.

Family Structure – Adoption – Nonfiction

185. McCutcheon, John. HAPPY ADOPTION DAY! Little Brown, 1996.
Parents celebrate the day on which they adopted their child and continue to reassure the new addition to their family that she is wanted, loved, and very special

186. Rogers, Fred. LET'S TALK ABOUT IT: ADOPTION. Paper Star, 1998 (pap).
Discusses what it means to be part of a family and examines some feelings that adopted children may have.

187. Rosenberg, Maxine. BEING ADOPTED. Lothrop, 1984.
Several young children recount their experiences as adopted members of their families.

188. Stein, Sara Bonnett. THE ADOPTED ONE: AN OPEN FAMILY BOOK FOR PARENTS AND CHILDREN TOGETHER. Walker, 1979.

Includes dual text, one for the adult reader, one for the child, explaining some of the conflicting feelings of an adopted child.

Family Structure – Foster Children – Fiction

189. Brown, Susan M. YOU'RE DEAD, DAVID BORELLI. Atheneum, 1995.

After his mother dies and his father disappears with company funds, David moves from wealth and comfort to a foster home, an inner-city school, an environment of bullies and uncaring teachers, and new opportunities.

190. Byars, Betsy. THE PINBALLS. Harper, 1977.

Three lonely foster children learn to care about themselves and each other.

191. Hermes, Patricia. HEADS, I WIN. Pocket, 1989 (pap).

Bailey runs for class president, hoping that popularity will secure her place in her current foster home.

192. Hughes, Dean. TEAM PICTURE. Atheneum, 1996.

Trying to hold onto the newfound stability of his life in a foster home, thirteen-year-old David worries about the growing moodiness of his guardian Paul.

193. Kidd, Diana. ONION TEARS. Orchard, 1991.

A little Vietnamese girl tries to come to terms with her grief over the loss of her family and adjust to her new life with the Australian family with whom she now lives.

194. L'Engle, Madeleine. MEET THE AUSTINS. Farrar, 1997; Dell, 1981 (pap).

The life of the Austin family is changed by the arrival of self-centered young Meggy Hamilton, orphaned by the sudden death of her pilot father.

195. MacLachlan, Patricia. BABY. Delacorte, 1993; Bantam, 1993 (pap).

Taking care of a baby left with them at the end of the tourist season helps a family come to terms with the death of their own infant son.

196. Paterson, Katherine. THE GREAT GILLY HOPKINS. Crowell, 1978.

An eleven-year-old foster child tries to cope with her longings and fears as she schemes against everyone who tries to be friendly.

197. Sebestyen, Ouida. OUT OF NOWHERE. Orchard, 1994.

When he no longer fits into his vagabond mother's life, thirteen-year-old Harley adopts an abandoned dog and falls in with an outspoken old woman, a junk collector, and an energetic and loving teenage girl.

198. Stevenson, Laura C. HAPPILY AFTER ALL. Houghton Mifflin, 1990.

When her father dies, ten-year-old Rebecca is sent to live with the mother she's been brought up to believe had abandoned her, and through her relationship with a troubled foster child begins to accept her mother.

199. Thesman, Jean. WHEN THE ROAD ENDS. Houghton Mifflin, 1992.

Sent to spend the summer in the country, three foster children and an older woman recovering from a serious accident are abandoned by their caretaker and must try to survive on their own.

Family Structure – Orphans – Picture Books

200. Bunting, Eve. TRAIN TO SOMEWHERE. Illus. by Ronald Himler. Clarion, 1996.
   In the late 1800's, Marianne travels westward on the Orphan Train in hopes of being placed with a caring family.

201. Stanley, Diane. SAVING SWEETNESS. Illus. by G. Brian Karas. Putnam, 1996.
   The sheriff of a dusty Western town rescues Sweetness, an unusually resourceful orphan, from nasty old Mrs. Sump and her terrible orphanage.

Family Structure – Orphans – Fiction

202. Buchanan, Jane. GRATEFULLY YOURS. Farrar Straus & Giroux, 1997; Puffin, 1999 (pap).
   In 1923, nine-year-old Hattie rides the Orphan Train from New York to Nebraska where she must adjust to a strange new life with a farmer and his wife, who is despondent over the loss of her own two children.

203. Burnett, Frances Hodgson. THE SECRET GARDEN. Grosset, 1996.
   Ten-year-old Mary comes to live in a lonely house on the Yorkshire moors and discovers an invalid cousin and the mysteries of a locked garden.

204. Dexter, Catherine. SAFE RETURN. Candlewick Press, 1996.
   In the early nineteenth century, a Swedish orphan worries that she will again lose someone she loves when her aunt sails to Stockholm during the stormiest season.

205. Nixon, Joan Lowery. AGGIE'S HOME. Delacorte, c1998; Yearling, 2000 (pap).
   A clumsy and unattractive twelve-year-old, Aggie is sure no one will want to adopt her when she rides the orphan train out west, but when she meets the eccentric Bradon family she begins to have some hope.

206. Nixon, Joan Lowery. WILL'S CHOICE. Delcorte, 1998; Dell, c1998 (pap).
   Sent away on an orphan train by his self-centered father Jessie, Will keeps hoping Jessie will claim him, even though the people he lives with care for him far more.

207. Wallace, Barbara Brooks. SPARROWS IN THE SCULLERY. Atheneum, c1997; Aladdin, 1999 (pap).
   Despite horrible conditions at the boys' home where kidnappers left him, eleven-year-old Colley, an orphan, finds a reason and a way to live.

Family Structure – Orphans – Nonfiction

208. Warren, Andrea. ORPHAN TRAIN RIDER. Houghton Mifflin, 1996.
   Discusses the placement of over 200,000 orphans or abandoned children in homes throughout the Midwest from 1854 to 1929 by recounting the story of one boy and his brothers.

Family Structure – Living in Home of Grandparent and Other Relatives – Picture Books

209. Cowley, Joy. GRACIAS, THE THANKSGIVING TURKEY. Illus. by Joe Cepeda. Scholastic, 1996.
   Trouble ensues when Papa gets Miguel a turkey to fatten up for Thanksgiving and Miguel develops an attachment to it.

210. Greenfield, Eloise. GRANDMAMA'S JOY. *SEE 52.*

211. Hickman, Martha. ROBERT LIVES WITH HIS GRANDPARENTS. Illus. by Tim Hinton. Whitman, 1995.
Robert is embarrassed to admit to his classmates that he has lived with his grandparents ever since his parents' divorce.

212. Steptoe, John. STEVIE. Trophy, 1969 (pap).
Robert wishes Stevie, a house guest, would go away, but when he does Robert realizes how much fun they had together.

Family Structure – Living in Home of Grandparent and Other Relatives – Fiction

213. Gardiner, John. STONE FOX. Harper, 1980; Trophy 1996 (pap).
Little Willie hopes to pay the back taxes on his grandfather's farm with the purse from a dog-sled race he enters.

214. Hahn, Mary Downing. AS EVER, GORDY. Clarion, c1998; Camelot, 2000 (pap).
When he and his younger sister move in with their older brother after their grandmother dies, thirteen-year-old Gordy finds himself caught between the boy he was when he lived with his abusive father and the boy his grandmother was helping him become.

215. Hahn, Mary. DAPHNE'S BOOK. Houghton, 1983.
As author Jessica and artist Daphne collaborate on a picture book for a seventh grade English class contest, Jessica becomes aware of conditions in Daphne's life that threaten her health and safety.

216. Hahn, Mary. FOLLOWING MY OWN FOOTSTEPS. Clarion, 1996; Avon, 1998 (pap).
Gordy's grandmother takes him and his family into her North Carolina home after his abusive father is arrested, and he just begins to respond to her loving discipline when his father returns.

217. Hahn, Mary. TALLAHASSEE HIGGINS. Avon, 1988 (pap).
Tallahassee enjoys the vagabond lifestyle she lives with her free-spirited mother, but when she is placed with her uncle, his conventional suburban lifestyle makes her question her mother's values - and her own.

218. Lisle, Janet Taylor. THE LOST FLOWER CHILDREN. Philomel, c1999.
After their mother's death, Olivia and Nellie go to live with their great aunt, where they slowly bring her overgrown and weedy old garden back to life, enabling them to adjust to a new life as well.

219. Little, Jean. THE BELONGING PLACE. Viking, 1997.
Elspet Mary is happy to be living with her kind aunt and uncle after her mother and father die, but worries when the family decides to go to Upper Canada from Scotland to own their own farm.

220. MacLachlan, Patricia. JOURNEY. Delacorte, 1991; Dell, 1991 (pap).
Left by their mother with their grandparents, two children feel as if their past has been erased, until Grandfather finds a way to restore it to them.

221. Peck, Richard. STRAYS LIKE US. Dial, c1998; Puffin, 2000 (pap).
When her drug-addict mother can no longer care for her, twelve-year-old Molly comes to stay with her great-aunt and slowly begins to realize that others in the small town also feel as if they don't belong.

222. Rylant, Cynthia. MISSING MAY. *SEE 113.*

223. Spyri, Johanna. HEIDI. Grosset, c1994; Puffin, 1994 (pap).
A Swiss orphan is heartbroken when she must leave her beloved grandfather and their happy home in the mountains to go to school and care for an invalid girl in the city.

224. Voigt, Cynthia. DICEY'S SONG. Atheneum, 1982; Bantam, 1997 (pap).
Now that the four abandoned Tillerman children are settled in with their grandmother, Dicey finds that their new beginnings require love, trust, humor and courage.

Family Structure – Youngest Child – Picture Books

225. Havill, Juanita. JAMAICA TAG-ALONG. Illus. by Ann Sibley O'Brien. *SEE 118.*

226. Hayes, Sarah. EAT-UP, GEMMA. Lothrop, 1988; Mulberry, 1988 (pap).
Baby Gemma refuses to eat, throwing her breakfast on the floor and squashing her grapes, until her brother gets an inspired idea.

227. Hutchins, Pat. YOU'LL SOON GROW INTO THEM, TITCH. Mulberry, 1992 (pap).
As the youngest child, Titch gets his brother's and sister's outgrown clothing, which don't really fit him.

228. McDaniel, Becky. KATIE DID IT. Illus. by Lois Axelman. Childrens, 1983.
Whenever something goes wrong, Katie's older brother and sister are quick to blame her.

Family Structure – Middle Child - Fiction

229. Blume, Judy. THE ONE IN THE MIDDLE IS THE GREEN KANGAROO. *SEE 126.*

Family Structure – Older Child – Picture Book

230. Cooke, Trick. SO MUCH. Illus. by Jan Ormerod. Candlewick, 1994.
Relatives arriving in succession give in to their desire to squeeze and kiss and play with the baby.

231. Dale, Penny. BIG BROTHER, LITTLE BROTHER. Candlewick, 1997.
When Little Brother is unhappy, Big Brother always knows why – and makes everything okay. But when Little Brother takes Big Brother's truck, who's turn is it to cry?

232. Hest, Amy. YOU'RE THE BOSS, BABY DUCK! Candlewick, 1997.
When her parents make such a fuss over the new baby, Baby Duck feels neglected, until Grandpa helps her to realize that she is still important.

233. Hiatt, Fred. BABY TALK. McElderry, c1999.
Joey finds that he can connect with hie new baby brother by speaking his own special language with him.

234. Kleven, Elisa. A MONSTER IN THE HOUSE. Dutton, 1998.
A little girl describes "the monster" who lives in her house to a new friend. The monster turns out to be her baby brother.

235. Keats, Ezra Jack. PETER'S CHAIR. *SEE 120.*

236. Schindel, John. FROG FACE. Holt, 1998.
A little girl describes the joys and frustrations of living with her little sister.

237. Ziefert, Harriet. WAITING FOR BABY. Illus. by Emily Bolam. Holt, 1998.
When Max learns that his mommy is going to have a baby, he talks and sings to his unborn sibling but he can't seem to make the baby come out sooner.

Family Structure – Older Child – Easy Reader

238. Hooks, William H. MR. BIG BROTHER. Gareth Stevens, 1999; Bantam, 2000 (pap).
Eli is disappointed when the new baby in his family is a little sister rather than the brother he had expected.

Family Structure – Older Child - Fiction

239. Byars, Betsy. THE NIGHT SWIMMERS. Dell, 1983.
With their mother dead and their father working nights, Retta tries to be mother to her two younger brothers, but somehow things just don't seem to be working right.

Family Structure – Older Child – Nonfiction

240. Green, Jen. OUR NEW BABY. Copper Beech, 1998.
Discusses the fun and frustration of coping with being a big brother or sister to a new baby, the disruption to the normal family life, and the sharing of the parents' time, attention, and love.

Family Structure – Only Child – Picture Books

241. Hazen, Barbara S. TIGHT TIMES. Illus. by Trina Shart Hyman. Puffin, 1983 (pap).
A small boy, not allowed to have a dog because "times are tight," finds a starving kitten in a trash can on the same day his father loses his job.

Family Structure – Only Child – Fiction

242. Fitzhugh, Louise. HARRIET THE SPY. Harper, 1964; Trophy, 1990 (pap).
Eleven-year-old Harriet, who is a spy and plans to be an author, keeps a secret notebook filled with thoughts and notes on her schoolmates, but when some of her classmates read the notebook, they seek revenge.

243. Gates, Doris. BLUE WILLOW. Viking, 1940.
A little girl, who wants most of all to have a real home and go to a regular school, hopes that the valley her family has come to will be their permanent home.

244. Hoover, H.M. ONLY CHILD. Dutton, 1992.
Twelve-year-old Cody discovers that the Terran Corporation, in colonizing the planet Patma, is illegally destroying the intelligent native inhabitants, giant insect-like creatures.

245. Lowry, Lois. ANASTASIA KRUPNIK. Houghton Mifflin, 1979; Dell, 1979 (pap).
Anastasia's tenth year has some good happenings, like really getting to know her grandmother, and some bad ones, like finding out about an impending baby brother!

Family Structure – Multiple Births – Picture Books

246. Cleary, Beverly. THE GROWING UP FEET. Illus. by DyAnne DiSalvo Ryan. Morrow, 1997.
The twins' feet haven't "grown up" enough for new shoes, so they get bright red boots instead.

247. Cleary, Beverly. TWO DOG BISCUITS. Illus. by DyAnne DiSalvo Ryan. Mulberry, 1996 (pap).
Four-year-old twins in search of a dog to eat their two dog biscuits find all the neighborhood dogs undeserving.

248. Doro, Ann. TWIN PICKLE. Illus. by Clare Mackie. Holt, 1996.
Rhyming text describes a day's activities for twins Ivory and Jenny.

249. Hutchins, Pat. WHICH WITCH IS WHICH? Greenwillow, 1989.
Although Ella and Emily look alike, their choices of food, games, and colors at a birthday party help the reader tell them apart.

Family Structure – Multiple Births – Fiction

250. Banks, Jacqueline Turner. THE NEW ONE. Houghton Mifflin, 1994.
Twelve-year old twin brothers fail to see eye to eye about whether or not to befriend the new girl in their class, and whether or not they should interfere with their mother's plans to marry her boyfriend.

251. Bradley, Kimberly Brubaker. ONE-OF-A-KIND MALLIE. Delacorte, 1999.
Living in Indiana during World War I, ten-year-old Mallie longs to be seen as different from her identical twin and finds an example of individuality in the gypsies who moved into her community.

252. Paterson, Katherine. JACOB HAVE I LOVED. *SEE 130.*

Family Structure – Multiple Births – Nonfiction

253. Aldape, Virginia Totorica. DAVID, DONNIE AND DARREN: A BOOK ABOUT IDENTICAL TRIPLETS. Lerner, c1997.
Eight-year-old identical triplets tell about the things they do together, their family, and how they are alike and yet different from each other.

254. Dilley, Becki. SIXTY FINGERS, SIXTY TOES: SEE HOW THE DILLEY SEXTUPLETS GROW. Walker, 1998.
Pictures show Brenna, Julian, Quinn, Claire, Ian and Adrian as they grow from babyhood to age four.

255. Landau, Elaine. MULTIPLE BIRTHS. Franklin Watts, 1998.
Explores the phenomenon of multiple births, including those of twins, triplets, and larger groupings, discussing possible causes, medical issues, effects on the families, and other moral and practical concerns.

Family Structure – Step-Families – Picture Books

256. Ballard, Robin. WHEN I AM A SISTER. Greenwillow, c1998.
Papa tells his daughter what will change and what will stay the same after he and his new wife have a baby.

257. Clifton, Lucille. EVERETT ANDERSON'S 1-2-3. Illus. by Ann Grifalconi. Holt, 1977.
As a small boy's mother considers remarriage, he considers the numbers one, two, and three—sometimes they're lonely, sometimes crowded, sometimes just right.

258. Cook, Jean Thor. ROOM FOR A STEPDADDY. Illus. by Martine Gourboult. Whitman, 1995.
Joey has trouble accepting his new stepfather, but the constant love of his father, mother and stepfather finally convince him that there is love enough to go around for everybody.

259. Hines, Anna G. WHEN WE MARRIED GARY. Greenwillow, 1996.
Beth still remembers the daddy who went away, although her younger sibling does not, but both of them accept Gary and call him Papa.

260. Hoffman, Mary. BOUNDLESS GRACE. Illus. by Caroline Binch. Dial, 1995.
Accompanied by Nana, Grace travels to Africa to visit her father, who left home when she was little, and learns that love can be without bounds even in divided families.

261. Jukes, Mavis. LIKE JAKE AND ME. Illus. by Lloyd Bloom. Knopf, 1984.
Alex feels that he does not have much in common with his stepfather Jake until a fuzzy spider brings them together.

Family Structure – Step-Families - Fiction

262. Auch, Mary Jane. OUT OF STEP. Holiday, 1992.
After his father remarries, twelve-year-old Jeremy begins to feel that there is no place for him in a family which now includes a stepsister his age, who is a superb athlete.

263. Boyd, Candy Dawson. CHEVROLET SATURDAYS. Macmillan, 1993; Puffin, 1993 (pap).
When he enters fifth grade after his mother's remarriage, Joey has trouble adjusting to his new teacher and to his new stepfather.

264. Brooks, Bruce. WHAT HEARTS. Harper, 1992; Trophy, 1995 (pap).
After his mother divorces his father and remarries, Asa's sharp intellect and capacity for forgiveness help him deal with the instabilities of his new world.

265. Delton, Judy. ANGEL'S MOTHER'S BABY. Houghton, 1989.
Twelve-year-old Angel has adjusted to her mother's remarriage and believes that she and her brother now live in the perfect family, until she discovers that her mother is going to have another baby.

266. Fine, Anne. STEP BY WICKED STEP. Little Brown, 1996; Yearling, 1996 (pap).
Five schoolmates share the stories of their parents' estrangements, divorces, and remarriages, and the effects these events have had on their lives.

267. Hahn, Mary Downing. SPANISH KIDNAPPING DISASTER. Clarion, 1991.
Forced to accompany their parents on their honeymoon in Spain, two new stepsisters find their animosity escalating.

268. Henkes, Kevin. TWO UNDER PAR. Greenwillow, 1987; Puffin, 1997 (pap).
When his mother's new marriage takes them into the household of a miniature golf course owner, ten-year-old Wedge struggles with feelings of resentment and dislike for his stepfather.

269. Lowry, Lois. SWITCHAROUND. Houghton Mifflin, 1985; Dell, 1991 (pap).
Forced to spend a summer with their father and his "new" family, Caroline and J.P. are given unpleasant responsibilities for which they are determined to get revenge.

270. MacLachlan, Patricia. SARAH, PLAIN AND TALL. *SEE 150.*

271. Park, Barbara. MY MOTHER GOT MARRIED AND OTHER DISASTERS. Random, 1990.
Twelve-year-old Charles experiences many difficulties in adjusting to a new stepfather, stepsister, and stepbrother.

272. Snyder, Zilpha. THE HEADLESS CUPID. Atheneum, 1971; Bantam, 1999 (pap).
Life is never quite the same again for eleven-year-old David after the arrival of his new stepsister, a student of the occult.

Family Structure – Step-Families – Nonfiction

273. Johnson, Julie. MY STEPFAMILY. Copper Beech, 1998.
Young people in stepfamilies describe how they cope with having stepbrothers, stepsisters, and stepparents and offer tips on dealing with change in your family.

274. Sanders, Pete. STEPFAMILIES. Copper Beech, 1995.
Explores the different nature of stepfamilies, examining the difficulties, pleasures, and issues involved in becoming part of a stepfamily.

Family Structure – Interfaith Families – Picture Books

275. Wing, Natasha. JALAPEÑO BAGELS. Atheneum, 1996.
While trying to decide what to take for his school's International Day, Pablo helps his Mexican mother and Jewish father at their bakery and discovers a food that represents both his parents' backgrounds.

Family Structure – Interfaith Families - Fiction

276. Blume, Judy. ARE YOU THERE, GOD? IT'S ME, MARGARET. Simon & Schuster, c1970; Dell, 1986 (pap).
Faced with the difficulties of growing up and choosing a religion, a twelve-year-old girl talks over the problems with her own private God.

277. Sussman, Susan. THERE'S NO SUCH THING AS A CHANUKAH BUSH, SANDY GOLDSTEIN. Whitman, 1983.
A wise, understanding grandfather helps Robin, a Jewish child, cope with Christmas, not an easy task when even her friend Sandy, who is also Jewish, is allowed to have a Christmas tree and Robin can't have one.

Family Structure – Interracial Families – Picture Books

278. Davol, Marguerite. BLACK, WHITE, JUST RIGHT. Illus. by Irene Trivas. Whitman, 1993.
    A girl explains how her parents are different in color, in their taste in art and food, in pet preferences, and how she herself is different too but just right.

279. Friedman, Ina R. HOW MY PARENTS LEARNED TO EAT. Illus. by Allen Say. Houghton Mifflin, 1984.
    An American sailor courts a Japanese girl and each tries, in secret, to learn the other's way of eating.

280. Girard, Linda. WE ADOPTED YOU, BENJAMIN KOO. *SEE 179.*

281. Igus, Toyomi. TWO MRS. GIBSONS. Illus. by Daryl Wells. Childrens Press, 1996.
    The biracial daughter of an African American father and a Japanese mother fondly recalls growing up with her mother and her father's mother, two very different but equally loving women.

282. Kasza, Keiko. A MOTHER FOR CHOCO. Putnam, 1992.
    A lonely little bird named Choco goes in search of a mother and finds Mrs. Bear and her multi-species adopted family.

283. Williams, Vera B. MORE MORE MORE SAID THE BABY. Mulberry, 1996 (pap).
    Three babies are caught up in the air and given loving attention by a father, grandmother and mother.

Family Structure – Interracial Families - Fiction

284. Bradman, Tony. THROUGH MY WINDOW. Silver Burdett, 1986.
    Staying home sick for the day, Jo waits eagerly for her mother to return from work with a promised surprise.

285. Dorris, Michael. THE WINDOW. Hyperion, c1997.
    When ten-year-old Rayona's Native American mother enters a treatment facility, her estranged father, a black man, introduces her to his side of the family, who are not at all what she expected.

286. Hamilton, Virginia. ARILLA SUN DOWN. Scholastic, 1995 (pap).
    A young girl, half Black and half Indian, lives in a small town where her life revolves around family, school and friends.

287. Hamilton, Virginia. PLAIN CITY. Scholastic, 1993.
    Twelve-year-old Buhlaire, a "mixed" child who feels out of place in her community, struggles to unearth her past and her family history as she gradually discovers more about her long-missing father.

288. Wyeth, Sharon Dennis. GINGER BROWN: TOO MANY HOUSES. Random, 1995.
    When her parents get a divorce, six-year-old Ginger lives for a while with each set of grandparents and begins to understand her mixed background and her new family situation.

Family Structure – Interracial Families – Nonfiction

289. Adoff, Arnold. ALL THE COLORS OF THE RACE. Lothrop Lee, 1982.
A collection of poems written from the point of view of a child with a black mother and a white father.

290. Adoff, Arnold. BLACK IS BROWN IS TAN. Harper, 1973.
Describes in verse the life of brown-skinned momma, white-skinned daddy, their children, and assorted relatives.

291. Katz, William Loren. BLACK INDIANS. Aladdin, 1997 (pap).
The role of Black Indians, largely omitted from or distorted in conventional history books, is traced with careful and committed research. General history is integrated with brief individual biographies.

Social Issues

Gender Roles • Sexual Orientation •
Religious Diversity • Series

Illustration from *The Kids' Around the World Cookbook* by Deri Robins, © 1994 by Deri Robins.
Reprinted by permission of Kingfisher Books.

Social Issues

Gender Roles (Nontraditional) – Picture Books

292. Beck, Andera. ELLIOT BAKES A CAKE. Kids Can Press, c1999.
Elliot Moose and his animal friends return as they plan a wonderful celebration for Lionel the Lion's birthday and find, to their disappointment, that Beaverton's cake recipe has some problems that they must fix.

293. Brown, Marc. ARTHUR BABYSITS. Little Brown, 1992.
Arthur's experience as babysitter for the terrible Tibble Twins is as challenging as he expected, but he finally gains control by telling them a spooky story.

294. Carlson, Nancy L. LOUANNE PIG IN MAKING THE TEAM. Carolrhoda, 1985.
Though she plans to try out for cheerleading, Louanne Pig helps her friend Arnie try out for football, with surprising results.

295. Cole, Babette. PRINCE CINDERS. Paper Star, 1997 (pap).
A fairy grants a small, skinny prince, who has been made to do all of the housework by his big and hairy brothers, a change in appearance and the chance to go to the Palace Disco.

296. Cole, Babette. PRINCESS SMARTYPANTS. Putnam, 1987.
Forced by her parents into looking for a husband, Princess Smartypants sets impossible tasks for her suitors to prove their worthiness, but when Prince Swashbuckle succeeds at every task, the Princess turns him into a frog with her kiss.

297. Ehrlich, Amy. LEO, ZACK AND EMMIE. Illus. by Steven Kellogg. Puffin, 1997 (pap).
The new girl in Zach and Leo's class wiggles her ears, plays ball and is a good runner.

298. Hamanaka, Sheila. I LOOK LIKE A GIRL. Morrow, c1999.
In her imagination, a young girl assumes many shapes and forms, from dolphin and condor to wolf and jaguar.

299. Hilton, Nette. THE LONG RED SCARF. Illus. by Margaret Power. Carolrhoda, 1990.
After all his female relatives refuse to knit him a scarf as they go on about their business, driving the cows and building a crib, Grandfather learns to knit by himself.

300. Hines, Anna Grossnickle. DADDY MAKES THE BEST SPAGHETTI. Clarion, 1986.
Not only does Corey's father make the best spaghetti, but he also dresses up as Batman and acts like a barking dog.

301. Hoffman, Mary. THREE WISE WOMEN. Phyllis Fogelman Books, 1999.
Three women from different parts of the world follow a star that leads to a small stable. They have gifts for the newborn Christ child like the wise men of tradition, gifts that will be remembered and used when the baby becomes a man.

302. Howard, Elizabeth. VIRGIE GOES TO SCHOOL WITH US BOYS. Simon & Schuster, 2000.
Virgie must convince her brothers that she can manage the seven-mile walk to school – and that girls need education too.

303. Isadora, Rachel. MAX. Aladdin, 1987 (pap).
Max finds a new way to warm up for his Saturday baseball game: participate in his sister's dancing class.

304. Kroll, Virginia L. A CARP FOR KIMIKO. Illus. by Katherine Roundtree. Charlesbridge, 1993.
Although the tradition is to present carp kites only to boys on Children's Day, Kimiko's parents find a way to make the day special for her.

305. Lattimore, Deborah Nourse. FRIDA MARIA: A STORY OF THE OLD SOUTHWEST. Browndeer Press, 1994.
Because she does not sew, cook, or dance like a proper señorita, Frida cannot please her mother until she saves the day at the fiesta with her special talent: she wins a horse race.

306. Lyon, George Ella. MAMA IS A MINER. Illus. by Peter Catalanotto. Orchard, 1994.
In a thoroughly researched evocation of life in the coal-mining country of Kentucky, featuring realistic paintings, chronicles the day of a little girl as she offers a tribute to her hard-working, coal-mining mother.

307. Munsch, Robert N. THE PAPER BAG PRINCESS. Illus. by Michael Martchenko. Annick, 1980.
After her castle and clothes are destroyed by a dragon, Princess Elizabeth, dressed only in a paper bag, sets out to rescue Prince Ronald, who was taken captive.

308. Numeroff, Laura. WHAT MOMMIES DO BEST; WHAT DADDIES DO BEST. Simon & Schuster, c1998.
Mothers and fathers, participating in everyday activities, show their love for their children in very similar ways.

309. O'Neill, Alexis. LOUD EMILY. Simon & Schuster, c1998.
A little girl with a big voice, who lives in a nineteenth century whaling town, finds a way to be useful and happy aboard a sailing ship.

310. Waber, Bernard. GINA. *SEE 57.*

311. Wild, Margaret. MR. NICK'S KNITTING. Illus. by Dee Huxley. Harcourt, 1989.
When knitting companion Mrs. Jolly, who rides with him every day on the train into the city, becomes ill, Mr. Nick finds a way to cheer her up.

312. Zolotow, Charlotte. WILLIAM'S DOLL. *SEE 162.*

Gender Roles (Nontraditional) – Easy and Intermediate

313. Avi. ABIGAIL TAKES THE WHEEL. Harper, c1999; Trophy, 2000 (pap).
When the first mate of the freight boat Neptune falls ill, it is up to Abigail, the captain's daughter, to steer the ship up the Hudson River from New Jersey to New York City.

314. Bulla, Clyde. SHOESHINE GIRL. Crowell, 1975; Trophy, 1989 (pap).
Disgruntled at having to spend the summer with her Aunt Claudia, ten-year-old Sarah Ida takes a job shining shoes as a source of money and independence.

315. Coerr, Eleanor. THE BIG BALLOON RACE. Illus. by Carolyn Croll. Harper, 1981.
Ariel almost causes her famous mother to lose a balloon race, and then helps her win it.

316. Cristaldi, Kathryn. BASEBALL BALLERINA. Illus. by Abby Carter. Random, 1992.
A baseball-loving girl worries that the ballet class her mother forces her to take will ruin her reputation with the other members of her baseball team.

317. Ernst, Lisa Campbell. SAM JOHNSON AND THE BLUE RIBBON QUILT. Lothrop, 1983; Mulberry, 1992 (pap).
While mending the awning over the pig pen, Sam discovers that he enjoys sewing the various patches together but meets with scorn and ridicule when he asks his wife if he can join her quilting club.

318. Jukes, Mavis. LIKE JAKE AND ME. Knopf, 1984.
Alex, who takes ballet lessons, feels that he does not have much in common with his stepfather, a cowboy, until a fuzzy spider brings them together.

319. Moss, Marissa. TRUE HEART. Silver Whistle, c1999.
At the turn of the century, a young woman, who works on the railroad, accomplishes her yearning ambition to become an engineer when a male engineer is injured and can't drive his train.

320. Papademetriou, Lisa. MY PEN PAL, PAT. Millbrook, c1998.
Pat Glenn and Pat Scott, pen pals who share a name and have many things in common, get a big surprise when they finally meet face to face.

321. Paterson, Katherine. THE KING'S EQUAL. Illus. by Vladimir Vagan. HarperCollins, 1992; Trophy, 1999 (pap).
In order to wear the crown of the kingdom, an arrogant young prince must find an equal in his bride; instead, he finds someone far better than he.

322. Quindlen, Anna. HAPPILY EVER AFTER. Puffin, 1999 (pap).
A tomboy gets transported back in time after reading a fairy tale, and realizes that being a princess is not that much fun.

323. Roop, Peter. KEEP THE LIGHTS BURNING, ABBIE. Carolrhoda, 1985.
In the winter of 1856, a storm delays the lighthouse keeper's return to an island off the coast of Maine, and his daughter Abbie must keep the lights burning by herself.

324. Sathre, Vivian. SLENDER ELLA AND HER FAIRY HOGFATHER. Yearling, c1999 (pap).
Slender Ella, a pig forced into servitude by her stepmother and two horrid stepsisters, goes to the hoedown with the help of her fairy Hogfather and marries the handsome son of the Golsnoots of Diamond Snout Hay Ranch.

Gender Roles (Nontraditional) – Fiction

325. Alexander, Lloyd. THE ILLYRIAN ADVENTURE. Dell, 1986 (pap).
Sixteen-year-old Vesper is a female action-adventure character living in the 1870s.

326. Avi. THE TRUE CONFESSIONS OF CHARLOTTE DOYLE. Orchard, 1990.
Thirteen-year-old Charlotte, sailing from England to Rhode Island in 1832, joins the crew, learns to climb the riggings, and shoulders her share of the work.

327. Banks, Lynne. FARTHEST-AWAY MOUNTAIN. Avon, 1992 (pap).
Young Dakin has watched the farthest away mountain mysteriously change colors since she was a child, and on the brink of her fifteenth birthday, she decides to brave witches, gargoyles, monsters, and ogres to discover the mountain's secrets.

328. Brink, Carol R. CADDIE WOODLAWN. Macmillan, 1973.
Chronicles the adventures of eleven-year-old Caddie growing up with her six brothers and sisters on the Wisconsin frontier in the mid-nineteenth century.

329. Byars, Betsy. THE MIDNIGHT FOX. Viking, 1968.
Tommy doesn't like sports, does not like animals, and would rather spend his time constructing models. He remains his own self and is content.

330. Collier, James L. WAR COMES TO WILLY FREEMAN. Dell, 1987.
A free black girl disguises herself as a boy, finds work at a tavern during the Revolutionary War, and reflects on women's lack of freedom.

331. Craig, Ruth. MALU'S WOLF. Orchard, 1995.
Malu, a stone-age girl, is gifted with the skills of the boys in her tribe. She survives a grueling and lonely wilderness experience with her pet wolf, and wins the respect and acceptance of her people.

332. Dahl, Roald. MATILDA. Viking, 1988; Puffin, 1998 (pap).
Matilda, a read-a-holic, proves that girls can do anything they put their minds to, including tasks that requires superhuman strength!

333. Dorris, Michael. SEES BEHIND TREES. Hyperion, 1996.
A Native American boy, who cannot make the rite of passage because blindness prohibits him from hunting, eventually wins his place of respect after a harrowing, life-threatening trek.

334. Duffy, James. RADICAL RED. Scribner, 1993.
A girl and her mother are ardent suffragettes despite strong opposition.

335. Fitzhugh, Louise. NOBODY'S FAMILY IS GOING TO CHANGE. Farrar Straus, 1974.
A well-to-do conservative Black family faces the decision of the daughter to become a lawyer and the son to study dance.

336. Garden, Nancy. DOVE AND SWORD. Farrar Straus, 1995; Scholastic, 1997 (pap).
In 1455 in France, Gabrielle is visited by Pierre d'Arc, a brother of Joan of Arc, and with him reminisces about their childhood together in Domremy and Joan's subsequent trial and burning at the stake at Rouen twenty-four years before.

337. George, Jean Craighead. JULIE OF THE WOLVES. Harper, 1972.
An Eskimo girl, who has left home because she objects to a marriage that has been arranged for her, finds herself lost on the tundra. She befriends a small pack of wolves, and with their aid tries to survive the light months until the north star becomes visible again.

338. George, Jean Craighead. THE TALKING EARTH. Harper, 1983.
A young Seminole girl survives in the Everglades by drawing on her knowledge of nature.

339. Giff, Patricia R. THE GIFT OF THE PIRATE QUEEN. Delacorte, 1982.
When young Grace's mother dies, Cousin Fiona comes from Ireland to care for her, bringing marvelous tales of Grania, an Irish pirate queen.

340. Gilson, Jamie. CAN'T CATCH ME, I'M THE GINGERBREAD MAN. Beech Tree, 1997 (pap).
When the family health food store burns down, twelve-year-old-Mitch is even more determined to win first prize in a Bake-a-thon with his special gingerbread.

341. Hahn, Mary D. THE GENTLEMAN OUTLAW AND ME - ELI. Clarion, 1996; Avon, 1997 (pap).
Eliza heads west to Colorado to find her father, and quickly discovers she is safer disguised as a boy.

342. Holm, Jennifer. OUR ONLY MAY AMELIA. HarperCollins, c1999; Trophy, 2000 (pap).
As the only girl in a Finnish American family of seven brothers in Washington State in 1899, May Amelia Jackson resents being expected to act like a lady.

343. Hyatt, Patricia R. COAST TO COAST WITH ALICE. Carolrhoda, 1995.
Sixteen-year-old Hermine accompanied Alice Ramsey on the first coast-to-coast automobile trip by a female driver in 1909.

344. Karr, Kathleen. GO WEST, YOUNG WOMEN! Trophy, 1997 (pap).
A group of resourceful women have a chance to conquer the West when most of the men are eliminated by a buffalo stampede.

345. Klass, Sheila S. A SHOOTING STAR: A NOVEL ABOUT ANNIE OAKLEY. Holiday, 1996; Bantam, 1998 (pap).
As one who prefers hunting to sewing, Annie Oakley breaks free from conventional behavior for girls and goes on to develop her talent as a sharpshooter and entertainer.

346. L'Engle, Madeleine. A WRINKLE IN TIME. Farrar Straus, 1962; Dell, 1984 (pap).
Meg, a misfit at her high school, gains confidence and learns to rely on herself rather than on the males around her.

347. Lord, Bette Bao. IN THE YEAR OF THE BOAR AND JACKIE ROBINSON. *SEE 69.*

348. Lunn, Janet. THE ROOT CELLAR. Puffin, 1996 (pap).
A lonely orphan travels through time to the Civil War period and disguises herself as a boy.

349. McKinley, Robin. THE BLUE SWORD. Greenwillow, 1982; Ace Books, 1982 (pap).
Harry leads an extraordinary group of women and men, including some experienced soldiers willing to follow a woman, into battle against a formidable enemy.

350. McKinley, Robin. THE HERO AND THE CROWN. Greenwillow, 1985; Ace Books, 1987 (pap).
Aerin is feared as a witch, but her cousin Tor, heir to the throne, teaches her the skills of hunting, fishing, riding, and swordplay.

351. Mikaelsen, Ben. STRANDED. Hyperion, 1995.
Twelve-year-old Koby, who has lost a foot in an accident, sees a chance to prove her self-reliance to her parents when she tries to rescue two stranded pilot whales near her home in the Florida Keys.

352. Neuberger, Anne E. THE GIRL-SON. Carolrhoda, 1995.
An autobiographical novel in which a young Korean girl received her schooling disguised as a boy because Korean schools did not admit girls in the early twentieth century.

353. Nixon, Joan Lowery. A FAMILY APART. Gareth Stevens, 2000; Bantam, 1987 (pap).
Sent westward on the Orphan Train, Frances is determined to stay with her six-year-old brother and disguises herself as a boy so they will be more likely to attract a farm family.

354. O'Dell, Scott. CARLOTA. Houghton Mifflin, 1977; Dell, 1989 (pap).
Carlota has been raised as a boy; her father taught her to ride, to wield a lance and a lasso, and to help run their large ranch in Spanish California.

355. O'Dell, Scott. ISLAND OF THE BLUE DOLPHINS. Houghton Mifflin, 1960; Dell 1984 (pap).
A twelve-year-old Native American girl is alone on an island for many years and learns to build shelters, fashion spears and a bow and arrows, and kill wild dogs in order to survive.

356. Speare, Elizabeth G. THE WITCH OF BLACKBIRD POND. Houghton Mifflin, 1958; Dell, 1987 (pap).
The role of the female in Colonial days, as well as the impact of politics and religion, is dramatically described through the tale of an orphan living with her Puritan uncle and his family.

357. Sorensen, Virginia. PLAIN GIRL. Harcourt, 1956.
Esther, a member of an Amish family, struggles with the conflict between the teachings of her group and the rest of the world.

358. Spinelli, Jerry. THERE'S A GIRL IN MY HAMMERLOCK. Simon & Schuster, 1993 (pap).
Maisie tries out for the wrestling team because she has a crush on one of its members, but finds she loves wrestling. In spite of grief from the coach, players, and friends, she sticks to her resolve to make the team.

359. Strasser, Todd. THE DIVING BELL. Apple, 1992 (pap).
To her mother's dismay, Culca wants to dive for shells like her brother does.

360. Voigt, Cynthia. BAD GIRLS. Scholastic, 1996.
Mikey, a talented and aggressive player, objects loudly to boys dominating the soccer field.

Gender Roles (Nontraditional) - Nonfiction

361. Asbjornsen, Peter C. THE MAN WHO KEPT HOUSE. McElderry, 1992.
Convinced that his work in the field is harder than his wife's work at home, a farmer trades places with her for a day.

362. Blashfield, Jean F. WOMEN AT THE FRONT: THEIR CHANGING ROLES IN THE CIVIL WAR. Franklin Watts, c1997.
Explores ways in which the various activities of women during the Civil War altered their role in society and led to new initiatives in women's rights.

363. Hooks, William H. THE THREE LITTLE PIGS AND THE FOX. Aladdin, 1997 (pap).
In this Appalachian version of the classic tale, Hamlet, the youngest pig, rescues her two greedy brothers from the clutches of the "mean, tricky old drooly-mouthed fox".

364. Levinson, Nancy Smiler. SHE'S BEEN WORKING ON THE RAILROAD. Lodestar, c1997.
Relates the story of women who have worked on the railroad in ever-increasing numbers and expanding the range of jobs from the mid-1800's to the present.

365. Macy, Sue. A WHOLE NEW BALL GAME: THE STORY OF THE ALL-AMERICAN GIRLS PROFESSIONAL BASEBALL LEAGUE. Holt, 1993; Puffin, 1995 (pap).
Describes the activities of the members of the All-American Girls Professional Baseball League, the women's professional baseball league that existed between 1943 and 1954.

366. Phelps, Ethel Johnston. TATTERHOOD AND OTHER TALES. Feminist Press, 1978.
A collection of traditional tales from Norway, England, China and many other countries that feature female characters.

367. San Souci, Robert D. THE SAMURAI'S DAUGHTER. Puffin, 1997 (pap).
A Japanese folktale about the brave daughter of a samurai warrior and her journey to be reunited with her exiled father.

Gender Roles (Nontraditional) – Biographies

368. Adler, David. OUR GOLDA: THE STORY OF GOLDA MEIR. Viking, 1984.
Describes the life of the Israeli prime minister and world leader, emphasizing her early childhood and youth in Russia and America.

369. Adler, David A. A PICTURE BOOK OF HELEN KELLER. Holiday, 1990.
Helen Keller struggled with the handicaps of being both blind and deaf and became a productive individual, an advocate for people with disabilities.

370. Adler, David A. A PICTURE BOOK OF HARRIET TUBMAN. Holiday, 1992.
The biography of the Black woman who escaped from slavery and became famous as a conductor on the Underground Railroad.

371. Banfield, Susan. JOAN OF ARC. Chelsea, 1985.
Chronicles the experiences of the peasant girl who led a French army against the English, was burned at the stake for witchcraft, and became a saint.

372. Fritz, Jean. YOU WANT WOMEN TO VOTE, LIZZIE STANTON? Putnam, 1995; Paper Star, 1999 (pap).
A biography of the suffragist who organized the first women's rights convention.

373. Hart, Philip S. UP IN THE AIR: THE STORY OF BESSIE COLEMAN. Carolrhoda, 1996.
Presents the story of Bessie Coleman, an American, who in 1920 traveled to France to become the first Black woman to earn a pilot's license.

374. Kendall, Martha E. NELLIE BLY: REPORTER FOR THE WORLD. Millbrook, 1992.
Profiles the woman whose exposé of the insane asylums in New York City in the late 1800's was the beginning of her journalistic career.

375. Lasky, Kathryn. THE LIBRARIAN WHO MEASURED THE EARTH. Little Brown, 1994.
The Greek geographer and astronomer who accurately measured the circumference of the earth is presented in this picture biography.

376. Lauber, Patricia. LOST STAR: THE STORY OF AMELIA EARHART. Scholastic, 1988.
Traces the life of the pilot who became the first woman to fly across the Atlantic Ocean and mysteriously disappeared in 1937 while attempting to fly around the world.

377. Levin, Pamela. SUSAN B. ANTHONY. Chelsea, 1993.
This crusader who, after being denied the right to speak at a temperance convention because she was a woman, dedicated the rest of her life to fighting for women's rights.

378. McGovern, Ann. THE SECRET SOLDIER: THE STORY OF DEBORAH SAMPSON. Four Winds, 1975.
A brief biography of the woman who disguised herself as a man and joined the Continental Army during the American Revolution.

379. McPherson, Stephanie. PEACE AND BREAD: THE STORY OF JANE ADDAMS. Carolrhoda, 1993.
Traces the life of the woman who founded Hull House, one of the first settlement houses in the United States.

380. McPherson, Stephanie. ROOFTOP ASTRONOMER: A STORY ABOUT MARIA MITCHELL. Carolrhoda, 1990.
Recounts the accomplishments of the first woman astronomer in America.

381. Martinez, Elizabeth. SOR JUANA: A TRAIL-BLAZING THINKER. *SEE 261.*

382. Naden, Corinne J. CHRISTA MCAULIFFE: TEACHER IN SPACE. Millbrook, 1991.
The first private American citizen chosen to go on a space flight, Christa McAuliffe lost her life when the Challenger exploded just after liftoff.

383. Parks, Rosa. I AM ROSA PARKS. Dial, 1997.
Rosa Parks, the Black woman whose act of civil disobedience led to the 1956 Supreme Court order to desegregate buses in Montgomery, Alabama, explains what she did and why.

384. Pinkney, Andrea Davis. ALVIN AILEY. Hyperion, 1993.
Describes the life, dancing and choreography of Alvin Ailey, who created his own modern dance company to explore the Black experience.

385. Poynter, Margaret. MARIE CURIE: DISCOVERER OF RADIUM. Enslow, 1994.
The first woman to win a Nobel Prize, Marie Curie is one of the most famous women of all time in the field of science.

386. Reit, Seymour. BEHIND REBEL LINES: INCREDIBLE STORY OF EMMA EDMONDS, CIVIL WAR SPY. Harcourt, 1988.
Recounts the story of the Canadian woman who disguised herself as a man and slipped behind Confederate lines to spy for the Union Army.

387. Stanley, Diane. CLEOPATRA. Morrow, 1994; Mulberry, 1997 (pap).
Chronicles Cleopatra's rule in Egypt, and tells how she persuaded Romans Julius Caesar and Mark Antony to help her make Egypt powerful.

Sexual Orientation – Picture Books

388. Jordan, Mary Kate. LOSING UNCLE TIM. Illus. by Judith Friedman. Whitman, 1989.
When his beloved Uncle Tim dies of AIDS, Daniel struggles to find reassurance and understanding, and finds that his favorite grown-up has left him a legacy of joy and courage.

389. Newman, Leslea. HEATHER HAS TWO MOMMIES. Illus. by Dyana Souza. Alyson Wonderland, 1989.
Heather loves the number two because she has two mommies, but when she realizes she doesn't have a daddy, she learns that all families are different, and all families are special.

390. Newman, Leslea. TOO FAR AWAY TO TOUCH. Illus. by Catherine Stock. Clarion, 1995.
Zoe's favorite uncle Leonard takes her to a planetarium and explains that if he dies he will be like the stars, too far away to touch, close enough to see.

391. Vigna, Judith. MY TWO UNCLES. Whitman, 1995.
Plans for Elly's grandparents' fiftieth wedding anniversary party are upset when Grampy refuses to invite Elly's Uncle Phil and his friend, Ned, who are gay.

392. Willhoite, Michael. DADDY'S WEDDING. Alyson Wonderland, 1996.
Nick tells about the wedding of his daddy to Frank, including the gathering of family and friends, the ceremony and the food.

Sexual Orientation – Fiction

393. Durant, Penny Raife. WHEN HEROES DIE. Atheneum, 1992; Aladdin, 1995 (pap).
Devastated that his hero uncle, Rob, is dying of AIDS, twelve-year-old Gary, in need of advice and guidance in his life, draws strength from Rob himself.

Sexual Orientation – Nonfiction

394. Greenberg, Keith Elliot. ZACK'S STORY: GROWING UP WITH SAME-SEX PARENTS. Illus. by Carol Halebian. Lerner, 1996.
An eleven-year-old boy describes life as part of a family made up of himself, his mother, and her lesbian partner.

395. Harris, Robie H. IT'S PERFECTLY NORMAL: CHANGING BODIES, GROWING UP, SEX, AND SEXUAL HEALTH. Candlewick, 1994.
This title describes all aspects of adolescence and sexuality, and includes homosexual relationships.

Religious Diversity – General – Nonfiction

396. Ganeri, Anita. OUT OF THE ARK: STORIES FROM THE WORLD'S RELIGIONS. Harcourt, 1996.
Retells stories from religions around the world, arranged in such categories as "Creation stories", "Flood stories" and "Animal stories".

397. GODDESSES, HEROES AND SHAMANS: THE YOUNG PEOPLE'S GUIDE TO WORLD MYTHOLOGY. Kingfisher, 1994.
Brief discussions of major characters found in world mythology.

398. Hamilton, Virginia. IN THE BEGINNING: CREATION STORIES FROM AROUND THE WORLD. Harcourt, 1988.
An illustrated collection of twenty-five myths from various cultures, explaining the creation of the world.

399. Ingpen, Robert R. A CELEBRATION OF CUSTOMS AND RITUALS OF THE WORLD. Facts on File, 1996.
Explores initiation rites, wedding feasts, harvest celebrations, religious rituals and many other customs used around the world to mark all kinds of special occasions.

400. Maestro, Betsy. THE STORY OF RELIGION. Clarion, 1996; Mulberry, 1999 (pap).
An introduction to the beginning of worship and to the beliefs of several world religions.

401. Ward, Hiley H. MY FRIEND'S BELIEFS: A YOUNG READER'S GUIDE TO WORLD RELIGIONS. Walker, 1988.
Visits some twenty religious groups around the United States, introducing at each stop a young member who shares with the reader his or her religion's history, its beliefs and practices, and aspects of everyday life.

402. Webb, Lois Sinaiko. HOLIDAYS OF THE WORLD COOKBOOK FOR STUDENTS. Oryx, 1995.
A collection of 388 recipes from more than 136 countries plus an introduction describing local holidays, customs and foods that are part of the holiday tradition.

Religious Diversity – American Indian Religions – Nonfiction

403. Swamp, Chief Jake. GIVING THANKS: A NATIVE AMERICAN GOOD MORNING MESSAGE. Lee and Low, 1994.
An Iroquois message showing appreciation for Mother Earth and her natural gifts.

Religious Diversity – Bibles and Bible Stories

404. Chaikin, Miriam. EXODUS. Illus. by Charles Mikolaycak. Holiday, 1987.
Retells the Biblical story of Moses leading his enslaved people out of Egypt.

405. de Regniers, Beatrice. DAVID AND GOLIATH. Illus. by Scott Cameron. Orchard, 1996.
The Biblical tale of the young shepherd who uses a slingshot to do battle with a giant, and eventually becomes a king.

406. Fisher, Leonard. MOSES. Holiday, 1995.
The life of the Old Testament prophet who led the enslaved Israelites to freedom.

407. Hastings, Selena. THE CHILDREN'S ILLUSTRATED BIBLE. Illus. by Eric Warwick and Amy Burch. Dorling Kindersley, 1994.
Stories from the Old and New Testaments are enhanced by background information, color photographs, and maps.

408. L'Engle, Madeleine. THE GLORIOUS IMPOSSIBLE. Simon & Schuster, 1990.
Describes the life of Jesus Christ and presents twenty-four paintings showing scenes from the life of Christ by the fourteenth century Italian artist Giotto.

409. Winthrop, Elizabeth. HE IS RISEN: THE EASTER STORY. Illus. by Charles Mikolaycak. Holiday, 1985.
An adaptation of the Bible story of Christ's crucifixion and resurrection.

410. Wolkstein, Diane. ESTHER'S STORY. Illus. by Juan Wijngaard. Mulberry, 1998 (pap).
This account of a Jewish girl who became Queen of Persia and risked her life to save her people is told in diary form.

Religious Diversity – Buddhism – Fiction

411. Coatsworth, Elizabeth. THE CAT WHO WENT TO HEAVEN. Aladdin, 1990 (pap).
A little cat comes to the home of a poor Japanese artist and, through humility and devotion, brings him good fortune.

Religious Diversity – Buddhism – Nonfiction

412. Demi. BUDDHA STORIES. Holt, 1997.
A retelling of several animal fables from the traditional Buddhist Jataka stories.

413. Ganeri, Anita. WHAT DO WE KNOW ABOUT BUDDHISM? Peter Bedrick, c1997.
Discusses the principles and practices of Buddhism, including information about holy people and places, art and architecture, and festivals.

Religious Diversity – Christianity – Picture Books

414. Bishop, Roma. EASTER SUNDAY. Simon & Schuster, 1996 (pop-up).
Celebrations and traditions are featured in this color pop-up book.

415. De Paola, Tomie. THE NIGHT OF LAS POSADAS. Putnam, 1999.
In a village high in the mountains above Santa Fe a snowstorm delays Lupe and Roberto who are to portray Mary and Joseph in the traditional procession. It seems that only a miracle can save Las Posadas this year.

416. Gibbons, Gail. CHRISTMAS TIME. Holiday, 1982.
A brief look at how and why Christmas is celebrated.

417. Houselander, Caryll. PETOOK: AN EASTER STORY. Illus. by Tomie dePaola. Holiday, 1988.
Petook the rooster witnesses the crucifixion of Christ and rejoices in the birth of new chicks three days later, on Easter morning.

418. Joseph, Lynn. AN ISLAND CHRISTMAS. Illus. by Catherine Stock. Clarion Books, 1992.
Rosie's preparations for Christmas on the island of Trinidad include picking red petals for the sorrel drink, mixing up the black currant cake, and singing along with the parang band.

419. Polacco, Patricia. JUST PLAIN FANCY. Bantam, 1990; Dell, 1990 (pap).
Naomi, an Amish girl whose elders have impressed upon her the importance of adhering to the simple ways of her people, is horrified when one of her hen eggs hatches into an extremely fancy bird.

420. Say, Allen. TREE OF CRANES. Houghton Mifflin, 1991.
A Japanese boy learns of Christmas when his mother decorates a pine tree with paper cranes.

421. Tornqvist, Rita. THE CHRISTMAS CARP. Illus. by Marit Tornqvist. Farrar Straus & Giroux, 1990.
A young boy doesn't want to eat the live fish he and his grandfather have been keeping in the bathtub for their Christmas dinner.

Religious Diversity – Christianity – Fiction

422. Delton, Judy. KITTY FROM THE START. *SEE 64.*

423. Garden, Nancy. DOVE AND SWORD: A NOVEL OF JOAN OF ARC. *SEE 336.*

424. Gilchrist, Jan Spivey. MADELIA. Dial, c1997.
Madelia would rather be painting with her new watercolors than going to church, but as she listens to her father's sermon, she is glad she came.

425. Rylant, Cynthia. A FINE WHITE DUST. Bradbury, c1986; Aladdin, 1996 (pap).
The visit of a traveling Preacher Man to his small North Carolina town gives new impetus to thirteen-year-old Peter's struggle to reconcile his own deeply felt religious belief with the beliefs and non-beliefs of his family and friends.

Religious Diversity – Christianity – Nonfiction

426. De Paola, Tomie. THE CLOWN OF GOD. Harcourt, 1978.
A once-famous Italian juggler, now old and a beggar, gives one final performance before a statue of Our Lady and the Holy Child.

427. De Paola, Tomie. FRANCIS, THE POOR MAN OF ASSISI. Holiday, 1982.
A biography of the wealthy young Italian who gave away all his possessions to become a wandering preacher and protector of animals.

428. De Paola, Tomie. THE LEGEND OF THE POINSETTIA. Putnam, 1994.
When Lucida is unable to finish her gift for the Baby Jesus in time for the Christmas procession, a miracle enables her to offer the beautiful flower we now call the poinsettia.

429. De Paola, Tomie. MARY: THE MOTHER OF JESUS. Holiday, 1995.
Using the Bible as well as legend, this noted author-illustrator presents fifteen major events in the life of the mother of Jesus Christ.

430. De Paola, Tomie. THE MIRACLES OF JESUS. Holiday, 1987.
Recounts the miracles performed by Jesus, such as calming a storm, walking on water, and raising the dead to life.

431. De Paola, Tomie. THE PARABLES OF JESUS. Holiday, 1987.
An illustrated retelling of seventeen parables used by Jesus Christ in his teachings; includes "The Good Samaritan", "The Lost Sheep", and "The Prodigal Son".

432. DePaola, Tomie. PATRICK: PATRON SAINT OF IRELAND. Holiday, 1992.
Relates the life and legends of St. Patrick.

433. Goody, Wendy. A PEEK INTO MY CHURCH. Whippersnapper Books, c1998.
A young Catholic girl and her brother explain some of the customs, practices, and beliefs of their religion.

434. Kenna, Kathleen. A PEOPLE APART. Illus. by Andrew Stawicki. Houghton Mifflin, 1995.
The Old Order Mennonite way of life, which rejects electricity, machines and other modern conveniences, is described through moving words and photographs.

435. Sabuda, Robert. SAINT VALENTINE. Atheneum, 1992.
Recounts an incident in the life of St. Valentine, a physician who lived some 200 years after Christ, in which he treated a small child for blindness.

Religious Diversity – Hinduism – Picture Book

436. Lewin, Ted. SACRED RIVER. Clarion, 1994.
The Ganges River, located in India and Bangladesh and holy to Hindus, is portrayed with full-color paintings.

Religious Diversity – Hinduism – Nonfiction

437. MacMillan, Dianne M. DIWALI: HINDU FESTIVAL OF LIGHTS. Enslow, 1997.
Discusses the history and traditions, as well as the symbols and current celebrations, of this Hindu holiday.

Religious Diversity – Islam – Picture and Easy Books

438. Matthews, Mary. MAGID FASTS FOR RAMADAN. *SEE 173.*

Religious Diversity – Islam – Fiction

439. Staples, Suzanne F. SHABANU, DAUGHTER OF THE WIND. Random, 1989.
When eleven-year-old Shabanu, the daughter of a nomad in the desert of present-day Pakistan, is pledged in marriage to an older man whose money will bring prestige to the family, she must either accept the decision or risk the consequences of defying her father's wishes.

Religious Diversity – Islam – Nonfiction

440. Ghazi, Suhaib Hamid. RAMADAN. Holiday, 1996.
Describes the celebration of the month of Ramadan by an Islamic family and discusses the meaning and importance of this holiday in the Islamic religion.

441. MacMillan, Dianne. RAMADAN AND ID AL-FITR. Enslow, 1994.
Information about a significant month-long event in the Muslim year.

Religious Diversity – Judaism – Picture and Easy Books

442. Kimmelman, Leslie. HOORAY! IT'S PASSOVER! Illus. John Himmelman. Harper, 1996.
A family celebrates this major Jewish festival through songs, stories, prayers, special foods and a traditional hide-and-seek game.

443. Krulik, Nancy E. PENNY AND THE FOUR QUESTIONS. Illus. Marion Young. Scholastic, 1993 (pap).
Although Penny is disappointed and angry at not being able at last to ask the ritual seder questions that reveal the history and meaning of the Passover holiday, she learns about the hardships of others and makes a new friend as well.

444. Oberman, Sheldon. THE ALWAYS PRAYER SHAWL. Illus. Ted Lewin. Boyds Mills, 1994; Puffin, 1997 (pap).
A prayer shawl is handed down from grandfather to grandson in this story of Jewish tradition and the passage of generations.

445. Sussman, Susan. THERE'S NO SUCH THING AS A CHANUKAH BUSH, SANDY GOLDSTEIN. *SEE 277.*

Religious Diversity – Judaism – Fiction

446. Cohen, Barbara. THE CARP IN THE BATHTUB. Kar-Ben, 1987.
Two children try to rescue the carp their mother plans to make into gefilte fish for the Seder.

447. Cohen, Barbara. FIRST FAST. Union of American Hebrew Congregations, 1987.
Two boys make a wager shortly before Yom Kippur, and Harry must fast in order to win the bet.

448. Goldin, Barbara Diamond. THE WORLD'S BIRTHDAY: A ROSH HASHANAH STORY. Harcourt, 1995.
Daniel is determined to have a birthday party for the world to celebrate Rosh Hashanah.

449. Levitin, Sonia. THE RETURN. Fawcett, 1987 (pap).
Desta and the other members of her Falasha family, Jews in Ethiopia, flee the country and attempt the dangerous journey to Israel.

450. Pearl, Sydelle. ELIJAH'S TEARS: STORIES FOR THE JEWISH HOLIDAYS. Holt, 1996.
The prophet Elijah appears in five stories about special Jewish days: Hanukkah, Yom Kippur, Sukkot, Pesach, and Shabbat.

451. Taylor, Sydney. ALL-OF-A KIND FAMILY. Dial, 1985 (pap).
The adventures of five sisters growing up in a Jewish family in New York City in the early twentieth century.

452. Yolen, Jane. THE DEVIL'S ARITHMETIC. Puffin, 1990 (pap).
Hannah resents hearing stories of the past and her Jewish heritage until, while opening the door during a Passover Seder, she finds herself in Poland during World War II and experiences the horrors of a concentration camp.

Religious Diversity – Judaism – Nonfiction

453. Chaikin, Miriam. MENORAHS, MEZUZAS, AND OTHER JEWISH SYMBOLS. Clarion, 1990.
Explains the history and significance of many Jewish symbols, such as the Shield of David, the menora, and the mezuza.

454. Fishman, Cathy. ON PASSOVER. Atheneum, 1997; Aladdin, 2000 (pap).
As her family prepares for Passover, a little girl learns about the many traditions which are part of the celebration of this holiday.

455. Goldin, Barbara. PASSOVER JOURNEY. Viking, 1994.
Retells the story of the Israelites' fight for liberation from slavery in Egypt, and explains the traditions of the Passover Seder.

456. Lamstein, Sarah. ANNIE'S SHABBAT. Whitman, 1997.
Shows how Annie and her family celebrate the Jewish Sabbath.

457. Schwartz, Howard. NEXT YEAR IN JERUSALEM: 3,000 YEARS OF JEWISH STORIES. Puffin, 1998 (pap).
Jewish stories set in Jerusalem, adapted from the Talmud and Midrash, Hasidic sources, and oral tradition.

Religious Diversity – Mexican – Nonfiction

458. Ancona, George. PABLO REMEMBERS: THE FIESTA OF THE DAY OF THE DEAD. Lothrop, 1993.
During the three-day celebration of the Days of the Dead, a young Mexican boy and his family make elaborate preparations to honor the spirits of the dead.

459. Hoyt-Goldsmith, Diane. DAY OF THE DEAD: A MEXICAN-AMERICAN CELEBRATION. Holiday, 1994.
Two Mexican-American sisters celebrate the Day of the Dead, which honors relatives and friends who are no longer living.

Religious Diversity – Mormonism– Fiction

460. Litchman, Kristin Embry. ALL IS WELL. Delacorte, c1998; Bantam, 1999 (pap).
In Salt Lake City in 1885, Emmy tries to maintain a friendship with Mariana, a Gentile or non-Mormon, even though Miranda's father works for a newspaper that says polygamists,like Emmy's father, should be jailed.

Religious Diversity – Sikhism – Nonfiction

461. Dhanjal, Beryl. WHAT DO WE KNOW ABOUT SIKHISM? Peter Bedrick, 1996.
An illustrated guide to the origins, history, practices, and beliefs of Sikhism.

Religious Diversity – Interfaith – Picture Book

462. Polacco, Patricia. MRS. KATZ AND TUSH. Dell, 1992 (pap).
A long-lasting friendship develops between Lernel, a young African-American, and Mrs. Katz, a lonely Jewish widow, when Lernel presents her with a scrawny kitten without a tail.

Religious Diversity – Interfaith – Fiction

463. Bishop, Claire. TWENTY AND TEN. Viking, 1952; Puffin, 1978 (pap).
Twenty school children hide ten Jewish children from the Nazis during the occupation of France during World War II.

464. Blume, Judy. ARE YOU THERE, GOD? IT'S ME, MARGARET. *SEE 276.*

465. Cohen, Barbara. MAKE A WISH, MOLLY. Illus. by Jon Maimo Jones. Dell, 1995.
Molly, who recently emigrated with her family from Russia to New Jersey, learns about birthday parties and who her real friends are.

466. Cohen, Barbara. MOLLY'S PILGRIM. Illus. by Michael J. Deraney. Lothrop, 1983; Bantam, 1985 (pap).
Told to make a Pilgrim doll for the Thanksgiving display at school, Molly is embarrassed when her mother creates a doll dressed as she herself was dressed before leaving Russia to seek religious freedom in the United States as a Jew.

467. Greene, Bette. SUMMER OF MY GERMAN SOLDIER. Puffin, 1999 (pap).
Sheltering an escaped German prisoner of war is the beginning of some shattering experiences for a twelve-year-old Jewish girl in Arkansas.

468. Hurwitz, Johanna. ONCE I WAS A PLUM TREE. Morrow, 1980.
Increasingly aware of the differences between her family, who are non-observant Jews, and their Catholic neighbors, ten-year-old Gerry begins to investigate her heritage.

469. Lowry, Lois. NUMBER THE STARS. Houghton, 1989; Dell, 1990 (pap).
In 1943, during the German occupation of Denmark, ten-year-old Annemarie learns how to be brave and courageous when she helps shelter her Jewish friend from the Nazis.

470. Rosen, Michael J. ELIJAH'S ANGEL. Harcourt, 1992.
At Christmas-Hanukkah time, a Christian woodcarver gives a carved angel to a young Jewish friend, who struggles with accepting the Christmas gift until he realizes that friendship means the same thing in any religion.

471. Sachs, Marilyn. PETER AND VERONICA. Puffin, 1969 (pap).
A twelve-year-old Jewish boy struggles to maintain his friendship with his tomboy classmate, Veronica, despite the opposition of their parents and disapproval of his other friends.

Religious Diversity – Interfaith – Nonfiction

472. Yolen, Jane. O JERUSALEM. Blue Sky Press, 1996.
A poetic tribute to Jerusalem, in honor of the 3000th anniversary of its founding, celebrates its history as a holy city for three major religions.

Social Issues – Series

473. BELIEFS AND CULTURES. Children's Press.
Introduces religions, describing the origins and traditions of each one. Includes related crafts and activities.

474. COMPARING RELIGIONS. Thomson Learning.
Describes the customs, rituals, ceremonies, and celebrations related to each life event in various cultures around the world.

475. MAKING THEIR MARK: WOMEN IN SCIENCE AND MEDICINE. PowerKids Press.
Biographies written for children in grades K-4 about successful women in a male dominated field.

Challenges

Physical Challenges • Mental Challenges •
Chronic Illness and Death • Physical Apperance •
Series

Illustration by Sean Murtha.

Challenges

Physical Challenges – Picture Books

476. Aseltine, Lorraine. I'M DEAF, AND IT'S OK. Illus. by Helen Coganberry. Whitman, 1986.
A young boy describes the frustrations caused by his deafness, and the encouragement he receives from a deaf teenager.

477. Carlson, Nancy L. ARNIE AND THE NEW KID. Puffin, 1992 (pap).
When an accident requires Arnie to use crutches, he begins to understand the limits and possibilities of his new classmate who requires a wheelchair.

478. Cohen, Miriam. SEE YOU TOMORROW, CHARLES. Illus. by Lillian Hoban. Dell, 1989 (pap).
The first graders learn to accept a new boy, Charles, who is blind.

479. Cowen-Fletcher, Jane. MAMA ZOOMS. Scholastic, 1993.
A boy's mother takes him zooming everywhere with her, because her wheelchair is a zooming machine.

480. Fassler, Joan. HOWIE HELPS HIMSELF. Illus. by Joe Lasker. Whitman, 1974.
Though he enjoys life with his family and attends school, Howie, a child with cerebral palsy, wants more than anything else to be able to move his wheelchair by himself.

481. Hoffman, Alice. FIREFLIES. Hyperion, c1997.
Jackie can't run and skate and throw as well as the other children, but his clumsiness eventually saves the villagers from a winter that would not end.

482. Lasker, Joe. NICK JOINS IN. Whitman, 1980.
When Nick, confined to a wheelchair, enters a regular classroom for the first time, he and his new classmates must resolve their initial apprehensions.

483. Martin, Bill. KNOTS ON A COUNTING ROPE. Illus. by Ted Rand. Holt, 1993.
A grandfather and his blind grandson reminisce about the young boy's birth, his first horse, and an exciting horse race.

484. Osofsky, Audrey. MY BUDDY. Illus. by Ted Rand. Holt, 1992.
A young boy with muscular dystrophy tells how he is teamed up with a dog trained to do things for him that he can't do for himself.

485. Rau, Dana Meachen. THE SECRET CODE. Children's Press, c1998.
Oscar, who is blind, teaches Lucy how to read his Braille book.

486. Strom, Maria Diaz. RAINBOW JOE AND ME. Lee & Low, c1999.
Eloise shares her love of colors with her blind friend Rainbow Joe, who makes his own colors when he plays beautiful notes on his saxophone.

Physical Challenges – Intermediate

487. Abbott, Deborah. ONE TV BLASTING AND A PIG OUTDOORS. Whitman, 1994.
Conan describes life with his father, who lost his hearing at age three.

488. Christopher, Matt. CATCH THAT PASS. Little, 1989.
Everyone knows Jim will be the star linebacker on the team if he can only conquer his fear of being tackled, but it takes a boy in a wheelchair to teach him that kind of courage.

489. Emmert, Michelle. I'M THE BIG SISTER NOW. Whitman, 1989.
A nine-year-old describes the joys, loving times, difficulties and special situations involved in living with her older sister, who was born severely disabled with cerebral palsy.

490. Griese, Arnold. AT THE MOUTH OF THE LUCKIEST RIVER. Boyds Mills, 1996 (pap).
A lame Athabascan Indian boy confronts his tribe's medicine man in an effort to prevent trouble with the Eskimos.

491. Hodges, Margaret. THE HERO OF BREMEN. Holiday, 1993.
Retells the German legend in which a shoemaker who cannot walk helps the town of Bremen, aided by the spirit of the great hero Roland.

492. Konigsburg, E.L. THE VIEW FROM SATURDAY. Atheneum, 1996; Aladdin, 1998 (pap).
Four students develop a special bond and attract the attention of their teacher, a paraplegic, who chooses them to represent their sixth-grade class in the New York State Academic Bowl competition.

493. Lee, Jeanne. SILENT LOTUS. Farrar Straus & Giroux, 1991.
Although she cannot speak or hear, Lotus trains as a Khmer court dancer and becomes eloquent in dancing out the legends of the gods.

494. MacLachlan, Patricia. THROUGH GRANDPA'S EYES. Harper, 1980.
A young boy learns a different way of seeing the world from his blind grandfather.

495. Moore, Eva. BUDDY, THE FIRST SEEING EYE DOG. Scholastic, 1996 (pap).
True account of the training and early work experiences of the German Shepherd who became the first seeing eye dog in America.

496. Nichol, Barbara. BEETHOVEN LIVES UPSTAIRS. Orchard, 1994.
The letters that ten-year-old Christoph and his uncle exchange show how Christoph's feelings for Mr. Beethoven, the eccentric boarder who shares his house and is losing his hearing, change from anger and embarrassment to compassion and admiration.

497. Warner, Sally. ACCIDENTAL LILY. Knopf, c1999.
With help from her mother and brother, six-year-old Lily begins to tackle her bed-wetting problem so that she can go to a sleepover party.

498. Weaver, Lydia. CLOSE TO HOME. Puffin, 1997 (pap).
In the summer of 1952, Betsy sees her vacation fun overshadowed by the spreading polio epidemic, while her mother and other scientists work frantically to develop a vaccine.

499. Weik, Mary. THE JAZZ MAN. Macmillan, 1993 (pap).
A nine-year old boy who is lame and living in Harlem finds new meaning in life when the Jazz Man with his wonderful music moves into a room across the court,

Physical Challenges – Nonfiction – Intermediate

500. Carter, Alden R. SEEING THINGS MY WAY. Whitman, 1998.
   A second-grader describes how she and other students learn to use a variety of equipment and methods to cope with their visual impairments.

501. Davidson, Margaret. LOUIS BRAILLE. Scholastic, 1997 (pap).
   The life of the nineteenth century Frenchman, who lost his sight in a tragic accident and invented an alphabet enabling the blind to read.

502. Davidson, Margaret. HELEN KELLER. Scholastic, 1997 (pap).
   The bestselling biography of Helen Keller describes how, with the commitment and lifelong friendship of Anne Sullivan, she learned to talk, read, and eventually graduate from college with honors.

503. McMahon, Patricia. LISTEN FOR THE BUS: DAVID'S STORY. Boyds Mills, 1995.
   A real-life look at David, who is blind, as he begins kindergarten.

504. O'Connor, Barbara. THE WORLD AT HIS FINGERTIPS: A STORY ABOUT LOUIS BRAILLE. Carolrhoda, c1997.
   A biography of the blind nineteenth-century Frenchman who created the dot system of reading and writing that is now used throughout the world.

505. Osinski, Alice. FRANKLIN D. ROOSEVELT. Childrens, 1987.
   A look at the life and career of the thirty-second president of the United States, who was a Polio victim.

506. Peterson, Jeanne. I HAVE A SISTER - MY SISTER IS DEAF. Harper, 1977.
   A young girl describes how her deaf sister experiences everyday life.

507. Powers, Mary E. OUR TEACHER'S IN A WHEELCHAIR. Whitman, 1986.
   Brian Hanson is able to lead an active existence as a nursery school teacher despite partial paralysis requiring the use of a wheelchair.

508. Sabin, Francene. COURAGE OF HELEN KELLER. Troll, 1982.
   After a childhood illness leaves her blind and deaf, Helen Keller learns to communicate through the efforts of her young teacher, Anne Sullivan.

Physical Challenges – Fiction

509. Blume, Judy. DEENIE. Bradbury, 1982; Dell, 1991 (pap).
   A thirteen-year-old girl seemingly destined for a modeling career finds she has a deformation of the spine called scoliosis.

510. Fleischman, Paul. HALF-A-MOON INN. Trophy, 1980 (pap).
   A mute boy is held captive by the strange proprietress of an inn.

511. Forbes, Esther. JOHNNY TREMAIN. Houghton, 1943; Dell, 1971.
   After his hand is permanently maimed in an accident, thirteen-year-old Johnny gets caught up in the events leading to the American Revolution.

512. Hartling, Peter. CRUTCHES. Lothrop Lee, 1988.
   A young boy, searching vainly for his mother in postwar Vienna, is befriended by a man on crutches.

513. Hermann, Spring. SEEING LESSONS; THE STORY OF ABIGAIL CARTER AND AMERICA'S FIRST SCHOOL FOR THE BLIND. Holt, 1998.
Two blind sisters attend the first school for the blind in America, located in Boston.

514. Little, Jean. FROM ANNA. Harper, 1972.
Anna cannot learn to read due to low vision. Her outlook improves when she gets glasses and goes to a special school.

515. McElfresh, Lynn E. CAN YOU FEEL THE THUNDER? Atheneum, 1999.
Thirteen-year-old Mic Parsons struggles with mixed feelings about his deaf and blind sister while at the same time he makes his way through the turmoil of junior high.

516. Paulsen, Gary. THE MONUMENT. Yearling, 1993 (pap).
Thirteen-year-old Rocky, self-conscious about the braces on her leg, has her life changed by the remarkable artist who comes to her small Kansas town to design a war memorial.

517. Robinet, Harriette. FORTY ACRES AND MAYBE A MULE. Atheneum, 1998; Aladdin, 1999 (pap).
Born with a withered leg and hand, Pascal, who is about twelve years old, joins other former slaves in a search for a farm and the freedom which it promises.

518. Rostkowski, Margaret I. AFTER THE DANCING DAYS. Harper, 1986; Trophy, 1988 (pap).
Thirteen-year-old Annie meets Andrew, a badly burned young veteran of World War I, whom she helps adjust to a new life.

519. Taylor, Theodore. THE CAY. Doubleday, 1969.
During World War II, Philip Enright, blinded by a blow to the head, is cast ashore on a barren cay with an old West Indian man, who helps Philip adjust to his blindness.

Physical Challenges – Nonfiction – Upper Elementary Grades

520. Freedman, Russell. FRANKLIN DELANO ROOSEVELT. Clarion, 1990 (pap).
Stricken by polio in early adulthood, Franklin D. Roosevelt utilized a wheelchair and crutches for most of his life.

521. Keller, Helen. THE STORY OF MY LIFE. Bantam, 1990 (pap).
Deaf and blind Helen Keller recounts how she came to function and succeed once she became educated through her own determination and the devotion of her teacher, Anne Sullivan.

Mental Challenges – Autism – Picture Books

522. Lears, Laurie. IAN'S WALK: A STORY ABOUT AUTISM. Whitman, 1998.
Ian, who is autistic, takes a walk with his sisters and demonstrates how he sees, hears, smells, and tastes things .

Mental Challenges – Autism – Fiction

523. Martin, Ann M. KRISTY AND THE SECRET OF SUSAN. Gareth Stevens, 1995.
The babysitters club has a new sitting charge, a baby who has autism.

Mental Challenges – Autism – Nonfiction

524. Gold, Phyllis. PLEASE DON'T SAY HELLO. Human Science Press, 1986. *SEE 495.*

525. Amenta, Charles A. RUSSELL IS EXTRA SPECIAL: A BOOK ABOUT AUTISM FOR CHILDREN. Magination, c1992.
    Describes the daily life, likes and dislikes, and habits of Russell Amenta, who is severely autistic.

Mental Challenges – Brain-Injured – Fiction

526. Emmert, Michelle. I'M THE BIG SISTER NOW. *SEE 489.*

Mental Challenges – Depression – Picture Books

527. Hamilton, DeWitt. SAD DAYS, GLAD DAYS. Illus. by Gail Owens. Whitman, 1995.
    Amanda Martha tries to understand her mother's depression, which sometimes makes her sleep all day, feel sad, or cry.

528. MacLachlan, Patricia. MAMA ONE, MAMA TWO. Illus. by Ruth Lercher Bornstein. Harper, 1982.
    A young child deals with depression as she lives with a foster family until her mother is well enough to care for her.

Mental Challenges – Depression – Fiction

529. Franklin, Kristine L. ECLIPSE. Candlewick Press, 1995.
    Trina's father falls into a severe depression after losing his job.

530. Oneal, Zibby. THE LANGUAGE OF GOLDFISH. Puffin, 1990 (pap).
    Unable to relate to her parents, make friends at her new school, or adjust to her family's new affluence, thirteen-year-old Carrie is gradually losing the desire to live.

531. Sachs, Marilyn. THE BEARS' HOUSE. Puffin, 1996 (pap).
    A classroom dollhouse with toy bears serves as Fran Ellen's fantasy, and helps her cope with her mother's depression.

532. Wright, Betty. ROSIE AND THE DANCE OF THE DINOSAURS. Holiday, 1989.
    Rosie discovers that having nine fingers can be an asset as she faces the challenges of an upcoming piano recital and the absence of her father, who moved away to find a new job.

Mental Challenges – Down Syndrome – Picture Books

533. Carter, Alden R. BIG BROTHER DUSTIN. Illus. by Dan Young and Carol Carter. Whitman, 1997.
    A boy with Down Syndrome helps his parents get ready for the birth of his baby sister, and chooses the perfect name for her.

534. Carter, Alden, R. DUSTIN'S BIG SCHOOL DAY. Whitman, 1999.
    Second-grader Dustin, who has Down Syndrome, anticipates the arrival of two very special guests at his school.

535. Fleming, Virginia. BE GOOD TO EDDIE LEE. Illus. by Floyd Cooper. Philomel, 1993; Paper Star, 1997 (pap).
    A boy with Down Syndrome shares special discoveries with a young girl.

536. Rabe, Berniece. WHERE'S CHIMPY? Illus. by Diane Schmidt. Whitman, 1988.
A little girl with Down Syndrome and her father review her day's activities while they search for a stuffed monkey.

537. Testa, Maria. THUMBS UP RICO. Whitman, 1994.
A boy with Down Syndrome makes a new friend, helps his sister with a difficult decision, and finally draws a picture he likes.

Mental Challenges – Down Syndrome – Fiction

538. Buchanan, Dawna L. THE FALCON'S WING. Orchard, 1992.
After her mother's death, a twelve-year-old girl moves in with her cousin, who has Down Syndrome.

539. Fox, Paula. RADIANCE DESCENDING: A NOVEL. DK, 1997; Laureleaf, 1999. (pap).
When he sees all the attention which his parents and people in the neighborhood give to Jacob, eleven-year-old Paul struggles with his feelings toward this younger brother who has Down Syndrome.

540. Stuve-Bodeen, Stephanie. WE'LL PAINT THE OCTOPUS RED. Illus. by Pam DeVito. Woodbine House, c1998.
Emma and her father discuss what they will do when the new baby arrives, but they adjust their expectations when he is born with Down Syndrome.

541. Wood, June R. THE MAN WHO LOVED CLOWNS. Putnam, 1992; Hyperion, 1995 (pap).
A young girl loves her uncle, but is sometimes ashamed of his behavior because he has Down Syndrome.

Mental Challenges – Eating Disorders – Nonfiction

542. Brooks, Bruce. VANISHING. *SEE 4.*

Mental Challenges – Eating Disorders – Nonfiction

543. Bode, Janet. FOOD FIGHT: A GUIDE TO EATING DISORDERS FOR PRE-TEENS AND THEIR PARENTS. Simon & Schuster, 1997; Aladdin, 1998 (pap).
A comprehensive guide to eating diosrders, discussing their causes, symptoms, and solutions.

Mental Challenges – Epilepsy – Fiction

544. Rylant, Cynthia. A BLUE-EYED DAISY. *SEE 8.*

Mental Challenges – Mental Illness – Fiction

545. Antle, Nancy. LOST IN THE WAR. Dial, c1998.
Twelve-year-old Lisa Grey struggles to cope with a mother whose traumatic experiences as a nurse in Vietnam during the war are still haunting her.

546. Hamilton, Virginia. THE PLANET OF JUNIOR BROWN. Macmillan, 1971; Aladdin, 1993 (pap).
Buddy Clark takes on the responsibility of protecting the overweight, emotionally disturbed friend with whom he has been playing hooky.

547. Hanson, Regina. THE FACE AT THE WINDOW. Clarion, 1997.
When Dora tries to take a mango from Miss Nella's tree, she is frightened by the woman's strange behavior.

548. Levoy, Myron. ALAN AND NAOMI. Trophy, 1987 (pap).
In New York during the 1940's, a boy tries to befriend a girl traumatized by Nazi brutality in France.

549. Martin, Patricia. MEMORY JUG. *SEE 111.*

Mental Challenges – Mental Retardation – Fiction

550. Byars, Betsy C. THE SUMMER OF THE SWANS. Viking, 1970.
A teenage girl gains new insight into herself and her family when her mentally retarded brother gets lost.

551. Carrick, Carol. STAY AWAY FROM SIMON. Clarion, 1985.
Lucy and her younger brother examine their feelings about a mentally handicapped boy whom they fear.

552. Mazer, Harry. THE WILD KID. Simon & Schuster, c1998.
Twelve-year-old Sammy, who is mildly retarded, runs away from home and becomes a prisoner of Kevin, a wild kid living in the woods.

553. Shyer, Marlene F. WELCOME HOME, JELLYBEAN. Aladdin, 1988.
A boy's life changes when his retarded sister leaves an institution to live at home.

554. Williams, Karen L. A REAL CHRISTMAS THIS YEAR. Clarion, 1995.
A twelve-year-old girl tries to provide a real Christmas for her multiply handicapped brother.

555. Wood, June R. WHEN PIGS FLY. Putnam, 1995.
A thirteen-year-old and her best friend do everything together, including taking care of her mentally retarded younger sister.

Mental Challenges – Mental Retardation – Nonfiction

556. McNey, Martha. LESLIE'S STORY. Lerner, 1996.
A description of the home and school life of a twelve-year-old girl who is mentally retarded.

Mental Challenges – Schizophrenia – Easy Reader

557. Kroll, Virginia. MY SISTER, THEN AND NOW. Illus. by Mary Worcester. Carolrhoda, 1992.
Ten-year-old Rachel describes how her twenty-year-old sister's schizophrenia has affected the family, and expresses her own feelings of sadness and anger.

Mental Challenges – Schizophrenia – Fiction

558. Rubalcaba, Jill. SAINT VITUS' DANCE. Clarion, 1996.
Thirteen-year-old Melanie feels angry and guilty because she is worried about herself instead of her mother, who has Huntington's chorea, a hereditary condition, until Melanie finds the strength to face her mother's illness and her own uncertain future.

Mental Challenges – Learning Disabilities – Picture Books

559. Carlson, Nancy. SIT STILL! Viking, 1996; Puffin, 1998 (pap).
Patrick, who exhibits symptoms of Attention Deficit Disorder, has difficulty sitting still until his mother comes up with a plan to help him.

560. Kraus, Robert. LEO THE LATE BLOOMER. Illus. by Jose Aruego. HarperCollins, 1971.
Leo, a young tiger, finally blooms under the anxious eyes of his parents.

561. Lasker, Joe. HE'S MY BROTHER. Whitman, 1974.
A young boy describes the experiences of his slow-learning younger brother at school and at home.

Mental Challenges – Learning Disabilities – Intermediate

562. Giff, Patricia Reilly. THE BEAST IN MS. ROONEY'S ROOM. Dell, 1984 (pap).
Held back for a year in second grade, Richard can't seem to help getting into trouble, until he gets interested in reading and helps his class in a special way.

563. Giff, Patricia Reilly. TODAY WAS A TERRIBLE DAY. Illus. by Susanna Natti. Viking, 1980.
Follows the mishaps of a second grader who is learning to read with difficulty.

564. Kline, Suzy. HERBIE JONES. Putnam, 1985.
Herbie's experiences in the third grade include finding bones in the boys' bathroom, wandering away from his class on their field trip, and being promoted to a higher reading group.

565. Shreve, Susan. THE FLUNKING OF JOSHUA T. BATES. Random, 1984.
Driving home from the beach on Labor Day, Joshua receives the shocking news from his mother that he must repeat third grade.

566. Smith, Mark. PAY ATTENTION, SLOSH! Whitman, 1997.
Eight-year-old Josh hates being unable to concentrate or control himself, but with the help of his parents, his teacher, and a doctor, he learns to deal with his condition, known as ADHD or Attention-Deficit Hyperactivity Disorder.

Mental Challenges – Learning Disabilities - Fiction

567. Avi. MAN FROM THE SKY. Beech Tree, 1992 (pap).
In an almost fool-proof scheme, a man parachutes from an airplane with a large amount of money, only to be seen by a dyslexic boy who has a reputation for seeing things in the clouds.

568. Banks, Jacqueline Turner. EGG-DROP BLUES. Houghton Mifflin, 1995.
Twelve-year-old Judge Jenkins has a low science grade because of his dyslexia, so he convinces his twin brother Jury to work with him in a science competition in order to earn extra credit.

569. Barrie, Barbara. ADAM ZIGZAG. Delacorte, 1994; Bantam, 1996 (pap).
Adam, who is dyslexic and has great difficulty with his homework, struggles to find the right school, resist the lure of drugs, and endure the jealousy of his older sister.

570. Betancourt, Jeanne. MY NAME IS ~~BRAIN~~ BRIAN. Scholastic, 1993 (pap).
Although he is helped by his new sixth grade teacher after being diagnosed as dyslexic, Brian still has some problems with school and with people he thought were his friends.

571. Cutler, Jane. SPACEMAN. Dutton, 1997; Puffin, 1999 (pap).
Ten-year-old Gary, who is failing the fifth grade and has trouble getting along with other students, tries to adjust to his learning disability and his assignment to a special education class.

572. DeClements, Barthe. SIXTH GRADE CAN REALLY KILL YOU. Viking, 1985.
Helen fears that lack of improvement in reading may leave her stuck in the sixth grade forever, until a good teacher recognizes her reading problem as dyslexia.

573. Gehret, Jeanne. THE DON'T-GIVE-UP KID AND LEARNING DIFFERENCES. Verbal Images Press, 1992.
Alex learns to cope with his reading disability once he discovers that his idol Thomas Edison had dyslexia.

574. Gehret, Jeanne. EAGLE EYES. Verbal Images Press, 1991.
Ben causes disruptions at school and at home until he learns to recognize and adapt to his Attention Deficit Disorder.

575. Hansen, Joyce. YELLOW BIRD AND ME. Clarion, 1986.
Doris becomes friends with Yellow Bird as she helps him with his studies and his part in the school play, and discovers he has a problem known as dyslexia.

576. Hesse, Karen. JUST JUICE. *SEE 29.*

577. Janover, Caroline. JOSH: A BOY WITH DYSLEXIA. Waterfront Books, 1988.
Josh struggles to live down the stigma of having a learning disability, and to receive both respect and friendship from his peers.

578. Schlieper, Anne. THE BEST FIGHT. Whitman, 1995.
Fifth-grader Jamie, who goes to a special class because he has difficulty reading, thinks he is stupid until the school principal helps him realize that he also has many talents.

Mental Challenges – Learning Disabilities - Nonfiction

579. Cummings, Rhoda. SCHOOL SURVIVAL GUIDE FOR KIDS WITH LD. Free Spirit Pub., 1991.
A guide for children with learning disabilities on how to get along in a school setting.

580. Dwyer, Kathleen M. WHAT DO YOU MEAN I HAVE ATTENTION DEFICIT DISORDER? Walker, 1996.
Follows eleven-year-old Patrick's difficulties at home and at school until he is diagnosed with Attention Deficit Hyperactivity Disorder and learns how to deal with it.

581. Fisher, Gary. SURVIVAL GUIDE FOR KIDS WITH LD. Free Spirit Pub., 1990.
A handbook for kids with learning disabilities that discusses different types of disorders, programs at school, coping with negative feelings, and making friends. Includes a section for parents and teachers.

582. Hall, David E. LIVING WITH LEARNING DISABILITIES: A GUIDE FOR STUDENTS. Lerner, 1993.
Describes various learning disabilities, such as Attention Deficit Disorder, fine motor problems, and difficulties with visual information.

583. KIDS EXPLORE THE GIFTS OF CHILDREN WITH SPECIAL NEEDS. John Muir, 1994.
Children in a writing workshop describe the lives of ten young people with special needs, including a boy with fetal alcohol syndrome, a girl with cerebral palsy, and a boy with dyslexia.

584. Roby, Cynthia. WHEN LEARNING IS TOUGH: KIDS TALK ABOUT THEIR LEARNING DISABILITIES. Whitman, 1994.
Children describe their learning disabilities, talents, learning techniques, and misconceptions associated with learning disabilities.

Chronic Illness and Death – AIDS – Picture Books

585. Jordan, Mary. LOSING UNCLE TIM. Illus. by Judith Friedman. *SEE 388.*

Chronic Illness and Death – AIDS – Fiction

586. Bantle, Lee F. DIVING FOR THE MOON. Macmillan, 1995.
The summer after they finish the sixth grade, Bird discovers that her best friend Josh is HIV positive.

587. Durant, Penny Ralfe. WHEN HEROES DIE. *SEE 393.*

588. Porte, Barbara A. SOMETHING TERRIBLE HAPPENED. Orchard, 1994; Troll, 1994 (pap).
Gillian is ten years old when her mother is diagnosed with AIDS, then dies. Sent to live with relatives in rural Tennessee that she has never met, she withdraws at first, then learns to move on with her life.

589. Zalben, Jane Breskin. UNFINISHED DREAMS. Simon & Schuster, 1996.
Jason, a nine-year old, pursues his dream of becoming a great violinist even as he deals with disappointments and the deaths of loved ones.

Chronic Illness and Death – AIDS – Non-Fiction

590. Brimner, Larry Dane. THE NAMES PROJECT: THE AIDS QUILT. Children's Press, 1999.
Describes the continually growing quilt that is being created as a memorial to those who have died of AIDS and to draw attention to this devastating disease.

591. Gedatus, Gustav Mark. HIV AND AIDS. Capstone, 2000.
Discusses the history of AIDS, its causes, stages, diagnosis, treatments, and related research.

Chronic Illness and Death – Alzheimer's Disease – Picture Books

592. Kibbey, Marsha. MY GRAMMY. Illus. by Karen Ritz. Carolrhoda, 1988.
When eight-year-old Amy has to share her bedroom with Grammy, an Alzheimer's patient, she is at first resentful, but eventually comes to accept Grammy's needs and helps out when she can.

593. Kroll, Virginia. FIREFLIES, PEACH PIES, AND LULLABIES. Illus. by Nancy Cote. Simon & Schuster, 1995.
When Francie's Great-Granny Annabel dies of Alzheimer's disease, Francie finds a way to help people remember the real person, rather than the shell she had become as the disease ran its course.

Chronic Illness and Death – Alzheimer's Disease - Fiction

594. Bahr, Mary. THE MEMORY BOX. Whitman, 1992.
    When Gramps realizes he has Alzheimer's disease, he starts a memory box with his grandson Zach, to keep memories of all the times they have shared.

595. Kehret, Peg. NIGHT OF FEAR. Cobblehill, 1994; Pocket, 1996 (pap).
    Thirteen-year-old T.J. and his grandmother, who has Alzheimer's disease, find their lives in danger when they discover a disturbed arsonist hiding in a bar.

Chronic Illness and Death – Alzheimer's Disease – Non-Fiction

596. Landau, Elaine. ALZHEIMER'S DISEASE. Franklin Watts, 1996.
    Discusses the degenerative disease of the nervous system, its effect on the patient's family members, and suggestions for coping and care.

Chronic Illness and Death – Asthma - Fiction

597. Harrison, Troon. AARON'S AWFUL ALLERGIES. Kids Can Press, 1998.
    When he starts sneezing and wheezing Aaron's mom takes him to the doctor who explains that he is allergic to animals and that he must give away all his dogs, cats and guinea pigs.

598. Kudlinski, Kathleen V. FACING WEST: A STORY OF THE OREGON TRAIL. Puffin, 1996 (pap).
    As his family sets out from Missouri to Oregon, young Ben wonders whether he will experience more trouble with the dangers of the journey, or his debilitating asthma.

599. London, Jonathan. THE LION WHO HAD ASTHMA. Whitman, 1992.
    Sean's nebulizer mask and his imagination aid in his recovery following an asthma attack.

Chronic Illness and Death – Asthma – Non-Fiction

600. Carter, Siri M. I'M TOUGHER THAN ASTHMA! Whitman, 1996.
    A young girl describes what it is like to live with asthma.

601. Gosselin, Kim. THE ABC'S OF ASTHMA: AN ASTHMA ALPHABET BOOK FOR KIDS OF ALL AGES. JayJo Books, 1998.
    Uses the individual letters of the alphabet to explain twenty six aspects of the disease.

602. Ostrow, William. ALL ABOUT ASTHMA. Whitman, 1989.
    The young narrator describes life as an asthmatic, explaining causes and symptoms, and also discusses ways to control the disorder in order to lead a normal life.

Chronic Illness and Death – Cancer – Picture Books

603. Krisher, Trudy. KATHY'S HATS. Illus. by Nadine Bernard Westcott. Whitman, 1992.
    Kathy's love of hats comes in handy when the chemotherapy treatments she has received for her cancer make her hair fall out.

604. Vigna, Judith. WHEN ERIC'S MOM FOUGHT CANCER. Whitman, 1993.
    A ski trip with his father helps a young boy, who copes with fear and anger when his mother is diagnosed with breast cancer.

Chronic Illness and Death – Cancer – Intermediate

605. Borden, Louise. GOOD LUCK, MRS. K! McElderry, c1999.
All the students in the third grade are affected when their beloved teacher, Mrs. Kempczinski, is suddenly hospitalized with cancer.

606. Carrick, Carol. UPSIDE-DOWN CAKE. Clarion, c1999.
A nine-year-old boy tries to come to terms with his grief and anger when his father develops cancer, gradually becomes weaker, and then dies.

Chronic Illness and Death – Cancer – Fiction

607. Bennett, Cherie. ZINK. Delacorte, 1999.
Becky's leukemia diagnosis has introduced her to a scary world of hospitals, blood counts, and chemotherapy. As least she's got a trio of singing zebras to keep her company and boost her spirits!

608. Brisson, Pat. SKY MEMORIES. Delacorte, 1999.
When ten-year-old Emily learns that her mother has cancer, the two of them begin a ritual that will help Emily remember her mother after she is dead.

609. Coerr, Eleanor. SADAKO AND THE THOUSAND PAPER CRANES. *SEE 105.*

610. Hermes, Patricia. YOU SHOULDN'T HAVE TO SAY GOOD-BYE. Scholastic, 1984.
During autumn, twelve-year-old Sarah learns that her mother is dying of cancer.

611. Tomlinson, Theresa. DANCING THROUGH THE SHADOWS. DK Ink, c1997.
When she learns that her mother has cancer, Ellen finds that preparing for a special dance and helping with an archaeological dig help her to cope.

612. Wallace, Bill. THE CHRISTMAS SPURS. Holiday, 1990; Pocket, 1991 (pap).
A small private miracle helps Nick accept the fate of his younger brother who is dying of leukemia, and go forward with renewed faith.

613. Warner, Sally. SORT OF FOREVER. Random, c1998; Knopf, 1999 (pap).
A look at the friendship between the needy and dependent twelve-year-old Cady and her independent, feisty best friend Nana, who is dying of cancer.

Chronic Illness and Death – Cancer – Nonfiction

614. Peacock, Judith. LEUKEMIA. Capstone, 2000.
Discusses the disease, its diagnosis and treatments, and related research.

Chronic Illness and Death – Cerebral Palsy – Nonfiction

615. Peacock, Judith. CEREBRAL PALSY. Capstone, 2000.
Presents the causes, diagnosis, symptoms, and treatment of cerebral palsy, as well as current research and possible ways of preventing this disorder.

Chronic Illness and Death – Cystic Fibrosis – Fiction

616. Grishaw, Joshua. MY HEART IS FULL OF WISHES. Raintree Steck-Vaughan, 1995.
A young boy with cystic fibrosis describes some of his fears and dreams for a better life.

Chronic Illness and Death – Death and Dying – Picture Books

617. Anaya, Rudolfo. FAROLITOS FOR ABUELO. Hyperion, c1998.
When Luz's beloved grandfather dies, she places luminaria around his grave on Christmas Eve as a way of remembering him.

618. Barron, T. A. WHERE IS GRANDPA? Philomel, 2000.
Confused about the death of his grandfather, a young boy begins to think that he may be lost and so tries to find him in this touching tale about coping with loss for beginning readers.

619. Brown, Margaret. THE DEAD BIRD. Harper, 1965.
The bird was dead when the children found it, so they dug a grave in the woods, buried it, and sang a song to it.

620. De Paola, Tomie. NANA UPSTAIRS AND NANA DOWNSTAIRS. Putnam, 1987.
A small boy enjoys his relationship with his grandmother and his great-grandmother, and learns to face their inevitable death.

621. Hickox, Ruth. GREAT-GRANDMOTHER'S TREASURE. Illus. by David Soman. Dial, c1998.
Great-Grandmother puts all the treasured experiences of her life into her apron and takes them with her when she dies.

622. Miles, Mishka. ANNIE AND THE OLD ONE. *SEE 100.*

623. Rudner, Barry. WILL I STILL HAVE TO MAKE MY BED IN THE MORNING? Illus by Peggy Trabalka. Tiny Thought, 1992.
A healthy boy and his terminally ill best friend hold fast to the dreams of childhood.

624. Schneider, Antonie. GOOD-BYE, VIVI! Illus. by Maja Dusikova. North-South Books, 1998.
When Granny's beloved canary Vivi dies, the family comes to accept it, as well as the idea that some day they will lose Granny as well.

625. Varley, Susan. BADGER'S PARTING GIFTS. Lothrop Lee, 1984.
Badger's friends are sad when he dies, but they treasure the legacies he left them.

626. Vigna, Judith. SAYING GOOD-BYE TO DADDY. *SEE 102.*

627. Viorst, Judith. THE TENTH GOOD THING ABOUT BARNEY. Illus. by Erik Blegvad. Atheneum, 1971.
In an attempt to overcome his grief, a boy tries to think of the ten best things about his dead cat.

628. Zalben, Jane Breskin. PEARL'S MARIGOLDS FOR GRANDPA. Simon & Schuster, c1997.
A young girls remembers all the things she loved about her grandfather after he dies. Includes information about funeral customs of various religions.

Chronic Illness and Death – Death and Dying - Fiction

629. Bacon, Katharine. FINN. McElderry, c1998.
Unable to speak after his parents and sister are killed in a plane crash, sixteen-year-old Finn comes to stay with his grandmother on her Vermont farm, where various situations force him to face his grief.

630. Bauer, Marion D. ON MY HONOR. Clarion, 1986; Dell, 1987 (pap).
When his best friend drowns swimming with him in a treacherous river that they had promised never to go near, Joel is devastated and terrified of having to tell both sets of parents the terrible consequences of their disobedience.

631. Brisson, Pat. SKY MEMORIES. *SEE 608.*

632. Buchanan, Jane. GRATEFULLY YOURS. *SEE 202.*

633. Byars, Betsy. GOOD-BYE, CHICKEN LITTLE. Trophy, 1990 (pap).
A boy discovers that he doesn't have to feel personally responsible for his uncle's drowning.

634. Carson, Jo. YOU HOLD ME AND I'LL HOLD YOU. Illus. by Annie Cannon. Orchard, 1992.
When a great-aunt dies, a young child is comforted when being held and when holding, too.

635. Caseley, Judith. DOROTHY'S DARKEST DAYS. Greenwillow, c1997.
Dorothy's boisterous life with her parents, two brothers, and sister is suddenly changed when something tragic happens to a classmate of hers, but she finds that things eventually do return to normal.

636. Conly, Jane. CRAZY LADY. Harper, 1993; Trophy, 1995.
As he tries to come to terms with his mother's death, Vernon develops a growing relationship with the neighborhood outcasts, an alcoholic and her mentally retarded son.

637. Greene, Constance. BEAT THE TURTLE DRUM. Puffin, 1994 (pap).
A young girl learns to cope with her feelings about her sister's accidental death.

638. Hickman, Janet. SUSANNAH. Greenwillow, c1998.
After her mother's death, fourteen-year-old Susannah is taken by her father to live in a Shaker community in Ohio, but she does not find the same sense of peace there that he does.

639. L'Engle, Madeleine. A RING OF ENDLESS LIGHT. Farrar, Straus & Giroux, 1981; Dell, c1980 (pap).
During the summer her grandfather is dying of leukemia and death seems all around, fifteen-year-old Vicky is occupied with the pod of dolphins with whom she has been doing research.

640. Martin, Patricia. MEMORY JUG. *SEE 111.*

641. Naylor, Phyllis R. THE AGONY OF ALICE. Atheneum, 1985; Aladdin, 1997 (pap).
Eleven-year-old, motherless Alice decides she needs a gorgeous role model who does everything right. When placed in homely Mrs. Plotkins's class she is greatly disappointed until she discovers it's what people are inside that counts.

642. Park, Barbara . MICK HARTE WAS HERE. Knopf, 1995; Random, 1996 (pap).
Thirteen-year-old Phoebe recalls her younger brother and his death in a bicycle accident.

643. Paterson, Katherine. BRIDGE TO TERABITHIA. Crowell, 1977; Harper, 1987 (pap).
The life of a ten-year-old boy in rural Virginia expands when he becomes friends with a newcomer who subsequently meets an untimely death.

644. Paulsen, Gary. CHRISTMAS SONATA. Bantam, 1992 (pap).
When a little boy spends Christmas with his dying cousin, they discover that Santa really does exist.

645. Rodowsky, Colby F. THE TURNABOUT SHOP. Farrar Straus & Giroux, 1998; Trophy, 2000 (pap).
In "conversations" with her dead mother, fifth-grader Livvy records her adjustment to living in Baltimore with a woman she had never met, and she comes to see the wisdom of her mother's choice as she gets to know the woman's large, loving family.

646. Smith, Doris B. A TASTE OF BLACKBERRIES. HarperCollins, 1992.
A young boy recounts his efforts to adjust to the accidental death of his best friend.

647. Spelman, Cornelia. AFTER CHARLOTTE'S MOM DIED. Whitman, 1996.
Because her mom's death causes six-year-old Charlotte to feel sad, mad and scared, she and her dad visit a therapist who helps them acknowledge and express their feelings.

648. Wilson, Nancy Hope. FLAPJACK WALTZES. *SEE 114.*

649. Wittbold, Maureen. MENDING PETER'S HEART. Portunus Pub., 1995.
Peter learns to handle his grief over the death of his dog, Mishka, with the assistance of his neighbor, Mr. MacIntire, who helps him express his feelings by telling Peter how he feels about the loss of his wife

Chronic Illness and Death – Death and Dying – Non-Fiction

650. Brown, Laurie K. WHEN DINOSAURS DIE: A GUIDE TO UNDERSTANDING DEATH. Illus. by Marc Tolon Brown. Little Brown, 1996.
Explains in simple language the feelings people may have regarding the death of a loved one, and the ways to honor the memory of someone who has died.

651. Gellman, Marc. LOST AND FOUND: A KIDS BOOK FOR LIVING THROUGH LOSS. Morrow, c1999.
Describes different kinds of losses – losing possessions, competitions, health, trust, and permanent loss because of death – and discusses how to handle these situations.

652. Johnston, Marianne. LET'S TALK ABOUT GOING TO A FUNERAL. PowerKids Press, 1997.
Gives an overview of what a funeral is, why our culture holds them, and what might happen at one.

653. Levete, Sarah. WHEN PEOPLE DIE. Copper Beech, 1998.
Describes how people feel about death, discussing what happens when someone dies, why people die, and how to cope with grief.

654. Rushton, Lucy. DEATH CUSTOMS. Thomson Learning, 1995.
Examines the customs associated with death in six major religions of the world, describing ritual practices, attitudes, and beliefs.

655. Simon, Norma. THE SADDEST TIME. Whitman, 1986.
Explains death as the inevitable end of life, and provides three situations in which children experience powerful emotions when someone close has died.

Chronic Illness and Death – Diabetes – Fiction

656. Giff, Patricia Reilly. THE GIFT OF THE PIRATE QUEEN. *SEE 339.*

657. Roberts, Willo Davis. SUGAR ISN'T EVERYTHING. Aladdin, 1988 (pap).
Eleven-year old Amy discovers that she has diabetes, learns to treat it and to deal with her anger, and finally accepts that she CAN live with it.

Chronic Illness and Death – Diabetes – Non-Fiction

658. Gosselin, Kim. TRICK-OR-TREAT FOR DIABETES. Jayjo, c1999 (pap).
Sarah knows how to live well with diabetes, but as Halloween approaches she wonders whether she will have to miss the holiday, until her mother shows her how she can enjoy the fun and friendship which are the best part of it without causing herself health problems

659. Peacock, Carol Antoinette. SUGAR WAS MY BEST FOOD: DIABETES AND ME. Whitman, 1998.
An eleven-year-old describes how he learned that he had diabetes, the effect on his life, and how he learned to cope.

660. Peacock, Judith. DIABETES. Capstone, 2000.
Discusses the nature, types, symptoms, diagnosis, treatment, control, and complications of diabetes.

661. Pirner, Connie. EVEN LITTLE KIDS GET DIABETES. Whitman, 1994.
A book for the very young child and her parents, telling the story of the author's daughter who was diagnosed with diabetes when she was two years old.

Chronic Illness and Death – Miscellaneous – Picture Books

662. Sgouros, Charissa. A PILLOW FOR MY MOM. Houghton Mifflin, 1998.
A girl misses her mother, who is sick in the hospital.

663. Sherkin-Langer, Ferne. WHEN MOMMY IS SICK. Illus by Kay Life. Whitman, 1995.
A little girl expresses her sadness when her mother, frequently ill, goes to the hospital and her joy when Mommy returns home.

Chronic Illness and Death – Miscellaneous – Non-Fiction

664. Hyde, Margaret O. KNOW ABOUT TUBERCULOSIS. Walker, 1994.
A close-up look at turberculosis discusses this potentially fatal illness. Once thought a disease of the past, it has reemerged with new drug-resistant strains that may affect about one third of the world's population, particularly in urban areas.

665. Landau, Elaine. LIVING WITH ALBINISM. Watts, 1998.
Describes albinism, the inherited condition in which the individual lacks or has a shortage of melanin, the substance responsible for the body's coloring.

Physical Appearance – General – Picture Books

666. De Paola, Tomie. BIG ANTHONY AND THE MAGIC RING. Harcourt, 1979.
When Big Anthony borrows Strega Nona's magic ring to turn himself into a handsome man, he gets more trouble than fun.

667. Ginsburg, Mirra. CHINESE MIRROR. Illus. by Margot Zemach. Harcourt, 1988.
A traditional Korean tale in which a mirror brought from China causes confusion within a family, as each member looks in it and sees a different stranger.

668. Schroeder, Alan. LILY AND THE WOODEN BOWL. Illus. by Yoriko Ito. Bantam, 1997.
A young girl who wears a wooden bowl over her face to hide her beauty overcomes a variety of trials and eventually finds love, riches and happiness.

Physical Appearance – General – Easy Reader

669. Yolen, Jane. SLEEPING UGLY. Illus. by Diane Stanley. Paper Star, 1997 (pap).
When beautiful Princess Miserella, Plain Jane, and a fairy all fall under a sleeping spell, a prince undoes the spell in a surprising way.

Physical Appearance – General – Fiction

670. Coerr, Eleanor. MIEKO AND THE FIFTH TREASURE. Putnam, 1993; Bantam, 1994 (pap).
After the bombing of Nagasaki, Mieko feels that the happiness in her heart has departed forever, and she will no longer be able to produce a beautiful drawing for the contest at school.

671. McGraw, Eloise. MOORCHILD. McElderry, 1996; Aladdin, 1998 (pap).
Being neither fully human or "folk," a changeling struggles with looking and being different from her human neighbors.

Physical Appearance – General – Folk and Fairy Tales

672. Andersen, Hans Christian. THE UGLY DUCKLING. Adapt. and Illus. by Jerry Pinkney. Morrow, 1999.
An ugly and unloved "duckling" turns out to be a beautiful swan.

Physical Appearance – Cleanliness and Hygiene – Picture Books

673. Zion, Gene. HARRY THE DIRTY DOG. Illus. by Margot Bloy Graham. Harper, 1956; Trophy, 1984.
When a white dog with black spots runs away from home, he gets so dirty his family doesn't recognize him.

Physical Appearance – Cleanliness and Hygiene - Fiction

674. Pearson, Kit. AWAKE AND DREAMING. Viking, 1996.
Theo, a nine-year-old bookworm, lives with her neglectful mother in Vancouver, where she is left alone for days with filthy clothes and matted hair.

675. Sachs, Marilyn. THE BEARS' HOUSE. *SEE 531.*

Physical Appearance – Clothing – Different or Unusual – Picture Books

676. Choi, Sook Nyul. HALMONI AND THE PICNIC. Illus. by Karen Malone. Houghton Mifflin, 1993.
Halmoni is worried that her classmates will make fun of her grandmother's traditional Korean dress and the Korean food that she has prepared for the class picnic.

677. Cohen, Barbara. MOLLY'S PILGRIM. *SEE 466.*

678. Hest, Amy. THE PURPLE COAT. Illus. by Amy Schwartz. Aladdin, 1992 (pap).
Despite her mother's reminder that "navy blue is what you always have," Gabby begs her tailor grandfather to make her a beautiful purple fall coat.

679. McKee, David. ELMER. Lothrop Lee, 1989.
All the elephants of the jungle were gray except Elmer, who was a patchwork of brilliant colors until the day he got tired of being different and making the other elephants laugh.

680. Mills, Lauren. THE RAG COAT. Little Brown, 1991.
Minna proudly wears her new coat made of clothing scraps to school. The other children laugh at her until she tells them the stories behind the scraps.

681. Munsch, Robert. THE PAPER BAG PRINCESS. *SEE 307.*

682. Parton, Dolly. COAT OF MANY COLORS. Illus. by Judith Sutton. Trophy, 1994 (pap).
A poor girl delights in her coat of many colors, made by her mother from rags, because despite the ridicule of other children she knows the coat was made with love.

683. Pfister, Marcus. THE RAINBOW FISH. North-South Books, 1992 (board).
The most beautiful fish in the entire ocean discovers the real value of personal beauty and friendship by sharing his shiny scales.

684. Rathmann, Peggy. RUBY THE COPYCAT. Scholastic, 1991.
Ruby insists on copying Angela, one of her classmates. She copies her dresses and her hairstyles, until her teacher helps her find her own creative way to be unique.

685. Sharratt, Nick. MY MOM AND DAD MAKE ME LAUGH. Candlewick, 1994.
Simon's mom likes spots and his dad likes stripes, but Simon likes something which is neither spotted or striped.

686. Surat, Michele Maria. ANGEL CHILD, DRAGON CHILD. Illus. by Vo-Dinh Mai. Raintree, 1983; Scholastic, 1989 (pap).
Ut has just come from Vietnam to the United States, and everyone laughs at the way she talks and the clothes she wears.

687. Whitcomb, Mary E. ODD VELVET. Illus. by Tara Calahan King. Chronicle, 1998.
Although she dresses differently from the other girls and does things that are unusual, Velvet eventually teaches her classmates that even an outsider has something to offer.

688. Ziefert, Harriet. A NEW COAT FOR ANNA. Random, 1986 (pap).
Even though there is no money, Anna's mother finds a way to make Anna a badly needed winter coat.

Physical Appearance – Clothing – Different or Unusual – Fiction

689. Cochrane, Patricia A. PURELY ROSIE PEARL. Bantam, 1997 (pap).
Rosie Pearl and her family of immigrants endure the hardships of the Great Depression as they find work picking fruit in the California valley; that is why Rosie cannot afford nice clothes.

690. Leverich, Kathleen. BRIGID BEWARE! Random, 1995 (pap).
When her eight-year-old fairy godmother grants Brigid's wish for a pair of "glass slippers," and also makes some of Brigid's other clothing disappear, Brigid learns something about fads and peer pressure.

691. Lisle, Janet Taylor. AFTERNOON OF THE ELVES. Orchard, 1989; Paper Star, 1999 (pap).
Everyone at school laughs at Sara-Kate's ill-fitting, wrinkly garments and she believes that she has elves in her backyard.

692. Paterson, Katherine. FLIP-FLOP GIRL. *SEE 112.*

Physical Appearance – Eyeglasses – Picture Books

693. Brown, Marc T. ARTHUR'S EYES. Little Brown, 1979.
His friends tease Arthur when he gets glasses, but he soon learns to wear them with pride.

694. Hest, Amy. BABY DUCK AND THE BAD EYEGLASSES. Illus. by Jill Barton. Candlewick, 1996.
Baby Duck is unhappy about the new eyeglasses she has to wear, until grandpa helps her realize that they are not so bad after all.

695. Patel, Yogesh. MAGIC GLASSES. Child's Play, c1995.
Teaches a lesson about how glasses can correct vision problems through the story of a stuffed bear with button eyes and his toy friends that are helped by Dr. Oza, an optician who happens to help real children too.

696. Rascal. SOCRATES. Illus. by Gert Bogaerts. Chronicle Books, 1992.
When Socrates, a homeless dog, finds a pair of eyeglasses in the street, the incident benefits him in more ways than one.

697. Smith, Lane. GLASSES: WHO NEEDS 'EM? Puffin, 1995 (pap).
A boy is unhappy about having to wear glasses, until his doctor provides an imaginative list of well-adjusted eyeglass wearers.

698. Wild, Margaret. ALL THE BETTER TO SEE YOU WITH. Whitman, 1993.
Because Kate is the quiet one compared to her four noisy brothers and sisters, her parents are slow to notice that she is near-sighted and needs glasses.

Physical Appearance – Eyeglasses – Intermediate

699. Cowley, Joy. AGAPANTHUS HUM AND THE EYEGLASSES. Philomel, c1999.
Agapanthus struggles to do handstands and other acrobatic tricks while wearing her eyeglasses, which have a tendency to fall off as she cavorts about.

700. Giff, Patricia Reilly. WATCH OUT, RONALD MORGAN! Puffin, 1986 (pap).
Ronald has many mishaps until he starts wearing eyeglasses.

Physical Appearance – Freckles – Fiction

701. Blume, Judy. FRECKLE JUICE. Illus. by Sonia O. Lisker. Dell, 1986 (pap).
Andrew wants freckles so badly that he buys Sharon's freckle recipe for fifty cents.

Physical Appearance – Hair – Picture Books

702. Herron, Carolivia. NAPPY HAIR. Knopf, 1997; Dragonfly, 1999 (pap).
Various people at a backyard picnic offer their comments on Brenda's knotted-up, tightly curled, "nappy" hair, in a lively, empowering story told in the African-American "call and response" tradition.

703. Parr, Todd. THIS IS MY HAIR. Little Brown, c1999.
Simple text and child-like drawings describe how hair can look in many different situations.

Physical Appearance – Hair – Easy Reader

704. Grimes, Nikki. WILD, WILD HAIR. Scholastic, 1997 (pap).
In this rhyming story, an African American girl hides when it's time to comb and braid her hair.

Physical Appearance – Hair – Fiction

705. Yarbrough, Camille. CORNROWS. Illus. by Carole Byard. Coward, 1979.
Explains how the hair style of cornrows, a symbol in Africa since ancient times, can today in this country symbolize the courage of outstanding Afro-Americans.

Physical Appearance – Left-Handed – Fiction

706. Giff, Patricia. LEFT-HANDED SHORTSTOP. Delacorte, 1980.
When his classmates brag that Walter is their star shortstop, Walter makes a cast for his left arm so the kids won't see what a terrible player he really is.

707. Ritter, John H. CHOOSING UP SIDES. Philomel, c1998; Puffin, 2000 (pap).
In 1921, thirteen-year-old Luke finds himself torn between accepting his left-handedness or conforming to the belief of his preacher father that such a condition is evil and must be overcome.

Physical Appearance – Noses – Picture Books

708. Brown, Marc T. ARTHUR'S NOSE. Little Brown, 1976.
Unhappy with his nose, Arthur visits the rhinologist to get a new one.

709. Caple, Kathy. THE BIGGEST NOSE. Houghton Mifflin, 1985.
Eleanor the elephant is self-conscious about her large nose after she is teased by Betty the hippopotamus. She overcomes her sensitivity when she realizes Betty has the biggest mouth.

Physical Appearance – Size – Picture Books

710. Anderson, Janet. SUNFLOWER SAL. Whitman, c1997.
Sal, a very big girl, cannot sew a quilt like Gran's no matter how hard she tries, but eventually she finds that her talents lie elsewhere.

711. Benjamin, A. H. A DUCK SO SMALL. Little Tiger Press, 1998.
When the other ducks laugh at Duffle for being too small to do anything at all, he tries unsuccessfully to imitate Kingfisher, Stork, and Woodpecker, but finally finds something useful he can do.

712. Benson, Patrick. THE LITTLE PENGUIN. Philomel, 1991.
Comparing herself to the Emperor penguins, Pip the penguin feels unhappy with her size until an encounter with a huge sperm whale puts things in a different perspective.

713. Chevalier, Christa. SPENCE IS SMALL. Whitman, 1987.
Spence finds he is too short to perform some tasks, but just the right size to help his mother do others.

714. Lurie, Morris. THE STORY OF IMELDA, WHO WAS SMALL. Illus. by Terry Denton. Houghton Mifflin, 1984.
A little girl who is so small she sleeps in a shoebox visits a doctor who prescribes a diet of long foods to help her grow.

715. Mitchell, Rita Phillips. HUE BOY. Illus. by Caroline Binch. Dial, 1993; Puffin, 1997 (pap).
Everyone in Hue Boy's island village has suggestions on how to help him grow, but he learns how to stand tall in a way all his own.

Size – Easy Reader

716. O'Connor, Jane. SIR SMALL AND THE DRAGONFLY. Illus. by John O'Brien. Random, 1988.
When a dragonfly swoops over the town of Pee Wee and carries Lady Teena away, brave Sir Small vows to rescue her.

Physical Appearance – Size – Fiction

717. Bliss, Corinne Demas. THE SHORTEST KID IN THE WORLD. Random, 1994.
Emily is unhappy with her size until a new girl in class helps her see that being short can have its advantages.

718. Honeycutt, Natalie. GRANVILLE JONES, COMMANDO. Farrar Straus & Giroux, 1998.
Eight-year-old Granville struggles to accept himself as the shortest kid in the whole third grade while also trying to convince his parents that they don't need a new baby.

719. Oppel, Kenneth. SILVERWING. Simon & Schuster, c1997; Aladdin, 1999 (pap).
When a newborn bat named Shade, sometimes called "Runt," becomes separated from his colony during migration he grows in ways that prepare him for even greater journeys.

720. Wisler, Clifton. JERICHO'S JOURNEY. Puffin, 1995.
As his family makes the long and difficult journey from Tennessee to their new home in Texas in 1852, twelve-year-old Jericho, teased about his size, learns there are many ways to grow.

Physical Appearance – Skin Color – Picture Book

721. Lionni, Leo. A COLOR OF HIS OWN. Knopf, 1977 (pap).
A chameleon is distressed that he doesn't have his own color like other animals.

Physical Appearance – Skin Color – Fiction

722. Flake, Sharon G. THE SKIN I'M IN. Hyperion, c1998.
Thirteen-year-old Maleeka, whose skin is extremely dark, meets a new teacher with a birthmark on her face and makes some discoveries about how to love who she is and what she looks like.

Physical Appearance – Skin Color – Nonfiction

723. Adoff, Arnold. BLACK IS BROWN IS TAN. *SEE 290.*

724. Landau, Elaine. LIVING WITH ALBINISM. *SEE 665.*

725. Walton, Darwin. WHAT COLOR ARE YOU. Johnson, 1973.
Describes the purpose of skin and the cause of various skin colors, and discusses the fact that skin color has no effect on basic human needs and feelings.

Physical Appearance – Teeth - Fiction

726. Giff, Patricia Reilly. RAT TEETH. *SEE 83.*

Physical Appearance – Weight – Fiction

727. Blume, Judy. BLUBBER. Dell, 1974.
Jill goes along with the rest of the fifth grade in tormenting a classmate, and then finds out what it's like when she, too, becomes a target.

728. DeClements, Barthe. NOTHING'S FAIR IN THE FIFTH GRADE. Illus. by Nancy Poydar. Puffin, 1990 (pap).
A fifth grade class, repelled by the overweight new student who has serious problems at home, finally learns to accept her.

729. Forward, Toby. PIE MAGIC. Tambourine, 1996; Beech Tree, 1998 (pap).
Bertie thinks that other kids will like him if he loses weight, and so he drinks a special remedy.

730. Peters, Julie Anne. REVENGE OF THE SNOB SQUAD. Little Brown, c1998; Puffin, 2000 (pap).
An overweight sixth-grader joins forces with three other gym class outcasts to plot revenge against the spoiled popular girl who has been tormented them.

731. Smith, Robert Kimmel. JELLY BELLY. Dell, 1982 (pap).
When his parents send him to a summer diet camp, a twelve-year-old boy realizes the problem is his low self-esteem and his grandmother's insistence on showing her affection by overfeeding him.

732. Todd, Pamela. PIG AND THE SHRINK. Delacorte, 1999.
Seventh-grader Tucker needs to come up with a winning science fair project in a hurry, so he uses his overweight friend Angelo as an experimental subject and in the process learns about more than just science.

Challenges – Series

733. DON'T TURN AWAY. Gareth Stevens.
Several titles highlight children with varied physical and mental challenges.

734. LET'S TALK ABOUT IT. Putnam.
Fred Rogers is featured in this series to help children cope with life's difficulties.

735. LET'S TALK LIBRARY. PowerKids Press.
Helps children in grades K-4 deal with personal problems or issues. Includes emotions, illness, family problems, and more.

Cultural, Racial and Ethnic Diversity

Immigration-General Titles • African American • Asian American • Middle Eastern • European • Hispanic American • Carribbean American • Indigenous Peoples-USA • Series

Illustration from *Black Like Kyra, White Like Me* by Judith Vigna, © 1992 by Judith Vigna. Reprinted by permission of Albert Whitman & Company.

Cultural, Racial & Ethnic Diversity

Immigration – General Titles – Picture Books – Nonfiction

736. Cox, Judy. NOW WE CAN HAVE A WEDDING! Holiday, c1998.
Because the guests invited to Sallie's wedding believe that a proper celebration requires their specific ethnic food, they prepare delicacies from around the world.

Immigration – General Titles – Nonfiction

737. Ashabranner, Brent K. OUR BECKONING BORDERS: ILLEGAL IMMIGRATION TO AMERICA. Cobblehill, 1996.
Examines the problems connected with illegal immigration in the United States, from the perspectives of the immigrant as well as that of law enforcement officials.

738. Birdseye, Debbie Holsclaw. UNDER OUR SKIN: KIDS TALK ABOUT RACE. Holiday, 1997.
Six young people discuss their feelings about their own ethnic backgrounds and about their experiences with people of different races.

739. Dooley, Norah. EVERYBODY COOKS RICE. Carolrhoda, 1991.
A child is sent to find a younger brother at dinnertime and is introduced to a variety of cultures through encountering the many different ways rice is prepared at the different households visited.

740. Freedman, Russell. IMMIGRANT KIDS. Puffin, 1995 (pap).
Text and contemporary photographs chronicle the life of immigrant children at home, school, work, and play during the late 1800's and early 1900's.

741. Hauser, Pierre N. ILLEGAL ALIENS. Chelsea House, 1996.
Examines the history of undocumented immigration to the United States, the hardships endured by illegal aliens, their motives in immigrating, and current efforts to control this situation.

742. Herda, D.J. ETHNIC AMERICA: THE NORTHWESTERN STATES. Millbrook, 1991.
Presents an overview of the history and contributions of major ethnic groups that shaped America yesterday and continue to change the American scene today.

743. I WAS DREAMING TO COME TO AMERICA; MEMORIES FROM THE ELLIS ISLAND ORAL HISTORY PROJECT. Viking, 1995; Puffin, 1997 (pap).
In their own words, coupled with hand-painted collage illustrations, immigrants recall their arrival to the United States.

744. Jenness, Aylette. COME HOME WITH ME: A MULTICULTURAL TREASURE HUNT. New Press, 1993.
Takes kids ages eight and up on a tour of homes and neighborhoods in African-American, Irish-American, Latino, and Cambodian communities.

745. Kroll, Steven. ELLIS ISLAND: DOORWAY TO FREEDOM. Holiday House, 1995.
Describes how the immigration station on Ellis Island served as a gateway into the United States for more than sixteen million immigrants between 1892 and 1954.

746. Kuklin, Susan. HOW MY FAMILY LIVES IN AMERICA. Bradbury, 1992.
African-American, Asian-American and Hispanic-American children describe their families' cultural traditions.

747. Littlechild, George. WE ARE ALL RELATED; A CELEBRATION OF OUR CULTURAL HERITAGE. Vancouver, George T. Cunningham Elementary School, 1996.
Catalogue of an exhibition.

748. Sandler, Martin W. IMMIGRANTS. Harper, 1995.
This addition to the "Library of Congress" series provides a look at the mass immigration that took place in the last two centuries as millions of people came from around the globe to the U.S. in search of new opportunities and new lives.

749. Strom, Yale. QUILTED LANDSCAPES: CONVERSATIONS WITH YOUNG IMMIGRANTS. Simon & Schuster, 1996.
Twenty-six young people of different ages and nationalities describe their experience of leaving their countries and migrating to the United States.

750. Thompson, Gare. IMMIGRANTS: COMING TO AMERICA. Children's Press, 1997.
Provides facts about immigrants from various countries and what life was like for them when they reached the United States

African and African American – Picture Books

751. Coleman, Evelyn. WHITE SOCKS ONLY. Illus. by Tyrone Geter. Whitman, 1996.
Grandma tells the story of her first trip alone into town during the days when segregation still existed in Mississippi.

752. English, Karen. NEENY COMING, NEENY GOING. Illus. by Synthis Saint James. Troll, 1998.
Set on one of the islands off the coast of South Carolina, this is the story of a girl whose favorite cousin is coming to visit from the mainland. The language and style of the story represent the blend of West Africa traditions that make the Sea Islands unique.

753. Ford, Juwanda G. K IS FOR KWANZAA: A KWANZAA ALPHABET BOOK. Illus. by Ken Wilson-Max. Cartwheel, 1997.
The African American holiday Kwanzaa is celebrated by introducing related words from A to Z.

754. Hoffman, Mary. AN ANGEL JUST LIKE ME. Dial, 1997 (pap).
An African-American child wonders why all Christmas tree angels look alike and sets out to find an angel that looks just like him.

755. Kroll, Virginia. FARAWAY DRUMS. Illus. by Floyd Cooper. Little Brown, 1998.
Jamila and her little sister are frightened by the loud city noises at their new apartment, but they find comfort in recalling the stories their great-grandma used to tell about life in Africa.

756. Meadearis, Angela S. TREEMONISHA. Illus. by Michael Bryant. Holt, 1995.
The daughter of freed slaves in the post Civil War South gets an education and devotes herself to lifting her people out of poverty and ignorance.

757. Mendez, Phil. THE BLACK SNOWMAN. Illus. by Carole Byard. Scholastic, 1989 (pap).
Through the powers of a magical kente, a black snowman comes to life and helps young Jacob discover the beauty of his Black heritage as well as his own self-worth.

758. Miller, William. NIGHT GOLF. Lee & Low, c1999.
Despite being told that only whites can play golf, James becomes a caddy and is befriended by an older African American man who teaches him to play on the course at night.

759. Mitchell, Rhonda. THE TALKING CLOTH. Orchard, 1997.
When she and her father go to visit her Aunt Phoebe, Amber wraps herself in cloth from Ghana and learns the significance of the colors and symbols of the Ashanti people.

760. Ringgold, Faith. AUNT HARRIET'S UNDERGROUND RAILROAD IN THE SKY. Crown, 1995.
With Harriet Tubman as her guide, Cassie retraces the steps escaping slaves took on the Underground Railroad, in order to reunite with her younger brother.

761. Shange, Ntozake. WHITEWASH. Illus. by Michael Sporn. Walker, 1997.
A young African American girl is traumatized when a gang attacks her and her brother on their way home from school, and spraypaints her face white.

762. Thomassie, Tynia . MIMI'S TUTU. Illus. by Jan Spivey Gilchrist. Scholastic, 1996.
Mimi longs to have a tutu that reflects her African heritage.

763. Van Steenwyk, Elizabeth. MY NAME IS YORK. Rising Moon, c1997.
A slave describes the journey he makes with his master, Captain William Clark, into the uncharted territory of the American West to find a water passageway to the Pacific Ocean.

764. Vigna, Judith. BLACK LIKE KYRA, WHITE LIKE ME. Whitman, 1996 (pap).
When a Black family moves to an all-white neighborhood, prejudice rears its ugly head as the white adults behave rudely, and children's friendships break up.

765. Williams, Sherley Anne. WORKING COTTON. Illus. by Carole Byard. Harcourt, 1992; Voyager, 1997 (pap).
A young Black girl relates the daily events of her migrant family's life in the cotton fields of central California.

766. Yarbrough, Camille. CORNROWS. *SEE 705.*

African and African American – Easy Readers

767. Brenner, Barbara. WAGON WHEELS. *SEE 148.*

768. Monjo, F.N. THE DRINKING GOURD. Illus. by Fred Brenner. Harper, 1993; Trophy 1993 (pap).
When he is sent home alone for misbehaving in church, Tommy discovers that his house is a station on the Underground Railroad.

African and African American – Intermediate

769. Brill, Marlene Targ. ALLEN JAY AND THE UNDERGROUND RAILROAD. Illus. by Janice Lee Porter. Carolrhoda, 1993; First Avenue, 1993 (pap).
Allen Jay, a young Quaker boy living in Ohio during the 1840's, helps a fleeing slave escape his master and make it to freedom through the Underground Railroad.

770. Lewis, Zoe. KEISHA DISCOVERS HARLEM. Magic Attic Press, c1998.
While trying to find a topic for her school assignment, Keisha visits Ellie's attic and discovers the excitement of the music and writing that flourished among African-Americans in Harlem during the 1920's.

771. Taylor, Mildred D. THE GOLD CADILLAC. Illus. by Michael Hays. Dial, 1987.
Two Black girls living in the North are proud of their family's new Cadillac until they take it on a visit to the South and encounter racial prejudice for the first time.

772. Taylor, Mildred D. MISSISSIPPI BRIDGE. Bantam, 1992 (pap).
During a heavy rainstorm in 1930's rural Mississippi, a ten-year-old white boy sees a bus driver order all the Black passengers off a crowded bus to make room for late-arriving white passengers.

773. Taylor, Mildred D. THE WELL: DAVID'S STORY. Dial, 1995; Puffin, 1998 (pap).
In Mississippi, during the early 1900's, ten-year-old David's family generously share their well water with both white and black neighbors, in an atmosphere of potential racial violence.

774. Walter, Mildred Pitts. HAVE A HAPPY..... Illus. by Carole Byard. Lothrop Lee, 1989; Camelot, 1996 (pap).
Upset because his birthday falls on Christmas and will therefore be eclipsed as usual, and worried that there is less money because his father is out of work, eleven-year-old Chris takes solace in the carvings he is preparing for Kwanzaa.

African and African American – Fiction

775. Armstrong, Robb. DREW AND THE HOMEBOY QUESTION. Harper, 1997.
Drew's oldest friends accuse him of snobbery when he wins a scholarship to an exclusive all-white school.

776. Blume, Judy. IGGIE'S HOUSE. Simon & Schuster, 1970; Dell, 1990 (pap).
When a Black family with three children moves into the white neighborhood, eleven-year-old Winnie learns the difference between a good neighbor and being a good friend.

777. Christopher, Matt. THE BASKET COUNTS. Little Brown, 1991 (pap).
Long practice improves Mel's value as a basketball player, but how does he surmount the prejudice of a teammate?

778. Curtis, Christopher, Paul. BUD, NOT BUDDY. Delacorte, c1999.
It's 1936, and ten-year-old Bud hits the road in search of his father and a home.

779. Hurmence, Belinda. A GIRL CALLED BOY. Clarion, 1990 (pap).
A pampered young Black girl, who has been mysteriously transported back to the days of slavery, struggles to escape her bondage.

780. Forrester, Sandra. MY HOME IS OVER JORDAN. Lodestar, c1997; Puffin, 2000 (pap).
No longer a slave now that the Civil War is over, fifteen-year-old Maddie dreams of getting an education and becoming a teacher, but she finds the reality of freedom harsh.

781. Hamilton, Virginia. COUSINS. Philomel, 1990; Scholastic, 1991 (pap).
Concerned that her grandmother may die, Cammy is unprepared for the accidental death of another relative.

782. Hamilton, Virginia. SECOND COUSINS. Blue Sky, 1998; Scholastic, 2000 (pap).
The friendship of twelve-year-old cousins Cammy and Elodie is threatened when the family reunion includes two other cousins near their age and Elodie is tempted to drop Cammie for a new companion.

783. Hearne, Betsy Gould. LISTENING FOR LEROY. McElderry, c1998.
Growing up in rural Alabama in the 1950's, ten-year-old Alice has no one to talk to but Leroy, the black farm hand. When Alice's father moves the family to Tennessee, she has trouble fitting in and she sorely misses Leroy.

784. Nelson, Vaunda Micheaux. MAYFIELD CROSSING. Camelot, 1994 (pap).
When the school in Mayfield Crossing is closed, the students are sent to larger schools, where the Black children encounter racial prejudice for the first time.

785. Rabe, Berniece. HIDING MR. MCMULTY. Harcourt, 1997.
In 1937 in southeastern Missouri, eleven-year-old Rass, son of a proud sharecropper, proves his worth when a flood destroys his family's home and forces an elderly Black man into hiding from the Ku Klux Klan.

786. Robinet, Harriette. IF YOU PLEASE, PRESIDENT LINCOLN. Atheneum, 1995.
Shortly after the Christmas of 1863, fourteen-year-old Moses thinks he is beginning a new free life when he becomes part of a group of former slaves headed for a small island off the coast of Haiti.

787. Shaik, Fatima. MELITTE. Dial, c1997; Puffin, 1999 (pap).
In 1772, years of mistreatment force thirteen-year-old Melitte to decide whether or not to run away from the Frenchman who has kept her as a slave on his poor Louisiana farm and leave the young girl who is the only person who ever loved her.

788. Taylor, Mildred D. ROLL OF THUNDER, HEAR MY CRY. *SEE 175.*

789. Winslow, Vicki. FOLLOW THE LEADER. Delacorte, 1997; Yearling, 1998 (pap).
In 1971, in a small North Carolina town, eleven-year-old Amanda must deal with being bussed to a newly integrated, formerly all-black school, and being separated from her best friend.

790. Woodruff, Elvira. DEAR AUSTIN: LETTERS FROM THE UNDERGROUND RAILROAD. Knopf, c1998.
In 1853, in letters to his older brother, eleven-year-old Levi describes his adventures in the Pennsylvania countryside with his African American friend Jupiter and his experiences with the Underground Railroad.

791. Woodson, Jacqueline. MAIZON AT BLUE HILL. Yearling, 1994 (pap).
After winning a scholarship to an academically challenging boarding school, Maizon finds herself one of only five Blacks there, and wonders if she will ever fit in.

792. Young, Ronder Thomas. LEARNING BY HEART. Houghton Mifflin, 1993.
In the early 1960's, ten-year-old Rachel sees changes in her family and her small Southern town, as she tries to sort out how she feels about her young Black maid and about racial prejudice.

African and African American - Nonfiction

793. Bial, Raymond. THE STRENGTH OF THESE ARMS: LIFE IN THE SLAVE QUARTERS. Houghton, 1997.
Describes how slaves were able to preserve some elements of their African heritage despite the often brutal treatment they experienced on Southern plantations.

794. Bridges, Ruby. THROUGH MY EYES. Scholastic, 1999.
Ruby Bridges recounts the story of her involvement, as a six-year-old, in the integration of an elementary school in New Orleans in 1960.

795. Dramer, Kim. NATIVE AMERICANS AND BLACK AMERICANS. Chelsea, 1997.
Describes the relationship between African Americans and Native Americans, both as adversaries and as partners.

796. Haskins, James. BLACK, BLUE AND GRAY: AFRICANS IN THE CIVIL WAR. Simon & Schuster, 1998.
An historical account of the role of African American soldiers in the Civil War.

797. Haskins, James. FREEDOM RIDES: JOURNEY FOR JUSTICE. Hyperion, 1995.
Describes the May 4, 1961 bus ride through the South to test Boynton vs. Virginia, and contributes insight into the importance of the Freedom Riders to the Civil Rights struggle.

798. Haskins, James. GET ON BOARD: THE STORY OF THE UNDERGROUND RAILROAD. Scholastic, 1997 (pap).
Discusses the Underground Railroad, the secret, loosely organized network of people and places that helped many slaves escape north to freedom.

799. Katz, William Loren. BLACK WOMEN OF THE OLD WEST. Atheneum, 1995.
Traces the history of African American women on the American frontier through old records, newspaper clippings, pioneer reminiscences and rare frontier photographs.

800. King, Casey. OH, FREEDOM! : KIDS TALK ABOUT THE CIVIL RIGHTS MOVEMENT WITH THE PEOPLE WHO MADE IT HAPPEN. Knopf, 1997.
Interviews between young people and people who took part in the Civil Rights Movement accompany essays that describe the history of efforts to make equality a reality for African Americans.

801. Lawrence, Jacob. THE GREAT MIGRATION: AN AMERICAN STORY. Trophy, 1995 (pap).
A series of paintings chronicle the journey of African Americans who, like the artist's family, left the rural South to find a better life in the industrial North.

802. Lester, Julius. FROM SLAVE SHIP TO FREEDOM ROAD. Dial, 1998.
A book of "imagination experiences," accompanied by paintings meant to encourage readers to visualize what it was like to be a slave.

803. Lester, Julius. TO BE A SLAVE. Dial, 1968; Scholastic, 1998 (pap).
A compilation of the reminiscences of slaves and ex-slaves about their experiences, from the leaving of Africa through the Civil War and into the twentieth century.

804. Lucas, Eileen. CRACKING THE WALL: THE STRUGGLES OF THE LITTLE ROCK NINE. Carolrhoda, 1997.
A brief introduction to the nine African American students who integrated Central High School in Little Rock, Arkansas, in 1957.

805. McKissack, Patricia. CHRISTMAS IN THE BIG HOUSE, CHRISTMAS IN THE QUARTERS. Scholastic, 1994.
Describes the customs, recipes, poems and songs used to celebrate Christmas in the big plantation houses and in the slave quarters just before the Civil War.

806. Myers, Walter Dean. NOW IS YOUR TIME!: THE AFRICAN AMERICAN STRUGGLE FOR FREEDOM. Harper, 1991.
A history of the African American struggle for freedom and equality, beginning with the capture of Africans in 1619, continuing through the American Revolution, the Civil War, and into contemporary times.

807. Reef, Catherine. BUFFALO SOLDIERS. Holt, 1994.
Recounts the deeds of the 9th and 10th Cavalry, comprised of African American soldiers, who kept peace between Indians and settlers on the western frontier, fought in the Spanish American War, and pursued the outlaw Pancho Villa through Mexico.

808. Saint James, Synthia. THE GIFTS OF KWANZAA. Whitman, 1994.
A celebration of the African American holiday Kwanzaa.

809. Schlissel, Lillian. BLACK FRONTIERS: A HISTORY OF AFRICAN AMERICAN HEROES IN THE OLD WEST. Simon & Schuster, 1995
Focuses on the experiences of Blacks as mountain men, soldiers, homesteaders, and scouts on the frontiers of the American West.

African and African American - Poetry

810. Giovanni, Nikki. EGO-TRIPPING AND OTHER POEMS FOR YOUNG PEOPLE. Lawrence Hill Books, 1993 (pap).
Thirty-two poems that reflect aspects of the African American experience.

811. Giovanni, Nikki. SPIN A SOFT BLACK SONG. Hill and Wang, 1987 (pap).
A poetry collection which recounts the feelings of Black children about their neighborhoods, American society, and themselves.

812. Greenfield, Eloise. HONEY, I LOVE AND OTHER LOVE POEMS. Crowell, 1978; Trophy, 1986 (pap).
Titles include "I Look Pretty," "Riding on the Train," "Harriet Tubman," and "By Myself."

813. Hughes, Langston. THE DREAM-KEEPER AND OTHER POEMS. Knopf, 1994.
A collection of sixty-six poems, selected by the author for young readers, including lyrical poems, songs and blues.

814. Myers, Walter D. BROWN ANGELS. HarperCollins, 1993; Trophy, 1996 (pap).
A collection of poems, accompanied by photographs, about African American children living around the turn of the century.

815. PASS IT ON: AFRICAN AMERICAN POETRY FOR CHILDREN. Scholastic, 1993 (pap).
An illustrated collection of poetry by such African American poets as Langston Hughes, Nikki Giovanni, Eloise Greenfield, and Lucille Clifton.

African and African American – Collective Biographies

816. Altman, Susan R. EXTRAORDINARY BLACK AMERICANS FROM COLONIAL TO CONTEMPORARY TIMES. Childrens, 1989.
Short biographies of ninety-five Black Americans, highlighting their personal achievements.

817. Burns, Khephra. BLACK STARS IN ORBIT: NASA'S AFRICAN AMERICAN ASTRONAUTS. Harcourt, 1995.
A history of African-American participation in the space program recounts NASA's campaign to recruit minority trainees, the space mission that included the first black crew member, and the achievements of three noted African-American astronauts.

818. Hacker, Carlotta. GREAT AFRICAN AMERICANS IN THE ARTS. Crabtree, 1997.
Profiles thirteen African Americans from the fields of dance, stage, opera, classical music, photography, and painting.

819. Hayden, Robert C. NINE AFRICAN AMERICAN INVENTORS. Twenty-first Century Books, 1992.
Chronicles the achievements of nine African Americans responsible for inventions related to important parts of modern life, such as refrigeration, electrical lighting, and transportation.

820. Hunter, Shaun. GREAT AFRICAN AMERICANS IN THE OLYMPICS. Crabtree, 1997.
Presents biographies of African American olympians such as Edwin Moses, George Foreman, Debi Thomas, and Florence Griffith-Joyner.

821. Rediger, Pat. GREAT AFRICAN AMERICANS IN ENTERTAINMENT. Crabtree, 1995.
Examines the lives of more than ten African American entertainers, including Josephine Baker, Sammy Davis Jr., And Spike Lee, and the obstacles they each overcame.

African and African American – Biographies

822. Biracree, Tom. ALTHEA GIBSON: TENNIS CHAMPION. Chelsea, 1989; Holloway, 1990 (pap).
Follows the life of the first Black woman to win the tennis competition at Wimbledon.

823. Coffey, Wayne R. WILMA RUDOLPH. Blackbirch, 1994.
This Olympic star overcame extraordinary adversity, including crippling polio, to become the fastest woman in the world by 1960.

824. Coles, Robert. THE STORY OF RUBY BRIDGES. Scholastic, 1995.
For months, six-year-old Ruby had to confront the hostility of white parents when she became the first African American girl to integrate an elementary school in New Orleans in 1960.

825. Colman, Penny. FANNIE LOU HAMER AND THE FIGHT FOR THE VOTE. Carolrhoda, 1989.
Biography of the civil rights activist who devoted her life to helping Black people register to vote.

826. Ferris, Jeri. ARCTIC EXPLORER; THE STORY OF MATTHEW HENSON. Lerner, 1989.
Traces the life of Henson, the Black explorer who accompanied the Perry expedition to the North Pole, and explains the reasons for the long delay in his recognition.

827. Finlayson, Reggie. COLIN POWELL: PEOPLE'S HERO. Lerner, 1996.
Traces the life and career of the Army general who became the country's first Black chairman of the Joint Chiefs of Staff in 1989.

828. Fleischner, Jennifer. I WAS BORN A SLAVE: THE STORY OF HARRIET JACOBS. Millbrook, 1997.
Traces the life of a slave who suffered mistreatment from her master, spent years as a fugitive in North Carolina, and was eventually released to freedom with her children.

829. Jakoubek, Robert E. JAMES FARMER AND THE FREEDOM RIDES. Millbrook, 1994.
Presents the life and times of the Black civil rights activist who formed CORE and organized the Freedom Rides.

830. Kent, Deborah. THURGOOD MARSHALL AND THE SUPREME COURT. Childrens Press, 1997.
Narrates the life of the first African American to serve as a Justice on the United States Supreme Court.

831. Nicholson, Lois P. OPRAH WINFREY: ENTERTAINER. Chelsea House, 1994.
The talk show host discusses her childhood of poverty and neglect, and her rise to the top of the entertainment world.

832. Pinkney, Andrea D. ALVIN AILEY. *SEE 384.*

833. Pinkney, Andrea D. DUKE ELLINGTON: THE PIANO PRINCE AND HIS ORCHESTRA. Disney Press, 1998.
Recounts the career of this jazz musician and composer, who along with his orchestra created music that was beyond category.

834. Wright, David K. ARTHUR ASHE: BREAKING THE COLOR BARRIER IN TENNIS. Enslow, 1996.
A biography of tennis champion Arthur Ashe, covering his personal life and his sports career, as well as his struggles with racism and AIDS.

Asian-American – Picture Books

835. Ashley, Bernard. CLEVERSTICKS. Illus. Derek Brazell. Crown, 1995.
Wishing he could be clever like each of the other children in his class, Ling Sung unexpectedly and happily discovers the others admire his prowess with chopsticks.

836. Chin, Steven A. DRAGON PARADE. Illus. by Mou-Sien Tseng. Raintree Steck-Vaughn, 1993.
A Chinese New Year story set in the United States that shows how people get ready for Chinese New Year.

837. Chin-Lee, Cynthia. ALMOND COOKIES AND DRAGON WELL TEA. Illus. by You Shan Tang. Polychrome, 1993.
Erica visits the home of Nancy, a Chinese American girl, and makes many delightful discoveries about her friend's cultural heritage.

838. Chinn, Karen. SAM AND THE LUCKY MONEY. Illus. by Cornelius Van Wright and Ying-Hwa Hu. Lee and Low, 1995.
Sam, a Chinese American boy, must decide how to spend the lucky money he's received for Chinese New Year.

839. Choi, Sook Nyul. HALMONI AND THE PICNIC. *SEE 676.*

840. Fisher, Iris L. KATIE-BO: AN ADOPTION STORY. Illus. by Miriam Shaer. Adama Books, 1987.
Relates the adoption of a Korean baby girl into an American family as seen through the eyes of her brother-to-be.

841. Friedman, Ina R. HOW MY PARENTS LEARNED TO EAT. *SEE 279.*

842. Garland, Sherry. MY FATHER'S BOAT. Scholastic, 1998.
A Vietnamese-American boy spends a day with his father on his shrimp boat, listening as he describes how his own father fishes on the South China Sea.

843. Gilmore, Rachna. LIGHTS FOR GITA. Illus. by Alice Priestley. Tilbury House, 1994.
Recently arrived from India, Gita is looking forward to celebrating her favorite holiday, Divali, a festival of lights, but things are so different here in the United States that she wonders if she will ever adjust.

844. Girard, Linda Walvoord. WE ADOPTED YOU, BENJAMIN KOO. *SEE 179.*

845. Heo, Yumi. FATHER'S RUBBER SHOES. Orchard, 1995.
Yungsu misses Korea terribly until he begins to make friends in America.

846. Igus, Toyomi. TWO MRS. GIBSONS. *SEE 281.*

847. Johnston, Tony. FISHING SUNDAY. Illus. by Barry Root. Tambourine, 1996.
A young boy is embarrassed by his grandfather's old-fashioned Japanese ways, but on one of their fishing Sundays, he learns to see Grandfather in a new light.

848. Lee, Milly. NIM AND THE WAR EFFORT. Illus. by Yangsook Choi. Farrar Straus, 1997.
A Chinese-American girl tries to do her patriotic best to help the war effort during World War II.

849. Levine, Ellen. I HATE ENGLISH. Illus. by Steve Bjorkman. Scholastic, 1989.
When her family moves to New York from Hong Kong, Mei finds it difficult to adjust to school and learn the alien sounds of English.

850. Low, William. CHINATOWN. Holt, 1997.
A boy and his grandmother wind their way through the streets of Chinatown, enjoying all the sights and smells of the Chinese New Year.

851. McKay, Lawrence. JOURNEY HOME. Illus. by Dom and Keunhee Lee. Lee and Low, 1998.
Mai returns to Vietnam, the land of her mother's birth, to discover something about her country and something about herself.

852. Mitsui Brown, Janet. THANKSGIVING AT OBAACHAN'S. Polychrome, 1994.
A Japanese-American girl describes Thanksgiving at her grandmother's house.

853. Mochizuki, Ken. HEROES. Illus. by Dom Lee. Lee and Low, 1995.
Japanese-American Donnie, whose playmates insist he be the "bad guy" in their war games, calls on his reluctant father and uncle to help him change that role.

854. Molnar-Fenton, Stephan . AN MEI'S STRANGE AND WONDROUS JOURNEY. Illus. by Vivienne Flesher. DK Ink, 1998.
Six-year-old An Mei tells the story of how she was born in China and came to live in America.

855. Nunes, Susan. THE LAST DRAGON. Illus. by Christ K. Soentpiet. Clarion, 1995.
While spending the summer in Chinatown with his great aunt, a young boy finds an old ten-man dragon in a shop and finds some people to help him repair it.

856. Pellegrini, Nina. FAMILIES ARE DIFFERENT. *SEE 181.*

857. Pomeranc, Marion Hess. THE AMERICAN WEI. Illus. by DyAnne DiSalvo Ryan. Whitman, 1998.
Many soon-to-be Americans join in the search when Wei Fong loses his first tooth on the way to his family's naturalization ceremony.

858. Porte, Barbara A. LEAVE THAT CRICKET BE, ALAN LEE. Illus. by Donna Ruff. Greenwillow, 1993.
Alan Lee tries to catch the singing cricket in his mother's office.

859. Rattigan, Jama K. DUMPLING SOUP. Illus. by Lillian Hsu-Flanders. Little Brown, 1993.
A young Hawaiian girl tries to make dumplings for her family's New Year's celebration.

860. Say, Allen. GRANDFATHER'S JOURNEY. Houghton Mifflin, 1993.
A Japanese American man recounts his grandfather's journey to America and reveals the feelings of being torn by a love for two different countries.

861. Say, Allen. STRANGER IN THE MIRROR. Houghton Mifflin, 1995.
When a young Asian-American boy who spends all of his time skateboarding wakes up one morning with the face of an old man, he has trouble convincing people that he is still himself.

862. Sing, Rachel. CHINESE NEW YEAR'S DRAGON. Ilus. by Shao Wei Liu. Modern Curriculum Press, 1992; Simon & Schuster, 1994 (pap).
This New Year, the Year of the Dragon, something magical happens. A young girl's grandmother tells her about dragons, and suddenly she finds herself on a dragon's back soaring over ancient China.

863. Surat, Michele Maria. ANGEL CHILD, DRAGON CHILD. *SEE 686.*

864. Uchida, Yoshiko. THE BRACELET. Illus. by Joanna Yarldley. Philomel, 1993; Paper Star, 1996 (pap).
Emi, a Japanese-American girl in the second grade, is sent with her family to an internment camp during World War II.

865. Vaughan, Marcia K. THE DANCING DRAGON. Illus. by Stanley Wong Hoo Foon. Mondo, 1996.
A rhyming story that describes a typical Chinese New Year celebration.

866. Wells, Rosemary. YOKO. Hyperion, c1998.
When Yoko brings sushi to school for lunch, her classmates make fun of what she eats – until one of them tries it for himself.

Asian-American – Easy Readers

867. Coerr, Eleanor. CHANG'S PAPER PONY. Illus. by Deborah Kogan Ray. Harper, 1988.
In San Francisco during the 1850's gold rush, the son of Chinese immigrants wants a pony but cannot afford one.

Asian-American – Intermediate

868. Bunting, Eve. SO FAR FROM THE SEA. Illus. by Chris Soentpiet. Clarion, 1998.
Japanese-American, seven-year-old Laura and her family visit Grandfather's grave at the Manzanar War Relocation Center.

869. Kline, Suzy. SONG LEE AND THE HAMSTER HUNT. Illus. by Frank Remkiewicz. Puffin, 2000 (pap).
When Korean-American Song Lee's hamster escapes from its cage in Room 2B, the students all become involved in the search.

870. Kline, Suzy. SONG LEE IN ROOM 2B. Viking, 1993; Puffin, 1999 (pap).
Spring becomes a memorable time for the second grade because of the special insights of shy Song Lee, who is Korean-American.

871. Kraus, Joanna Halpert. TALL BOY'S JOURNEY. Illus. by Karen Ritz. Carolrhoda, 1992.
When Kim Moo Yong, an orphaned Korean boy, is adopted by an American couple and makes the long journey by plane to their house, he finds it a strange and terrifying experience.

872. Mochizuki, Ken. BASEBALL SAVED US. Illus. by Dom Lee. Lee & Low, 1993.
A Japanese American boy learns to play baseball when he and his family are forced to live in an internment camp during World War II, and his ability to play helps him after the war is over.

Asian-American – Fiction

873. Balgassi, Haemi. TAE'S SONATA. Clarion, 1997.
Tae, a Korean American eighth grader, tries to sort out her feelings when she has a argument with her best friend.

874. Blakeslee, Ann R. A DIFFERENT KIND OF HERO. Marshall Cavendish, c1997.
In 1881 twelve-year-old Renny, who resists his father's efforts to turn him into a rough, tough, brawling boy, earns the disapproval of the entire mining camp when he befriends a newly arrived Chinese boy.

875. Lord, Bette. IN THE YEAR OF THE BOAR AND JACKIE ROBINSON. *SEE 69.*

876. Myers, Anna. ROSIE'S TIGER. Walker, 1994.
Sixth-grader Rosie enlists the aid of her best friend in trying to get rid of the Korean wife and stepson her older brother has brought back from Korea after the Korean War.

877. Namioka, Lensey. YANG THE THIRD AND HER IMPOSSIBLE FAMILY. *SEE 164.*

878. Namioka, Lensey. YANG THE YOUNGEST AND HIS TERRIBLE EAR. *SEE 71.*

879. Paterson, Katherine. PARK'S QUEST. *SEE 152.*

880. Shalant, Phyllis. BEWARE OF KISSING LIZARD LIPS. Dutton, 1995.
Zach is small and the girls at school make fun of him, but things begin to change when one girl starts showing him some tae kwon do moves and teaches him about martial arts.

881. Terris, Susan. THE LATCHKEY KIDS. Farrar Straus, 1986.
Callie tries to cope with her new responsibilities when, due to changed family circumstances, she is left in charge of her younger brother.

882. Uchida, Yoshiko. THE BEST BAD THING. Atheneum, 1983; Aladdin, 1986.
Rinko has some pleasant surprises when she spends her summer vacation helping out in the household of recently widowed Mrs. Hata.

883. Uchida, Yoshiko. A JAR OF DREAMS. Atheneum, 1981; Aladdin, 1993.
A young girl grows up in a closely-knit Japanese American family in California during the 1930's, a time of great prejudice.

884. Yep, Laurence. THE CASE OF THE GOBLIN PEARLS. HarperCollins, 1997.
Lily and her aunt, a Chinese American movie actress, join forces to solve the theft of some priceless pearls.

885. Yep, Laurence. THE CASE OF THE LION DANCE. HarperCollins, c1998; Trophy, 1999 (pap).
When $2000 is stolen during the opening day of a restaurant, Lily and her aunt, a Chinese-American movie actress, search for the thief throughout San Francisco's Chinatown.

886. Yep, Laurence. CHILD OF THE OWL. HarperCollins, 1977.
A twelve-year-old girl who knows little about her Chinese heritage is sent to live with her grandmother in San Francisco's Chinatown.

887. Yep, Laurence. THE COOK'S FAMILY. Putnam, c1998; PaperStar, 1999 (pap).
As her parents' arguments become more frequent, Robin looks forward to the visits that she and her grandmother make to Chinatown, where they pretend to be an elderly cook's family, giving Robin new insights into her Chinese heritage.

888. Yep, Laurence. THE IMP THAT ATE MY HOMEWORK. HarperCollins, 1998.
Jim teams up with his grandfather, who is known as the meanest man in Chinatown, to defeat a powerful demon.

889. Yep, Laurence. RIBBONS. Putnam, 1996.
A promising young ballet student cannot afford to continue lessons when her Chinese grandmother emigrates from Hong Kong, creating jealousy and conflict among the entire family.

890. Yep, Laurence. SEA GLASS. Harper, 1979.
A Chinese-American boy whose father wants him to be good in sports asserts his right to be himself.

891. Yep, Laurence. THE STAR FISHER. Morrow, 1991; Puffin, 1992 (pap).
A Chinese American family encounters difficulties and prejudice when they move to West Virginia in the 1920's.

892. Yep, Laurence. THIEF OF HEARTS. HarperCollins, 1995.
When Stacy is paired with a Chinese girl at school who is accused of theft, she must come to terms with her own Chinese and American heritage.

Asian-American – Nonfiction

893. Behrens, June. GUNG HAY FAT CHOY. Illus. by Terry Behrens and Ronnie Ramos. Childrens Press, 1982.
Explains the significance of the Chinese New Year and describes its celebration by Chinese Americans.

894. Brown, Tricia. CHINESE NEW YEAR. Illus. by Fran Ortiz. Holt, 1987.
Text and photographs depict the celebration of Chinese New Year by Chinese Americans living in San Francisco's Chinatown.

895. Cha, Dia. DIA'S STORY CLOTH. Illus. by Chue and Nhia Thao Cha. Lee & Low, 1996.
The story cloth made for her by her aunt and uncle chronicles the life of the author and her family in their native Laos, and their eventual emigration to the United States.

896. Demi. HAPPY NEW YEAR! KUNG-HSI FA-TS'AI! Crown, 1997.
Examines the customs, traditions, foods, and lore associated with the celebration of Chinese New Year.

897. Gogol, Sara. A MIEN FAMILY. Lerner, 1996.
Describes the experiences of one Mien family driven from their home in Laos, who moved to a new life in Portland, Oregon.

898. Hamanaka, Sheila. THE JOURNEY: JAPANESE AMERICANS, RACISM AND RENEWAL. Orchard, 1990.
Text and photographed details of a mural depicting the history of the Japanese people in America.

899. Hoyt-Goldsmith, Diane. HOANG ANH: A VIETNAMESE AMERICAN BOY. Holiday, 1992.
A Vietnamese American boy describes the daily activities of his family in San Rafael, California, and the traditional culture and customs that shape their lives.

900. Kilborne, Sarah S. LEAVING VIETNAM: THE JOURNEY OF TUAN NGO, A BOAT BOY. Simon & Schuster, c1999; Aladdin, 1999 (pap).
Tells the story of a boy and his father who endure danger and difficulties when they escape by boat from Vietnam, spend days at sea, and then months in refugee camps before making their way to the United States.

901. Murphy, Nora. A HMONG FAMILY. Lerner, 1997.
Depicts the history and culture of the Hmong, a unique ethnic group living in Southeast Asia, and describes the experiences of a Hmong family who left Laos to rebuild their lives in America.

902. O'Connor, Karen. A KURDISH FAMILY. Lerner, 1996.
Describes the experiences of one Kurdish family that was driven from their home in northern Iraq and moved to a new life in California.

903. Stepanchuk, Carol. RED EGGS AND DRAGON BOATS: CELEBRATING CHINESE FESTIVALS. Pacific View, 1994.
The celebration of such Chinese festivals as Chinese Lunar New Year, Clear Brightness Festival, Full-Month Red Egg and Ginger Party, Dragon Boat Festival and Moon Festival.

904. Waters, Kate. LION DANCER: ERNIE WAN'S CHINESE NEW YEAR. Illus. by Martha Cooper. Scholastic, 1990.
Describes six-year-old Ernie Wong's preparations, at home and in school, for the Chinese New Year celebrations and his first public performance of the lion dance.

Asian-Americans – Biographies

905. Chin, Steven A. WHEN JUSTICE FAILED: THE FRED KOREMATSU STORY. Raintree, 1993.
Relates the life and experience of the Japanese American who defied the order of internment during World War II and took his case as far as the Supreme Court.

906. Donohue, Shiobhan. KRISTI YAMAGUCHI: ARTIST ON ICE. Lerner, 1994.
A biography of the Japanese American figure skater who won the National, Olympic and World Championships in 1992.

907. Kwan, Michelle. MICHELLE KWAN, HEART OF A CHAMPION: AN AUTOBIOGRAPHY. Scholastic, 1997.
The Chinese American 1996 World champion discusses the rigors of competition, the importance of a strong support group, her love of ice skating, and her Olympic dream.

908. Ling, Bettina. MAYA LIN. Raintree, 1997.
Describes the life and work of the Chinese American architect who designed the Vietnam Veterans Memorial in Washington, D.C., and the Civil Rights Memorial in Montgomery, Alabama.

909. Morey, Janet. FAMOUS ASIAN AMERICANS. Puffin, 1999 (pap).
Chronicles the lives and accomplishments of fourteen Asian Americans including Jose Aruego, Michael Chang, An Wang and Ellison Onizuka.

910. Riley, Gail Blasser. WAH MING CHANG: ARTIST AND MASTER OF SPECIAL EFFECTS. Enslow, 1995.
The life of artist Wah Ming Chang, who is best known for his special effects for Disney films and the Star Trek series.

911. Uchida, Yoshiko. THE INVISIBLE THREAD: AN AUTOBIOGRAPHY. Beech Tree, 1995 (pap).
Children's author Yoshiko Uchida describes growing up in Berkeley as a Nisei, second generation Japanese American, and her family's internment in a Nevada internment camp during World War II.

912. Yep, Laurence. THE LOST GARDEN. Beech Tree, 1996, (pap).
The author describes how he grew up as a Chinese American in San Francisco and how he came to use his writing to celebrate his family and his ethnic heritage.

913. Yokoe, Lynn. MAYA LIN: ARCHITECT. Modern Curriculum Press, 1995.
Easy biography of the architect of the Vietnam Veterans Memorial in Washington, D.C.

Middle Eastern – Picture Books

914. Matze, Claire Sighom. THE STARS IN MY GEDDOH'S SKY. Whitman, 1999.
Alex's Arabic-speaking grandfather comes to visit the United States, and Alex learns about his father's Middle Eastern homeland.

915. Nye, Naomi Shihab. SITTI'S SECRETS. Four Winds, c1994; Aladdin, 1997 (pap).
A young Arab-American girl describes a visit to see her grandmother in a Palestinian village on the West Bank.

European Immigrants – Picture Books

916. Bartoletti, Susan C. DANCING WITH DZIADZIU. Illus. by Annika Nelson. Harcourt, 1997.
A young Polish-American girl shares her ballet dancing with her dying grandmother, and the grandmother shares memories of her family's immigration from Poland and of dancing with the girl's grandfather.

917. Bartone, Elisa. PEPPE THE LAMPLIGHTER. *SEE 21.*

918. Bliss, Corinne D. ELECTRA AND THE CHARLOTTE RUSSE. Illus. by Michael Garland. Boyds Mills, 1997.
A misadventure ensues when a young Greek-American girl goes to the bakery to buy dessert for her mother's tea party.

919. Cech, John. MY GRANDMOTHER'S JOURNEY. Illus. by Sharon McGinley-Nally. Simon & Schuster, 1991; Aladdin, 1998 (pap).
A grandmother retells the story of her eventful life in early twentieth-century Europe and her arrival in the United States after World War II.

920. Harvey, Brett. IMMIGRANT GIRL: BECKY OF ELDRIDGE STREET. Illus. by P. J. Lynch. Holiday, 1987.
Becky, whose family emigrated from Russia to avoid being persecuted as Jews, finds growing up in New York City in 1910 a vivid and exciting experience.

921. Hest, Amy. WHEN JESSIE CAME ACROSS THE SEA. Candlewick, 1997; Camelot, 1998 (pap).
A thirteen-year-old Jewish orphan reluctantly leaves her grandmother in Europe and immigrates to New York City, where she works for three years sewing lace and earning money to bring her grandmother to the United States, too.

922. Joosse, Barbara M. THE MORNING CHAIR. Illus. by Marcia Sewall. Clarion, 1995.
Bram and his family leave their small brick house in Holland and travel to New York City.

923. Khalsa, Dayal Kaur. TALES OF A GAMBLING GRANDMA. Tundra, 1986.
Reminiscences of a grandmother who came to the U.S. from Russia, married a plumber, gambled to earn extra money, and formed a strong bond with her young granddaughter.

924. Krulik, Nancy E. PENNY AND THE FOUR QUESTIONS. *SEE 443.*

925. Nelson, Nan F. MY DAY WITH ANKA. Illus. by Bill Farnsworth. Lothrop, 1996.
When Anka comes each week on Thursday, young Karrie enjoys her Czech cooking and helps her with the housework.

926. Polacco, Patricia. THE TREES OF THE DANCING GOATS. Illus. by Marjorie Priceman. Simon & Schuster, 1996.
During a scarlet fever epidemic one winter in Michigan, a Jewish family helps make Christmas special for their sick neighbors by making their own Hanukkah miracle.

927. Rael, Elsa O. WHAT ZEESIE SAW ON DELANCEY STREET. Illus. by Marjorie Priceman. Simon & Schuster, 1996.
A young Jewish girl living on Manhattan's Lower East Side attends her first "package party," where she learns about the traditions of generosity, courage and community among Jewish immigrants in the early 1900's.

928. Rael, Elsa O. WHEN ZAYDEH DANCED ON ELDRIDGE STREET. Simon & Schuster, 1997.
While staying with her grandparents in New York City in the mid-1930's, eight-year-old Zeesie joins in the celebration of Simḥat Torah and sees a side of her stern grandfather she never knew.

929. Ray, Mary L. SHAKER BOY. Illus. by Jeanette Winter. Browndeer, 1994.
Having come to live among the Shakers at the age of six, Caleb spends the rest of his life learning their songs and their ways.

930. Smucker, Barbara. SELINA AND THE BEAR PAW QUILT. Illus. by Janet Wilson. Dragonflyer, 1999 (pap).
When her Memmonite family moves to Upper Canada to avoid involvement in the Civil War, Selina is given a special quilt to remember the grandmother she left behind.

931. Yezerski, Thomas. TOGETHER IN PINECONE PATCH. Farrar Straus, 1998.
A girl from Ireland and a boy from Poland overcome the prejudices held by the residents of the small American town to which they have emigrated.

European Immigrants – Easy and Intermediate Fiction

932. Armstrong, Jennifer. PATRICK DOYLE IS FULL OF BLARNEY. Illus. by Krista Brauckmann-Towns. Random, 1997.
Irish American nine-year-old Patrick promises his buddies that his baseball hero will come to their playground in Hell's Kitchen and bat for him.

933. Cohen, Barbara. MOLLY'S PILGRIM. *SEE 466.*

934. Kudlinski, Kathleen V. SHANNON. Illus. by Bill Farnsworth. Simon & Schuster, 1996.
Newly arrived in Victorian San Francisco from Ireland, Shannon plans the daring rescue of a young Chinese slave.

935. Littlefield, Holly. FIRE AT THE TRIANGLE FACTORY. Illus. by Mary O'Keefe Young. Carolrhoda, 1995.
Two fourteen-year-old girls, one Jewish and one Italian-American and both sewing machine operators at the Triangle Shirtwaist Company, are caught in the Triangle fire of 1911.

936. Machlin, Mikki. MY NAME IS NOT GUSSIE. Houghton Mifflin, 1999.
A young girl describes the difficulties and joys that she and her family experience when they come from Russia to settle in New York City in the early twentieth century.

937. Mayerson, Evelyn. THE CAT WHO ESCAPED FROM STEERAGE: A BUBBEMEISER. Atheneum, 1990.
Living in the steerage section of a steamship bound for America, Chanah, a European Jew, tries to keep her newly found cat a secret.

938. Orgel, Doris. DON'T CALL ME SLOB-O. Illus. by Bob Dorsey. Hyperion, 1996 (pap).
Shrimp must decide whether to befriend the new boy in his neighborhood, who is a Croatian American, or join the kids who make fun of his name and his accent.

939. Reynolds, Marilynn. THE NEW LAND: A FIRST YEAR ON THE PRAIRIE. Illus. by Stephen McCallum. Orca Book Publisher, 1997.
Tells the story of the European pioneer family's first year in the United States, from their journey by boat, train, and wagon to their own plot of land, through the task of finding water, building the homestead, plowing the land, and surviving their first winter.

940. Sandin, Joan. THE LONG WAY TO A NEW LAND. Trophy, 1986 (pap).
Carl Erik journeys with his family from Sweden to America during the famine of 1868.

941. Sandin, Joan. THE LONG WAY WESTWARD. Harper, 1992 (pap).
In a continuation of "The Long Way to a New Land", Carl Erik and his family travel from New York to their new home in Minnesota.

942. Shaw, Janet B. MEET KIRSTEN: AN AMERICAN GIRL. Pleasant Company, 1986 (pap).
Nine-year-old Kirsten and her family experience many hardships as they travel from Sweden to the Minnesota frontier in 1854.

Shaw, Janet B.
943. HAPPY BIRTHDAY, KIRSTEN. Pleasant, 1987.
944. KIRSTEN LEARNS A LESSON. Pleasant, 1986.
945. KIRSTEN SAVES THE DAY. Pleasant, 1988.
946. KIRSTEN'S SURPRISE. Pleasant, 1986.

European Immigrants - Fiction

947. Christiansen, C.B. I SEE THE MOON. Atheneum, 1995.
Twelve-year-old Norwegian American Bitte learns the answer to the question "what is love" when her older sister decides to place her unborn child for adoption.

948. Denenberg, Barry. SO FAR FROM HOME: THE DIARY OF MARY DRISCOLL, AN IRISH MILL GIRL. Scholastic, 1997.
In the diary account of her journey from Ireland in 1847 and of her work in a mill in Lowell, Massachusetts, fourteen-year-old Mary reveals a great longing for her family.

949. Giff, Patricia Reilly. THE GIFT OF THE PIRATE QUEEN. *SEE 339.*

950. Giff, Patricia Reilly. LILY'S CROSSING. Doubleday, 1997; Yearling, 1999 (pap).
During a summer spent at Rockaway Beach in 1944, Lily's friendship with a young Hungarian refugee causes her to see the war and her own world differently.

951. Holland, Isabelle. PAPERBOY. Holiday, c1999.
In 1881, in New York City, teenager Kevin O'Donnell, conscious of the prejudice against the Irish poor, struggles to support his sick father and young sister by working as a messenger for a prominent newspaper, but finds his job threatened when he is falsely accused of stealing from his employer.

952. Holm, Jennifer L. OUR ONLY MAY AMELIA. *SEE 342.*

953. Karr, Kathleen. MAN OF THE FAMILY. Farrar Straus & Giroux, 1999.
During the 1920's, life for Istvan, the eldest child of a Hungarian-American family, holds both joy and sadness.

954. Levitin, Sonia. SILVER DAYS. Aladdin, 1992 (pap).
After escaping from Hitler's Germany and living in a New York City tenement, Papa decides to move the family to California.

955. Paulsen, Gary. THE WINTER ROOM. Orchard, 1989; Yearling, 1996 (pap).
A young boy growing up on a northern Minnesota farm describes the scenes around him and recounts his old Norwegian uncle's tales of an almost mythological logging past.

956. Rinaldi, Ann. KEEP SMILING THROUGH. Harcourt, 1996.
A ten-year-old Irish-American girl living in middle-class America during World War II learns the painful lesson that doing what is right is not always an easy thing to do.

957. Snyder, Zilpha Keatley. THE GYPSY GAME. Bantam, 1997; Yearling, 1998 (pap).
Six imaginative schoolmates embark on a game in which they pretend to be gypsies, but when one of the boys runs away and takes up with a group of homeless people, the game threatens to become too real.

958. Sorenson, Henri. NEW HOPE. Puffin, 1998 (pap).
Jimmy's Grandpa tells him the same wonderful story each time he visits, the story of how Jimmy's great-great-great grandfather, a European immigrant turned pioneer, started the town of New Hope because his axle broke.

959. Springer, Nancy. THE BOY ON A BLACK HORSE. Atheneum, 1994; Troll, 1995 (pap).
Intrigued by the mysterious and angry Roma (gypsy) boy who joins her class, thirteen-year-old Gray finds that he shares her love of horses.

960. Thomassie, Tynia. FELICIANA FEYDRA LEROUX: A CAJUN TALL TALE. Little, 1995.
Even though Feliciana, a Cajun girl, is her grandfather's favorite, he refuses to allow her to go alligator hunting with him, so one night she sneaks out and joins the hunt anyway.

961. Woodruff, Elvira. THE ORPHAN OF ELLIS ISLAND: A TIME TRAVEL ADVENTURE. Scholastic, 1997.
During a school trip to Ellis Island, a ten-year-old foster child travels back in time to 1908 Italy and accompanies two young emigrants to America.

European Immigrants – Nonfiction

962. Bial, Raymond. CAJUN HOME. Houghton Mifflin, 1998.
Discusses the history and culture of the Cajuns, French-speaking people who settled deep in the woods and bayous of Louisiana.

963. Cavan, Seamus. THE IRISH AMERICAN EXPERIENCE. Millbrook, 1993.
Traces the history of Irish immigration to the United States, discussing why the Irish emigrated, their problems in a new land, and their contributions to American culture.

964. DiFranco, J. Phillip. THE ITALIAN AMERICANS. Chelsea, 1995.
Discusses the history, culture and religion of the Italians, factors encouraging their emigration, and their acceptance as an ethnic group in North America.

965. Galicich, Anne. THE GERMAN AMERICANS. Chelsea, 1995.
Presents German-American culture and history as the United States' largest ethnic group.

966. Leder, Jane M. RUSSIAN JEWISH FAMILY. Lerner, 1996.
Describes one Jewish family's fourteen-year struggle to emigrate from Leningrad to Chicago, and the adjustments they have had to make.

967. Moscinski, Sharon. TRACING OUR POLISH ROOTS. John Muir, 1994.
Offers a brief look at Polish history and culture, and describes the experiences and accomplishments of Polish immigrants.

968. Sewall, Marcia. THE PILGRIMS OF PLIMOTH. Atheneum, 1987; Aladdin, 1996 (pap).
Chronicles, in text and illustrations, the day-to-day life of the early Pilgrims in the Plimouth Colony.

969. Watts, J.F. THE IRISH AMERICANS. Chelsea, 1995.
Provides an overview of immigration and acceptance of Irish-Americans, including explanations of the group's culture, history and religion.

Hispanic American – Picture Books

970. Anaya, Rudolfo A. FAROLITOS FOR ABUELO. *SEE 617.*

971. Cordova, Amy. ABUELITA'S HEART. Simon & Schuster.
Before returning to the city with her parents, a young girl walks with her grandmother, learning about the special feelings, places, and plants that are part of her heritage and the Southwestern desert where Abuelita lives.

972. Cowley, Joy. BIG MOON TORTILLA. Boyds Mills, 1998.
When Marta ruins her homework and breaks her glasses, Grandmother sooths her with an ancient story and one of her delicious tortillas.

973. Dorros, Arthur. ABUELA. Illus. by Elisa Kleven. Dutton, 1991; Puffin, 1997 (pap).
While riding on the bus with her grandmother, a little girl imagines that they are carried up into the sky and fly over the sights of New York City.

974. Estes, Kristyn Rehling. MANUELA'S GIFT. *SEE 24.*

975. Kleven, Elisa. HOORAY, A PIÑATA. Dutton, 1996.
Little Clara falls in love with a piñata dog bought for her birthday.

976. Markel, Michelle. GRACIAS, ROSA. Illus. by Diane Paterson. Whitman, 1995.
At first Kate does not like her new babysitter, Rosa, but as time goes by they learn from each other through cultural and language exchanges.

977. Mora, Pat. A BIRTHDAY BASKET FOR TÍA. Illus. by Cecily Lang. Simon & Schuster, 1992; Aladdin, 1997 (pap).
Cecilia prepares a basket of birthday surprises for her great-aunt's ninetieth birthday.

978. Mora, Pat. THE RAINBOW TULIP. Viking, c1999.
A Mexican-American first-grader experiences the difficulties and pleasures of being different when she wears a tulip costume with all the colors of the rainbow for the school May Day parade.

979. Soto, Gary. SNAPSHOTS FROM THE WEDDING. Illus. by Stephanie Garcia. Putnam, 1997; Paper Star, 1998 (pap).
Maya, the flower girl, describes a Mexican American wedding through snapshots of the day's events, beginning with the procession to the altar and ending with her sleeping under a table.

980. Torres, Leyla. SATURDAY SANCOCHO. Farrar, 1995; Sunburst, 1999 (pap).
Maria Lili and her grandmother barter a dozen eggs at the market square to get the ingredients to cook their traditional Saturday chicken sancocho.

981. Wing, Natasha. JALAPEÑO BAGELS. *SEE 275.*

Hispanic American – Easy Readers and Intermediate

982. Bunting, Eve. GOING HOME. Illus. by David Diaz. HarperCollins, 1996; Trophy, 1998 (pap).
Although a Mexican family comes to the United States to work as farm laborers so that their children will have greater opportunities, the parents still consider Mexico their home.

983. Giff, Patricia Reilly. HO, HO, BENJAMIN, FELÍZ NAVIDAD. Bantam-Doubleday, 1995.
Benjamin's Christmas is not turning out well – until he catches some of the season's spirit from Senora Sanchez, his new neighbor from Ecuador.

984. Giff, Patricia Reilly. SAY HOLA, SARAH. Illus. by DyAnne DiSalvo-Ryan. Gareth Stevens, 1998.
Sarah is too embarrassed to speak Spanish in front of her friends at the Columbus Day party until Anna's cousin from Colombia explains her own secret fear.

985. Tamar, Erika. THE GARDEN OF HAPPINESS. Illus. by Barbara Lambase. Harcourt Brace, 1996.
Marisol and her ethnically diverse neighbors turn a vacant New York City lot into a lush community garden; the plants die when the season changes, but are reborn again in the art of a neighborhood wall.

Hispanic American – Fiction

986. Krumgold, Joseph. ....AND NOW MIGUEL. Crowell, 1953; Trophy, 1995 (pap).
A young boy tries to prove he is man enough to help his family drive their sheep into the Sangre de Cristo mountains.

987. Reeve, Kirk. LOLO AND RED-LEGS. Rising Moon, c1998.
When eleven-year-old Lolo catches a tarantula, it turns an ordinary summer into a series of adventures that take him and his friends beyond their Mexican-American neighborhood in East Los Angeles.

988. Soto, Gary. BASEBALL IN APRIL AND OTHER STORIES. Harcourt Brace, 1990.
A collection of eleven short stories focusing on the everyday adventures of young Hispanic people growing up in Fresno, California.

989. Soto, Gary. TAKING SIDES. Harcourt Brace, 1991.
A fourteen-year-old aspiring basketball player must come to terms with his divided loyalties when he moves from the Hispanic inner city to a white suburban neighborhood.

Hispanic American – Nonfiction

990. Ancona, George. BARRIO: JOSE'S NEIGHBORHOOD. Harcourt Brace, 1998.
Presents life in a barrio in San Francisco, describing the school, recreation, holidays, and family life of an eight-year-old boy who lives there.

991. Ancona, George. FIESTA U.S.A. Lodestar Books, 1995.
In a tribute to the customs and traditions of Latinos in the United States, photographs depict four fiestas: the Day of the Dead in San Francisco, Las Posadas and the Dance of the Matachines in New Mexico, and Three Kings' Day in New York City.

992. Brimmer, Larry Dane. A MIGRANT FAMILY. Lerner, 1992.
Portrays the life of twelve-year-old Juan Medina and his family, migrant workers living in Encinitas, California.

993. Gonzalez, Ralkfa. MY FIRST BOOK OF PROVERBS. Children's, 1995.
Humorous contemporary illustrations of traditional Mexican American proverbs, which appear in both English and Spanish.

994. Howlett, Bud. I'M NEW HERE. Houghton Mifflin, 1993.
Jazmin Escalante arrives in California from El Salvador with her family. Although she speaks no English, through perseverance she is accepted into the fifth grade and begins to make new friends.

995. Hoyt-Goldsmith, Diane. MIGRANT WORKER. *SEE 31.*

996. Malone, Michael. A GUATEMALAN FAMILY. Lerner, 1996.
Describes a Guatemalan family's struggle to emigrate from their country to the United States, and the adjustments they have made.

997. Palacios, Argentina. STANDING TALL: THE STORIES OF TEN HISPANIC AMERICANS. Scholastic, 1994 (pap).
A collection of mini-biographies follows the achievements of U. S. Navy Admiral David Farragut, baseball player Roberto Clemente, singer Gloria Estefan, schoolteacher Jaime Escalante, and six other notable Hispanic Americans.

998. Soto, Gary. NEIGHBORHOOD ODES. Harcourt Brace, 1992; Point, 1994 (pap).
Twenty-one poems about growing up in an Hispanic neighborhood, highlighting the delights in such everyday items as sprinklers, the parks, the library, and pomegranates.

999. Westridge Young Writers Workshop. KIDS EXPLORE AMERICAN HISPANIC HERITAGE. John Muir, 1996.
Presents writing by students in grades three to seven on topics of Hispanic culture, including dance, cooking, games, history, art, songs, and role models.

Hispanic American – Biographies

1000. Amdur, Melissa. LINDA RONSTADT. Chelsea, 1993.
Examines the life and musical career of the singer whose performances have included rock, opera, and Mexican folk music.

1001. Byers, Ann. JAMIE ESCALANTE: SENSATIONAL TEACHER. Enslow, 1996.
Presents the life of the Bolivian-born teacher who immigrated to the United States, where he inspired and motivated his inner city students to excel in mathematics.

1002. Cole, Melanie. JIMMY SMITS. Mitchell Lane, 1998.
Presents a biography of the talented and versatile actor best known for his television roles in "L.A. Law" and "NYPD Blue."

1003. Collins, David R. FARMWORKER'S FRIEND: THE STORY OF CESAR CHAVEZ. Carolrhoda, 1996.
Examines the life and accomplishments of the Mexican-American labor activist who helped organize migrant farm workers and establish a union to fight for their rights.

1004. Cooper, Martha. ANTHONY REYNOSO: BORN TO ROPE. Clarion, 1996.
Documents the experiences of nine-year-old Tony as he follows in the Mexican trick rope tradition handed down to him by his father, grandfather, and great-grandfather.

1005. Martinez, Elizabeth C. EDWARD JAMES OLMOS: MEXICAN AMERICAN ACTOR. Millbrook, 1994.
Traces the life and career of the award-winning actor, looks at his roles in television and motion pictures, and describes his efforts to help the Hispanic community.

1006. Martinez, Elizabeth C. HENRY CISNEROS: MEXICAN AMERICAN LEADER. Millbrook, 1993.
A biography of the first Hispanic mayor of a major United States city.

1007. Marvis, Barbara . J. ROBERT RODRIGUEZ. Mitchell Lane, 1998.
Presents a biography of the young Latino filmmaker who made "El Mariachi" for $7,000 and went on to direct "Desperado" and "From Dusk till Dawn."

Caribbean-American – Picture Books

1008. Cohen, Miriam. DOWN IN THE SUBWAY. DK Pub., 1998.
While riding on a hot subway train in New York City, Oscar and his family meet the Island Lady and experience the sights, smells, tastes, and sounds of the Caribbean Islands.

Caribbean-American – Intermediate

1009. Ada, Alma Flor. MY NAME IS MARIA ISABEL. Illus. by Dyble K. Thompson. Atheneum, 1993; Aladdin, 1995 (pap).
A third grader, born in Puerto Rico and now living in the US, wants to fit in at school. The writing assignment "My Greatest Wish" gives her that opportunity.

1010. Schecter, Ellen. THE BIG IDEA. Illus. by Bob Dorsey. Hyperion, 1996 (pap).
Eight-year-old Luz Mendez is determined to turn a run-down vacant lot into a garden like the one her grandmother had in Puerto Rico, but first she must convince the neighbors to help.

1011. Tamar, Erika. ALPHABET CITY BALLET. Trophy, 1997 (pap).
Marisol, a ten-year-old Puerto Rican girl, wins a scholarship to attend ballet school along with a Haitian-born classmate.

1012. Steptoe, John. CREATIVITY. Illus. by E. B. Lewis. Clarion, 1997.
Charles helps Hector, a student who has just moved from Puerto Rico, adjust to his new life.

Caribbean-American – Fiction

1013. Bernardo, Anil'u. FITTING IN. Arte Publico, 1996 (pap).
A collection of stories about young girls who, as Cuban immigrants to the United States, grow in confidence and spirit as they confront painful challenges.

1014. Hyppolite, Joanna. SETH AND SAMONA. Yearling, 1997 (pap).
A quiet Haitian-American boy and the wildest girl in fifth grade are accomplices in every adventure, until Seth decides that he has to stop Samona from entering the Little Miss Dorchester pageant.

Caribbean-American – Nonfiction

1015. Greenberg, Keith Elliot. A HAITIAN FAMILY. Lerner, 1997.
Chronicles the history of Haiti and the efforts of one Haitian family to emigrate to the United States and rebuild their lives in Brooklyn.

1016. Halliburton, Warren J. THE WEST-INDIAN AMERICAN EXPERIENCE. Millbrook Press, 1994.
Traces the history of West Indian immigration to the United States, discussing why people emigrated, their problems in a new land, and their contributions to American culture.

1017. McKenley, Yvonne. A TASTE OF THE CARIBBEAN. Thomson, 1995.
Provides a brief introduction to the culture of the Caribbean islands, describes common foods and dishes from the region, and includes representative recipes.

Caribbean-American – Biography

1018. Hawxhurst, Joan C. ANTONIA NOVELLO, US SURGEON GENERAL. Millbrook, 1993.
A biography of President Bush's Surgeon General, focusing on her childhood in Puerto Rico, personal medical problems, training and practice as a pediatrician, and opinions on health issues.

Indigenous People, U.S. – Picture Books

1019. Conway, Diana C. NORTHERN LIGHTS; A HANUKKAH STORY. Illus. by Shelley O. Haas. Kar-Ben, 1994.
When a storm grounds their plane, a Jewish family celebrates Hanukkah with a Yupik Eskimo family and discovers that they share many customs.

1020. Fellows, Rebecca Nevers. A LEI FOR TUTU. Whitman, 1998.
Nahoa loves making leis with her grandmother and looks forward to helping her create a special one for Lei Day, until her grandmother becomes very ill.

1021. Littlesugar, Amy. A PORTRAIT OF SPOTTED DEER'S GRANDFATHER. Whitman, 1997.
When Spotted Deer's grandfather dreams that one white man can keep the Indians from blowing away forever, Moose Horn agrees to let George Catlin paint his portrait.

1022. McCain, Becky R. GRANDMOTHER'S DREAMCATCHER. Whitman, 1998.
While spending a week with her grandmother who is a Chippewan Indian, Kimmy learns to make a dreamcatcher which helps a sleeper to have only good dreams.

1023. Medearis, Angela S. DANCING WITH THE INDIANS. Holiday, 1991.
A young African American girl goes to a Seminole powwow with the descendents of the tribe who rescued her grandfather from slavery and accepted him as one of their own years before.

1024. Momaday, N. Scott. CIRCLE OF WONDER; A NATIVE AMERICAN CHRISTMAS STORY. Clear Light, 1993.
A mute Indian child has an extraordinary experience one Christmas when, following a figure who seems to be his beloved dead grandfather, he becomes part of a circle in which he, animals, nature and all the world join in a moment of peace and good will.

1025. Polacco, Patricia. BOAT RIDE WITH LILLIAN TWO-BLOSSOM. Philomel, 1988.
A mysterious Indian woman takes William and Mabel on a strange boat ride and answers their questions about the wind, the rain, and the changing nature of the sky.

1026. Raczek, Linda Theresa. RAINY'S POWWOW. Rising Moon, c1999.
A Native American girl attends the traditional powwow where she is expected to choose for herself a specific form of dance and receive her special name.

1027. Schick, Eleanor. MY NAVAJO SISTER. Simon & Schuster, 1996.
A white girl lives for a short time on an Indian reservation and forms a close bond with a Navajo girl.

1028. Schick, Eleanor. NAVAJO WEDDING DAY: A DINE MARRIAGE CEREMONY. Marshall Cavendish, c1999.
When a young girl attends the wedding of her best friend's cousin, she learns many things about the customs of the Navajo Indians living in the American Southwest.

1029. Scott, Ann H. BRAVE AS A MOUNTAIN LION. Illus. by Glo Coalson. Houghton Mifflin, 1996.
Spider is afraid to get up on stage in the school spelling bee, but after listening to his father's advice, decides that he too will try to be as brave as his Shoshoni ancestors.

Indigenous Peoples, U.S. – Easy and Intermediate Fiction

1030. Bruchac, Joseph. EAGLE SONG. Illus. by Dan Andreason. Dial, 1997.
After moving from a Mohawk reservation to Brooklyn, eight-year-old Danny Bigtree encounters stereotypes about his Native American heritage.

1031. Dowd, John. RING OF TALL TREES. Alaska Northwest Books, 1992.
Dylan and his Native American friends call on ancient rituals and Raven the trickster for help in stopping a logging company from clearing the old-growth forest near Dylan's farm.

1032. Roop, Peter. AHYOKA AND THE TALKING LEAVES. Illus. by Yoshi Miyake. Morrow, 1994.
Ahyoka helps her father Sequoyah in his quest to create a system of writing for his people.

1033. Stewart, Elisabeth Jane. ON THE LONG TRAIL HOME. Clarion, 1994.
Meli and her brother escape from the Cherokee people being herded westward on the Trail of Tears, determined to return to their beloved mountain home.

Indigenous Peoples, U.S. – Fiction

1034. Ackerman, Ned. SPIRIT HORSE. Scholastic, 1998.
When a Siksika boy living on the Plains during the 1770's becomes separated from a raiding party, he discovers the legendary spirit horse which he attempts to track down and tame.

1035. Bruchac, Joseph. THE HEART OF A CHIEF: A NOVEL. Dial, c1998.
An eleven-year-old Penacook Indian boy living on a reservation faces his father's alcoholism, a controversy surrounding plans for a casino on a tribal island, and insensitivity toward Native Americans in his school and nearby town.

1036. Durrant, Lynda. THE BEADED MOCCASINS. Clarion, c1998.
After being captured by a group of Delaware Indians and given to their leader as a replacement for his dead granddaughter, twelve-year-old Mary Campbell is forced to travel west with them to Ohio.

1037. Erdich, Louise. THE BIRCHBARK HOUSE. Hyperion, c1999.
Omakayas, a seven-year-old Native American girl of the Ojibwa tribe, lives through the joys of summer and the perils of winter on an island in Lake Superior in 1847.

1038. George, Jean Craighead. THE TALKING EARTH. *SEE 338.*

1039. Griese, Arnold A. ANNA'S ATHABASKAN SUMMER. Boys Mills Press, 1995.
A young Athabaskan girl and her family make the annual return to their fish camp, where they prepare for the long winter ahead.

1040. Griese, Arnold. AT THE MOUTH OF THE LUCKIEST RIVER. *SEE 490.*

1041. Hobbs, Will. FAR NORTH. Avon, 1997.
After the destruction of their floatplane, sixteen-year-old Gabe and his Dene friend struggle to survive a winter in the wilderness of the Northwest Territories.

1042. Martin, Nora. THE EAGLE'S SHADOW. Scholastic, 1997.
In 1946, while her emotionally distant father is in occupied Japan, a twelve-year-old girl spends a year with her mother's relatives in a Tlingit Indian village in Alaska and begins to love and respect her heritage as she confronts the secret of her mother's disappearance.

1043. McKissack, Pat. RUN AWAY HOME. Scholastic, 1997.
In 1886 in Alabama, an eleven-year-old African American girl and her family befriend and give refuge to a runaway Apache boy.

1044. Oughton, Jerrie. MUSIC FROM A PLACE CALLED HALF MOON. Houghton, 1995; Bantam, 1996 (pap).
In 1956 in Half Moon, North Carolina, thirteen-year-old Edie Jo comes to terms with her own prejudice and the death of a friend.

1045. Strete, Craig. THE WORLD IN GRANDFATHER'S HANDS. Clarion, 1996.
Eleven-year-old Jimmy is upset when he and his mother must move from the pueblo to the city after his father's death, but his grandfather's patient philosophy helps Jimmy slowly adjust.

Indigenous Peoples, U.S. – Nonfiction

1046. Bruchac, Joseph. THIRTEEN MOONS ON TURTLE'S BACK: A NATIVE AMERICAN YEAR OF MOONS. Illus. by Thomas Locker. Philomel, 1992; Putnam, 1997 (pap).
Celebrates the seasons of the year through poems from the legends of such tribes as the Cherokee, Cree and Sioux.

1047. Claro, Nicole. THE CHEROKEE INDIANS. Chelsea, 1991.
Examines the history, culture, and future prospects of the Cherokee people.

1048. Dailey, Robert. THE CODE TALKERS; AMERICAN INDIANS IN WORLD WAR II. Watts, 1995.
Describes how Navajo soldiers in World War II used their languages as unbreakable codes to transmit information between American units.

1049. DANCING TEEPEES; POEMS OF AMERICAN INDIAN YOUTH. Illus. by Stephen Gammell. Holiday, 1989.
An illustrated collection of poems from the oral tradition of American Indians.

1050. Dolan, Terrance. THE SHAWNEE INDIANS. Chelsea, 1996.
Examines the history and present status of the Shawnee Indians, discussing their fight to retain their native lands.

1051. Force, Roland W. THE AMERICAN INDIANS. Chelsea, 1996.
Looks at the history and culture of the North American Indians.

1052. Greene, Jacqueline Dembar. POWWOW: A GOOD DAY TO DANCE. Franklin Watts, c1998.
Follows the activities of a young boy as his family attends a Wampanoag powwow, describing the significance of some of the events at the gathering, particularly the dances.

1053. Hazen-Hammond, Susan. THUNDER BEAR AND KO: THE BUFFALO NATION AND NAMBE PUEBLO. Dutton, 1999.
Describes the life of Thunder Bear Yates and his family in Nambe Pueblo, where they are trying to preserve the traditions of their ancestors as well as the buffalo that are sacred to their people.

1054. Kalman, Bobbie. CELEBRATING THE POWWOW. Crabtree, 1998.
Examines American Indian powwow celebrations, discussing the preparation, grand entry, competitions, traditional costumes, instruments, and symbols.

1055. Klausner, Janet. SEQUOYAH'S GIFT; A PORTRAIT OF THE CHEROKEE LEADER. HarperCollins, 1993.
A biography of the Cherokee Indian who created a method for his people to write and read their own language.

1056. Miller, Jay. AMERICAN INDIAN GAMES. Children's Press, c1996.
Briefly describes some of the toys and games used by various North American Indian cultures to amuse their children and teach lessons about life.

1057. Philip, Neil. EARTH ALWAYS ENDURES: NATIVE AMERICAN POEMS. Illus. by Edward S. Curtis. Viking, 1996.
A collection of sixty poems, accompanied by more than forty photographs, provides a portrait of the worlds of Native Americans, their beliefs, lifestyles, traditions, and views on various topics.

1058. Rendon, Marcie R. POWWOW SUMMER: A FAMILY CELEBRATES THE CIRCLE OF LIFE. Lerner, 1996.
Follows the Downwind family as the parents pass on their heritage to their children by attending a series of weekend powwows. Includes explanation of the Native American view of life cycles, especially as it corresponds to the seasons.

1059. Staub, Frank J. CHILDREN OF THE TLINGIT. Carolrhoda, c1999.
Introduces the history, geography, and culture of the Tlingit people in Southeast Alaska through the daily lives of children who live there.

1060. Stein, R. Conrad. THE BATTLE OF LITTLE BIGHORN. Childrens, 1997.
The story of the worst defeat ever suffered by the United States Army at the hands of the American Indians near the Little Bighorn River in Montana on June 25, 1876.

1061. Stein, R. Conrad. THE TRAIL OF TEARS. Childrens, 1993.
Describes the Federal government's seizure of Cherokee lands in Georgia and the forced migration of the Cherokee nation to Oklahoma along the route that came to be called the Trail of Tears.

1062. Williams, Jeanne. TRAILS OF TEARS: AMERICAN INDIANS DRIVEN FROM THEIR LANDS. Hendrick-Long, 1992.
A discussion of the white man's treatment and forcible displacement of five Indian nations of the Southwest: the Comanche, Cheyenne, Apache, Navajo and Cherokee.

Cultural, Racial & Ethnic – Series

1063. CULTURES OF AMERICA. Published by Marshall Cavendish.
A look at the historical background of the cultures that make up the American population of today, and the ways in which each culture has contributed to the mainstream.

1064. ETHNIC ANSWER BOOKS. Chelsea House.
In two broadly arranged sections, presents questions and answers covering the history, culture and social life, religion, political activities, economic life, and accomplishments of of various ethnic groups.

1065. FOOTSTEPS TO AMERICA. New Discovery Books, Parsippany, New Jersey.
This series looks at the reasons why groups leave their homelands, and the reasons they give for choosing the United States for their new home. Emphasis on understanding the immigrant culture and the cultureal prejudices each group encounters.

1066. IN AMERICA. Lerner Publications.
A discussion of the contributions of many different ethnic groups to the history and civilization of the United States. Includes a discussion of the historical reasons for migrating.

1067. JOURNEY BETWEEN TWO WORLDS. Lerner.
Chronicles the history of immigrant groups and describes the experience of one family from each group that left their native country to rebuild their lives in America.

1068. LIBRARY OF AFRICAN AMERICAN HISTORY. Facts on File.
Discusses important issues in different stages of history of special interest to African Americans.

1069. NATIVE PEOPLES. Bridgestone Books.
Provides an overview of the past and present lives of selected Native American tribes, covering daily life, customs, relations with the United States government, and so on.

1070. ORIGINS. Franklin Watts.
Discusses the history of emigration from various countries, detailing accounts of the emigrants' experiences and emphasizing their positive input to their new countries.

1071. OUR AMERICAN FAMILY. PowerKids Press.
Briefly discusses an immigrant American's heritage, including clothing, food, holidays, and famous immigrants.

1072. THE PEOPLE OF NORTH AMERICA. Published by Chelsea House.
The wide variety of ethnic groups which make up the population of the United States, Canada and Mexico are examined with insight and attention to detail. A look at each culture and the contributions that have enhanced the everyday life of North Americans receive recognition.

1073-1094. COOKING THE ... WAY. Lerner.
Features titles that provide recipes from all corners of the earth.

Settings

Geographical • Historical • City/Country •
Education & Learning • Series

Settings

Geographical Settings – General – Nonfiction

1095. Ajmera, Maya. CHILDREN FROM AUSTRALIA TO ZIMBABWE: A PHOTOGRAPHIC JOURNEY AROUND THE WORLD. Charlesbridge, c1997.
Text and photographs depict how children live in nations across the alphabet from Australia to Zimbabwe.

1096. Ajmera, Maya. TO BE A KID. Charlesbridge, c1999.
Illustrates some of the activities children everywhere have in common.

1097. Albyn, Carole Lisa. THE MULTICULTURAL COOKBOOK FOR STUDENTS. Oryx, 1993.
Presents a collection of recipes from over 120 countries and briefly discusses the culture and culinary habits of each country.

1098. Badt, Karin Luisa. GOOD MORNING, LET'S EAT! Childrens, 1994.
Discusses the different types of food and drink that people from around the world have for breakfast.

1099. Badt, Karin Luisa. HAIR THERE AND EVERYWHERE. Childrens, 1994.
Photographs and text show how people throughout the world wear their hair. Discusses various cultures' customs and celebrations that call for special hairstyles.

1100. Badt, Karin Luisa. LET'S GO! Childrens, 1995.
Explores various forms of transportation throughout the world.

1101. Badt, Karin Luisa. ON YOUR FEET! Childrens, 1994.
Photographs and text discuss the types of footwear worn around the world, their uses, and their history.

1102. Badt, Karin Luisa. PASS THE BREAD! Childrens, 1994.
Discusses the bread eaten by people of various cultures.

1103. Bernhard, Emery. HAPPY NEW YEAR! Lodestar, 1996.
Describes the origins of New Year traditions and ways in which the coming of the New Year is celebrated around the world.

1104. Chandler, Clare. HARVEST CELEBRATIONS. Millbrook, c1997.
Discusses the significance of harvest festivals worldwide and describes how they are celebrated.

1105. Cook, Deanna F. THE KIDS' MULTICULTURAL COOKBOOK: FOOD AND FUN AROUND THE WORLD. Williamson, 1995.
A selection of seventy-five international recipes and local customs of the countries from which the recipes originate.

1106. Gelber, Carol. LOVE AND MARRIAGE AROUND THE WORLD. Millbrook, c1998.
Discusses customs around the world relating to the taboos and societal conventions surrounding love and marriage.

1107. Greising, Cynthia David. TOYS EVERYWHERE. Childrens, 1996.
Describes a variety of toys, including the Australian boomerang, South American knobkerrie and Chinese shuttlecock.

1108. HOLIDAY COOKING AROUND THE WORLD. Lerner, 1988.
A collection of holiday recipes from fifteen different countries, including a variety of dishes such as Thai egg rolls, Passover layer cake, paella, and Danish rice pudding.

1109. Kindersley, Barnabas. CELEBRATIONS. DK, 1997.
A calendar of celebrations which describes holidays and festivals of a variety of major religions and cultures.

1110. Kindersley, Barnabas. CHILDREN JUST LIKE ME. DK, 1995.
Photographs and text depict the homes, schools, family life and culture of young people around the world.

1111. Markham, Lois. HARVEST. Blackbirch, c1999.
Describes how people in various countries give thanks for the harvest.

1112. Milord, Susan. HANDS AROUND THE WORLD: 365 CREATIVE WAYS TO BUILD CULTURAL AWARENESS AND GLOBAL RESPECT. Williamson, 1992.
Presents a variety of games and other activities to promote awareness of different cultures.

1113. Simon, Norma. ALL KINDS OF CHILDREN. Whitman, 1999.
Presents the things that all children have in common, including their need for food, clothes, people to love them, and the opportunity to play.

1114. Spirn, Michele. BIRTH. Blackbirch, c1999.
Describes how people in different regions of the world celebrate the birth of babies.

1115. Steele, Philip. THE WORLD OF FESTIVALS. Rand McNally, 1996.
Covers a variety of world festivals, holidays and celebrations.

1116. Swain, Ruth Freeman. BEDTIME! Holiday, c1999.
Relates a variety of facts about beds, sleepwear, and sleeping from different cultures and periods of history, from ancient Egypt and China to the contemporary world of astronautics.

1117. Vezza, Diane Simone. PASSPORT ON A PLATE: A ROUND-THE-WORLD COOKBOOK FOR CHILDREN. Simon & Schuster, 1997.
Describes the culinary styles of twelve regions and provides recipes for each, including Africa, the Caribbean, and China.

Geographical Settings – Africa – Picture Books

1118. Chocolate, Deborah M. Newton. KENTE COLORS. Illus. by John Ward. Walker, 1996.
A rhyming description of the Kente clothing of the Ashanti and Ewe people of Ghana.

1119. Greenfield, Eloise. AFRICA DREAM. Illus. by Carole Byard. HarperCollins, 1992 (pap).
A black child's dreams are filled with the images of the people, animals, and places of Africa.

1120. Isadora, Rachel. A SOUTH AFRICAN NIGHT. Greenwillow, 1998.
The animals in Kruger National Park go about their business at night, while the people of Johannesburg sleep, and then lie down in the shade as the people wake up.

1121. Kroll, Virginia. JAHA AND JAMIL WENT DOWN THE HILL: AN AFRICAN MOTHER GOOSE. Illus. by Katherine Roundtree. Charlesbridge Pub., 1995.
Forty-nine original verses written in the tradition of Mother Goose and set in Africa.

1122. MacDonald, Suse. NANTA'S LION. Morrow, 1995.
A Masai child is curious to see the lion that her father and the other villagers are hunting.

1123. Sisulu, Elinor B. THE DAY GOGO WENT TO VOTE. *SEE 171.*

1124. Stock, Catherine. WHERE ARE YOU GOING, MANYONI? Morrow, 1993.
A child living near the Limpopo river in Zimbabwe encounters several wild animals on her way to school.

1125. Watson, Pete. THE MARKET LADY AND THE MANGO TREE. Illus. by Mary Watson. Tambourine, 1994.
A sly West African merchant gets rich when she devises a contraption for collecting mangos, but a dream teaches her a valuable lesson about greed.

1126. Williams, Karen L. GALIMOTO. Illus. by Catherine Stock. Mulberry, 1991 (pap).
Walking through his village in Africa, a young boy finds the materials he needs to make a special toy.

Geographical Settings – Africa – Fiction

1127. Farmer, Nancy. THE EAR, THE EYE AND THE ARM. Orchard, 1994; Puffin, 1995 (pap).
Three children are kidnapped and put to work in a plastic mine in Zimbabwe.

1128. Farmer, Nancy. DO YOU KNOW ME? Orchard, 1993; Puffin, 1994 (pap).
Tapiwa's uncle becomes her best friend when he comes to live with her family in Zimbabwe, after his village in Mozambique is burned by bandits.

1129. Hansen, Joyce. CAPTIVE. Scholastic, 1994; Apple, 1995 (pap).
An African boy recounts his journey from Africa to America as a slave.

1130. Kurtz, Jane. THE STORYTELLER'S BEADS. Gulliver, 1998.
Two girls, one Christian and one Jewish and blind, struggle to overcome their prejudices about each other as they make the dangerous journey out of Ethiopia during political strife and famine in 1980.

1131. Naidoo, Beverley. JOURNEY TO JO'BURG. HarperCollins, 1986; Trophy 1988 (pap).
Separated from their mother by the harsh social and economic conditions prevalent among Black people in South Africa, thirteen-year-old Naledi and her younger brother make a journey of over 300 kilometers to find her in Johannesburg.

1132. Naidoo, Beverley. CHAIN OF FIRE. Trophy 1993 (pap).
Sequel to Journey to Jo'burg. When the villagers of Bophelong are forced to leave their houses and resettle in a barren homeland, thirteen-year-old Naledi and her younger brother join in a school demonstration and learn that the South African government treats even children who dissent with brutality.

1133. Naidoo, Beverley. NO TURNING BACK. HarperCollins, 1997.
When the abuse at home becomes too much for twelve-year-old Sipho, he runs away to the streets of Johannesburg and learns to survive in the post-apartheid world.

Geographical Settings – Middle East – Picture Books

1134. Heide, Florence P. THE DAY OF AHMED'S SECRET. Illus. by Ted Lewis. Mulberry, 1995 (pap).
A young Egyptian boy goes about his daily work in the streets of Cairo, and waits for the evening to share a special surprise with his family.

1135. Khan, Rukhsana. THE ROSES IN MY CARPETS. Illus. by Ronald Himler. Holiday, 1998.
When a young boy and his mother and sister come to a refugee camp to escape the war in Afghanistan, he finds comfort in the beauty of the carpets he is learning to weave.

1136. Lewin, Ted. THE STORYTELLERS. Lothrop, 1998.
Abdul and Grandfather pass through the streets of Fez, Morocco, and stop at an old gate, where grandfather performs as a storyteller.

1137. McKay, Lawrence. CARAVAN. Illus. by Darryl Ligasan. Lee & Low, 1995.
A ten-year-old boy accompanies his father, for the first time, on a caravan trip through the mountains of Afghanistan to the city below to trade their goods at market.

1138. Oppenheim, Shulamit Levey. THE HUNDREDTH NAME. Boyds Mills Press, 1995.
Salah, a boy living in Egypt, wants to eliminate his camel's sadness, so he prays that the camel will learn Allah's hundredth name, which is unknown to humans.

Geographical Settings – Middle East – Fiction

1139. Dalokay, Vedat. SISTER SHAKO AND KOLO THE GOAT. Illus. by Guner Ener. Lothrop Lee, 1994.
Sister Shako describes village life in Eastern Turkey.

1140. Feder, Harriet K. THE MYSTERY OF THE KAIFENG SCROLL. Lerner, 1995.
Fifteen-year-old Aviva travels to Istanbul to vacation with her mother, but when she arrives she finds her mother missing. She must trust an Arab girl, as well as her knowledge of Torah, to unravel the mystery.

1141. Fletcher, Susan. SHADOW SPINNER. Atheneum, 1998; Aladdin, 1999 (pap).
Marjan, a thirteen-year-old crippled girl who joins the Sultan's harem in Persia, gathers for Shahrazad the stories which will save the queen's life.

Geographical Settings – Asia – Picture Books

1142. Bond, Ruskin. CHERRY TREE. Illus. by Allan Eitzen. Boyds Mills Press, 1996.
A girl learns about life and growth as she raises a cherry tree in the foothills of the Himalayas.

1143. Chin, Charlie. CHINA'S BRAVEST GIRL: THE LEGEND OF HUA MU LAN. Illus. by Tomie Arai. Children's, 1993.
The Chinese legend of Mu Lan, who goes to war disguised as a man to save her family's honor, and becomes a great general.

1144. Garland, Sherry. MY FATHER'S BOAT. *SEE 842.*

1145. Kroll, Virginia. A CARP FOR KIMIKO. *SEE 304.*

1146. Lewin, Ted. SACRED RIVER. *SEE 436.*

1147. Reeser, Michael. HUAN CHING AND THE GOLDEN FISH. Illus. by Dick Sakahara. Raintree Steck-Vaughn, 1988.
A grandfather competes against his grandson in a kite-flying contest on Chung Yang Chiesh, the Chinese kite-flying holiday.

1148. Russell, Christina. MOON FESTIVAL. Illus. by Christopher Zhong-Yuan Zhang. Boyd Mills Press, 1997.
This story of children celebrating the traditional autumn Moon Festival is based on the author's memories of her childhood in China.

1149. Say, Allen. TREE OF CRANES. *SEE 420.*

1150. Shea, Pegi Deitz. THE WHISPERING CLOTH: A REFUGEE'S STORY. Illus. by You Yang. Boyds Mills Press, 1996 (pap).
A young girl in a Thai refugee camp finds the story within herself to create her own pa'ndau, a brightly colored story cloth.

1151. Steckman, Elizabeth. SILK PEONY, PARADE DRAGON. Illus. by Carol Inouye. Boyds Mills Press, 1997.
The story of how Mrs. Ming's pet dragon, Silk Peony, becomes the official parade dragon of China.

1152. Wettasinghe, Sybil. UMBRELLA THIEF. Kane-Miller, 1987.
When each of the umbrellas he brings back to his village in Sri Lanka disappears, Kiri Mama devises a plan to track down the thief.

Geographical Settings – Asia – Fiction

1153. Axworthy, Ann. ANNI'S INDIA DIARY. Whispering Coyote Press, 1992.
A ten-year-old's diary entries chronicle the magical sights and sounds she and her family encounter as they explore India.

1154. Balgassi, Haemi. PEACEBOUND TRAINS. Clarioin, 1996.
Sumi's grandmother tells the story of her family's escape from Seoul during the Korean War.

1155. Choi, Sook Nyul. ECHOES OF THE WHITE GIRAFFE. Houghton Mifflin, 1993; Yearling, 1995 (pap).
Fifteen-year-old Sookan adjusts to life in the refugee village in Pusan, Korea, but continues to hope that the Korean War will end and her family will be reunited in Seoul.

1156. Choi, Sook Nyul. YEAR OF IMPOSSIBLE GOODBYES. Houghton Mifflin, 1991; Yearling, 1993 (pap).
A young girl survives the oppressive Japanese and Russian occupation of North Korea during the 1940's, and later escapes to freedom in South Korea.

1157. Coerr, Eleanor. SADAKO AND THE THOUSAND PAPER CRANES. *SEE 105.*

1158. De Jong, Meindert. THE HOUSE OF SIXTY FATHERS. Harper, 1956; Trophy, 1987 (pap).
Alone in a sampan with his pig and three ducklings, a little Chinese boy is whirled down a raging river, back to the town from which he and his parents escaped the invading Japanese.

1159. Fritz, Jean. HOMESICK, MY OWN STORY. Illus. by Margot Tomes. Putnam, 1982; Paper Star, 1999 (pap).
The author's fictionalized version, based on true events, of her childhood in China in the 1920's.

1160. Godden, Rumer. PREMLATA AND THE FESTIVAL OF LIGHTS. HarperCollins, 1999 (pap).
Premlata's family is too poor to celebrate the Indian Festival of Lights until fate and an elephant step in.

1161. Jiang, Ji-Li. RED SCARF GIRL; A MEMOIR OF THE CULTURAL REVOLUTION. HarperCollins, 1997; Trophy, 1998 (pap).
The story of a twelve-year-old girl growing up in China in 1966, the year that Chairman Mao launched the Cultural Revolution, and the changes it brought to her and her family.

1162. Lewis, Elizabeth. YOUNG FU OF THE UPPER YANGTZE. Dell, 1990 (pap).
During the 1920's, a Chinese youth comes to Chungking from the country, and his apprenticeship to a coppersmith brings good fortune.

1163. Neuberger, Anne E. THE GIRL-SON. *SEE 352.*

1164. Russell, Ching Yeung. FIRST APPLE. Illus. by Christopher Zhong-Yuan Zhang. Boyd Mills Press, 1994; Puffin, 1996 (pap).
Living in China during the late 1940's, a young girl works to save enough money to buy an apple for her grandmother's birthday, since neither of them have ever tasted an apple.

1165. Russell, Ching Yeung. LICHEE TREE. Illus. by Christopher Zhong-Yuan Zhang. Boyd Mills Press, 1997.
In the late 1940's in southeastern China, ten-year-old Ying can't wait for her lichee tree to bloom so she can sell the fruit for money to help her family.

1166. Say, Allen. INK-KEEPER'S APPRENTICE. Houghton Mifflin, 1994.
A fourteen-year-old boy lives on his own in Tokyo and becomes apprenticed to a famous Japanese cartoonist.

1167. Schaeffer, Edith. MEI FUH: MEMORIES FROM CHINA. Houghton Mifflin, 1997.
An account of the lives of an American girl and her family, living in China in the early 1900's.

1168. Schlein, Miriam. THE YEAR OF THE PANDA. Crowell, 1990; Trophy, 1992 (pap).
A Chinese boy rescues a starving baby panda, and in the process learns why pandas are endangered.

1169. Whelan, Gloria. GOODBYE, VIETNAM. Random, 1993 (pap).
Thirteen-year-old Mai and her family embark on a dangerous sea voyage from Vietnam to Hong Kong to escape the unpredictable and often brutal Vietnamese government.

1170. Wu, Priscilla. The ABACUS CONTEST: STORIES FROM TAIWAN AND CHINA. Illus. by Xiao-Jun Li. Fulcrum, 1996.
In a small city in southern Taiwan, six children with a traditional background experience different changes in their outlook.

Geographical Settings – Asia – Nonfiction

1171. Cheneviaere, Alain. PAK IN INDONESIA. Lerner, 1996.
Describes the work of a young Indonesian bull driver who trains and races his animals.

1172. Huynh, Quang Nhuong. THE LAND I LOST: ADVENTURES OF A BOY IN VIETNAM. Peter Smith, 1982; Trophy, 1986 (pap).
A collection of personal reminiscences of the author's youth in a hamlet on the central highlands of Vietnam.

1173. Lee, Jeanne M. THE SONG OF MU LAN. Front Street Press, 1995.
Translation of a Chinese folk song about a girl who joined the army to substitute for her father.

1174. Matthews, Jo. I REMEMBER VIETNAM. Steck-Vaughn, 1994.
Han, one of the Vietnamese boat people, describes life in his country, compares it to life in developed countries, and discusses the changes that have occured since the end of the Vietnam War.

1175. McMahon, Patricia. CHI-HOON: A KOREAN GIRL. Illus. by Michael F. O'Brien. Boyd Mills Press, 1998.
The story of a young Korean girl, her family, and their life in Seoul, Korea.

1176. Park, Frances. MY FREEDOM TRIP. Illus by Debra Reid Jenkins. Boyds Mills, 1998.
Soo, a young child living in North Korea prior to the start of the Korean War, must leave her mother behind in order to make a dangerous journey to cross into South Korea and be reunited with her father.

1177. Schmidt, Jeremy. TWO LANDS, ONE HEART: AN AMERICAN BOY'S JOURNEY TO HIS MOTHER'S VIETNAM. Illus. by Ted Rand. Walker, 1995.
Text and photographs record the visit to Vietnam of American-born TJ and his Vietnamese mother, who came to America twenty years ago, and the emotions and cultural disparities involved.

1178. Viesti, Joseph F. CELEBRATE IN SOUTH ASIA. Illus. by Diane Hall. Lothrop Lee, 1996.
Describes religious festivals and sacred days celebrated in India, Sri Lanka, Bangladesh, Pakistan, Bhutan, Burma, and Nepal.

1179. Viesti, Joe E. CELEBRATE IN SOUTHEAST ASIA. Illus. by Diane Hall. Lothrop Lee, 1996.
Describes a variety of holiday celebrations in Southeast Asia, including Thailand's Elephant Round-Up, Singapore's Moon Cake Festival, and the Vietnamese New Year.

Geographical Settings – Australia – Picture Books

1180. Winch, John. THE OLD WOMAN WHO LOVED TO READ. Holiday, 1997.
An old woman moves to the country in order to have a peaceful life with lots of time to read, but she soon finds that each season brings other tasks to keep her busy.

Geographical Settings – Australia – Fiction

1181. Crew, Gary. ANGEL'S GATE. Simon & Schuster, 1995.
Kimmy encounters two wild children who have grown up in the hills of Australia.

1182. Disher, Gary. BAMBOO FLUTE. Ticknor and Fields, 1993.
In a rural Australian community, twelve-year-old Paul has his predictable life brightened when a drifter helps him make a flute and teaches him how to play it.

1183. Gleitzman, Morris. BLABBER MOUTH. Harcourt Brace, 1995.
An Australian schoolgirl, who is unable to speak, is embarrassed by her father's outlandish dress and behavior.

1184. Hill, Anthony. THE BURNT STICK. Illus. by Mark Sofilas. Houghton Mifflin, 1995.
Growing up in a missionary home run by white men, John Jogamarra, who is part aborigine and part white, misses his mother and the culture of his own people.

1185. Rubinstein, Gillian. FOXSPELL. Illus. by Steve Michaels. Simon & Schuster, 1996.
Twelve-year-old Tod's mystical links with a spirit, and with the natural world around his grandmother's Australian home, interfere with his ability to adjust to the real world.

Geographical Settings – Australia – Nonfiction

1186. Crofford, Emily. HEALING WARRIOR: A STORY ABOUT SISTER ELIZABETH KENNY. Carolrhoda, 1989.
A biography of the Australian nurse who developed a successful method of treating and rehabilitating polio patients.

Geographical Settings – Europe – Picture Books

1187. Aliki. MARIANTHE'S STORY, PAINTED WORDS; MARIANTHE'S STORY, SPOKEN MEMORIES. Greenwillow, 1998.
This second story in a series describes the village in Greece that Marianthe and her family eventually leave in search of a better life.

1188. Bemelmans, Ludwig. MADELINE. Viking, 1963.
Madeline, the smallest and naughtiest of the twelve little charges of Miss Clavel, wakes up one night with an attack of appendicitis.

1189. Bemelmans, Ludwig. MADELINE IN LONDON. Viking, 1977 (pap).
The twelve little girls under Miss Clavel's charge go to visit the Ambassador's son in London.

1190. Bingham, Mindy. MINOU. Illus. by Itoko Maeno. Advocacy Press, 1987.
A cat who does not know how to take care of herself is abandoned in the streets of Paris and discovers self-reliance by working as a mouser at the Notre Dame Cathedral.

1191. Bresnick-Perry, Roslyn. LEAVING FOR AMERICA. Illus. by Mira Reisberg. Children's Book Press, 1992.
The author recalls her early years in a small Jewish town in western Russia, and the last days there as she and her mother prepare to join her father in the United States.

1192. Bunting, Eve. MARKET DAY. Illus. by Holly Berry. HarperCollins, 1996.
Tess and Wee Boy observe the farm animals, watch the sword-swallower, hear the playing of pipes, and experience all the excitement of a country fair in Ireland.

1193. De Paola, Tomie. DAYS OF THE BLACKBIRD: A TALE OF NORTHERN ITALY. Putnam, 1997.
At the request of a kind duke's loving daughter, La Colomba, a pure white bird braves the bitter winter of the northern Italian mountains to sing for the gravely ill man.

1194. Leaf, Munro. THE STORY OF FERDINAND. Viking, 1938.
In a story set in Spain, Ferdinand likes to sit quietly and smell the flowers, but one day he gets stung by a bee, and his snorting and stomping convince everyone that he is the fiercest of bulls.

1195. Levine, Arthur. ALL THE LIGHTS IN THE NIGHT. Illus. by James E. Ransome. Tambourine Books, 1991; Mulberry, 1997 (pap).
Moses and his little brother Benjamin find a way to celebrate Hanukkah during their dangerous emigration from Europe to Palestine.

1196. McCully, Emily Arnold. MIRETTE ON THE HIGH WIRE. Putnam, 1992.
Mirette, a French girl, learns tightrope walking from a guest in her mother's boarding house, not knowing that he is a celebrated tightrope artist who withdrew from performing because of fear.

1197. Nerlove, Miriam. FLOWERS ON THE WALL. McElderry Books, 1996.
Rachel, a Jewish girl living in Nazi-occupied Warsaw, struggles to survive with her family and maintains hope by painting colorful flowers on the dingy apartment walls.

1198. Oppenheim, Shulamith Levey. THE LILY CUPBOARD. Trophy, 1995 (pap).
Miriam, a young Jewish girl, is forced to leave her parents and hide with strangers in the country during the German occupation of Holland.

1199. Strevens, Biddy. TOTO IN ITALY: A FIRST TASTE OF ITALY AND THE ITALIAN LANGUAGE. Passport, 1992.
While visiting Rome, Toto befriends a lost cat who joins a sightseeing tour and causes a commotion before being reunited with his owner.

Geographical Settings – Europe – Fiction

1200. Ackerman, Karen. THE NIGHT CROSSING. Illus. by Elizabeth Sayles. Random, 1995 (pap).
In 1938, having begun to feel the persecution that all Jews are experiencing in their Austrian city, Clara and her family escape over the mountains into Switzerland.

1201. Alcock, Vivian. THE CUCKOO SISTER. Houghton Mifflin, 1997 (pap).
A scruffy, undernourished teenager appears at the door of Kate's parents' London home, bearing a note that she is their long-lost child who was stolen as a baby.

1202. Bunting, Eve. SPYING ON MISS MULLER. Clarion, 1995; Juniper, 1996 (pap).
At a boarding school in Belfast at the start of World War II, thirteen-year-old Jessie must deal with her suspicions about a teacher whose father was German, and her worries about her own father's drinking problems.

1203. Burnett, Frances Hodgson. A LITTLE PRINCESS(a.k.a. SARA CREWE). HarperCollins, 1999 (pap).
Sara Crewe, a pupil at a London school, is left in poverty when her father dies, but is later rescued by a mysterious benefactor.

1204. Carlson, Natalie Savage. THE FAMILY UNDER THE BRIDGE. *SEE 34.*

1205. Cooper, Susan. THE BOGGART. McElderry, 1993; Aladdin, 1995 (pap).
After visiting the castle in Scotland which her family has inherited, twelve-year-old Emily finds that she brought back home to Canada an invisible and mischievous spirit.

1206. DeJong, Meindert. THE WHEEL ON THE SCHOOL. Harper, 1924.
The children of Stora succeed in bring storks to every roof of their little Dutch town.

1207. Dodge, Mary Mapes. HANS BRINKER OR THE SILVER SKATES. Troll, 1988 (pap).
A Dutch boy and girl work toward two goals – finding a doctor who can restore their father's memory, and winning the competition for the silver skates.

1208. Hartling, Peter. CRUTCHES. *SEE 512.*

1209. Hautzig, Esther. A GIFT FOR MAMA. Peter Smith, 1992.
Sick and tired of making presents for various holidays and occasions, Sara, a Polish girl, decides that for this Mother's Day she will do something different.

1210. Hesse, Karen. LETTERS FROM RIFKA. Holt, 1992; Puffin, 1993 (pap).
In letters to her cousin, a young Jewish girl chronicles her family's flight from Russia in 1919 and her own experiences when she must be left in Belgium for a while when the others emigrate to America.

1211. Jimenez, Juan R. PLATERO Y YO = PLATERO AND I. Houghton Mifflin, 1994.
Presents a picture of life in the town of Moguer, in Andalusia, Spain, as seen through the eyes of a wandering poet and his faithful donkey.

1212. Kerr, Judith. WHEN HITLER STOLE PINK RABBIT. Paper Star, 1997 (pap).
Recounts the adventures of a nine-year-old Jewish girl and her family in the 1930's as they travel from Germany to England via Switzerland.

1213. King-Smith, Dick. SOPHIE'S TOM. Candlewick, 1994 (pap).
Befriending a stray cat helps a very determined five-year-old English girl adjust to school, learn about friends, and pursue her dream of someday becoming a farmer.

1214. Levitin, Sonia. JOURNEY TO AMERICA. Aladdin, 1987 (pap).
A Jewish family fleeing Nazi Germany in 1938 endures innumerable separations before they are once again united.

1215. Lowry, Lois. NUMBER THE STARS. *SEE 469.*

1216. McKay, Hilary. DOG FRIDAY. McElderry, 1995; Aladdin, 1997 (pap).
Ten-year-old Robin, an English child, is determined to keep the dog that he found abandoned on the beach from being impounded by the police.

1217. Mead, Alice. ADEM'S CROSS. Farrar Straus, 1996; Laureleaf, 1998 (pap).
Thirteen-year-old Adem's life is changed after he sees his sister shot to death for reading a poem at a demonstration against Serbian control of largely Albanian Kosovo.

1218. Mooney, Bel. THE VOICES OF SILENCE. Delacorte, 1997; Laureleaf, 1998 (pap).
Thirteen-year-old Floria and her family are caught up in the events leading to the overthrow of the repressive regime of Nicholas Ceausescu in Romania in 1989.

1219. Morpurgo, Michael. WAITING FOR ANYA. Viking, 1990; Puffin, 1997 (pap).
A reclusive widow's farm has become a haven for Jewish children hiding from the Nazis in the French Alps.

1220. Nichol, Barbara. BEETHOVEN LIVES UPSTAIRS. *SEE 496.*

1221. Seredy, Kate. THE GOOD MASTER. *SEE 223.*

1222. Spyri, Johanna. HEIDI. Grosset, 1994.
A Swiss orphan is heartbroken when she must leave her beloved grandfather in the Swiss mountains to go to school and to care for an invalid girl in the city.

1223. Vos, Ida. HIDE AND SEEK. Houghton Mifflin, 1991.
A young Jewish girl living in Holland tells of her experiences during the Nazi occupation, and after the war ends.

1224. Wojciechowska, Maia. SHADOW OF A BULL. Atheneum, 1964; Aladdin, 1992 (pap).
Manolo, a Spanish boy, has to make a decision: whether to follow in his famous father's footsteps and become a bullfighter, or to follow his heart and become a doctor.

Geographical Settings – Europe – Nonfiction

1225. Buettner, Dan. SOVIETREK: A JOURNEY BY BICYCLE ACROSS RUSSIA. Lerner, 1994.
Four American cyclists made a 7,353-mile bicycle journey across southern Russia from June 1990 through November 1990 and accompany their description with full-color photographs.

1226. Hautzig, Esther. THE ENDLESS STEPPE. Trophy, 1995 (pap).
The author describes how she and her family were arrested in Poland, during World War II by the Russians and exiled to Siberia when she was eleven years old.

1227. Herriot, James. ONLY ONE WOOF. St. Martins, 1993 (pap).
When Gyp, a sheepdog living in the English countryside, attends the sheepdog championship trials he sees his brother Seep for the first time since they were separated, and the silent sheepdog barks once, surprising everyone.

1228. Kossman, Nina. BEHIND THE BORDER. Lothrop, 1994; Beech Tree, 1996 (pap).
The author describes her childhood in the Soviet Union during the 1960's.

1229. Lewin, Ted. THE REINDEER PEOPLE. Macmillan, 1994.
Portrays the life of the Sami people in Lapland.

1230. McMillan, Bruce. NIGHTS OF THE PUFFLINGS. Houghton Mifflin, 1995.
Halla, a girl living in Iceland, describes how for two weeks she and her friends spend each night searching for stranded pufflings who haven't made it to the water, so that they will be able to leave for their winter at sea.

1231. Pitkanen, Matti R. THE GRANDCHILDREN OF THE VIKINGS. Illus. by Matti Pitkanen. Carolrhoda, 1996.
Describes the history of the Vikings and the locations and lifestyles of their descendants.

1232. Silverman, Robin Landew. A BOSNIAN FAMILY. Lerner, 1997.
Describes the events that led to war in the former Yugoslavia and the efforts of one family to escape from Bosnia and make a new life in Grand Forks, North Dakota.

Geographical Settings – Latin America – Picture Books

1233. Ada, Alma Flor. THE GOLD COIN. Illus. by Neil Waldman. Atheneum, 1991; Aladdin, 1994 (pap).
Determined to steal an old woman's gold coin, a young thief follows her all around the Central American countryside, and finds himself involved in a series of unexpected activities.

1234. Bulla, Clyde Robert. THE POPPY SEEDS. Puffin, 1994 (pap).
A little boy's attempt to grow poppy seeds in his drought-parched Mexican village softens the heart of the grouchy old man who has the village's only spring in his back yard.

1235. Cameron, Ann. THE MOST BEAUTIFUL PLACE IN THE WORLD. Illus. by Thomas B. Allen. Random, 1993 (pap).
Growing up with his grandmother in a small Guatemalan town, seven-year-old Juan discovers the value of hard work, the joy of learning, and the location of the most beautiful place in the world.

1236. Estes, Kristyn Rehling. MANUELA'S GIFT. *SEE 24.*

1237. Ets, Marie Hall. NINE DAYS TO CHRISTMAS. Illus. by Aurora Labastida. Puffin, 1991 (pap).
Ceci anxiously awaits her first posada, the special Mexican Christmas party, and the opportunity to select a piñata for it.

1238. Fine, Edith Hope. UNDER THE LEMON MOON = BAJO LA LUNA DE LIMON. Lee & Low, 1999 (pap).
The theft of all the lemons from her lemon tree leads Rosalinda to an encounter with la Anciana, the Old One, who walks the Mexican countryside helping things grow, and to an understanding of generosity and forgiveness.

1239. Flora, James. THE FABULOUS FIREWORK FAMILY. McElderry, 1994.
A Mexican family prepares a grand fireworks display for the festival of the village's patron saint.

1240. Franklin, Kristine L. IGUANA BEACH. Illus. by Lori Lohstoeter. Crown, 1997.
Though little Reina has promised not to swim in the waves during her first trip to the ocean, it becomes very difficult for her to keep that promise.

1241. Gage, Amy Glasser. PASCUAL'S MAGIC PICTURES. Illus. by May Gage. Carolrhoda, 1996.
Having saved enough money to buy a disposable camera, Pascual goes into the Guatemalan jungle to take pictures, but the results are not what he expected.

1242. Geeslin, Campbell. HOW NANITA LEARNED TO MAKE FLAN. Atheneum, c1999.
The cobbler in a tiny Mexican town is so busy that he cannot make shoes for his daughter, so she makes her own shoes, which take her far away to a rich man's home where she must clean and cook all day.

1243. Geeslin, Campbell. ON RAMON'S FARM: FIVE TALES OF MEXICO. Illus. by Petra Mathers. Atheneum, 1998.
The animals that Ramon tends on his family's farm in Mexico include sheep that weep when they are shorn, and a goat that climbs to the top of a windmill.

1244. Jendresen, Erik. THE FIRST STORY EVER TOLD. Simon & Schuster, 1996.
An explorer goes in search of the Inca's legendary lost city of gold in Peru, but discovers instead a spiritual treasure.

1245. Johnston, Tony. DAY OF THE DEAD. Illus. by Jeanette Winter. Harcourt Brace, 1997.
A Mexican family prepares for and celebrates the Day of the Dead.

1246. Johnston, Tony. THE MAGIC MAGUEY. Illus. by Elisa Kleven. Harcourt Brace, 1996.
Miguel figures out a way to save the beloved maguey plant in his Mexican pueblo.

1247. Krull, Kathleen. MARIA MOLINA AND THE DAYS OF THE DEAD. Illus. by Enrique O. Sanchez. Simon and Schuster, 1994.
In Mexico, Maria and her family celebrate Los Obias de los Muertos, the Days of the Dead.

1248. Madrigal, Antonio Hernandez. ERANDI'S BRAIDS. Putnam, c1999.
In a poor Mexican village, Erandi surprises her mother by offering to sell her long, beautiful hair in order to raise enough money to buy a new fishing net.

1249. Palacios, Argentina. A CHRISTMAS SURPRISE FOR CHABELITA. Illus. by Lori Lohstoeter. Troll, 1994 (pap).
While living with her grandparents when her mother goes to work in the city, a young Panamanian girl memorizes her mother's favorite poem for the school's Christmas pageant.

1250. Riecken, Nancy. TODAY IS THE DAY. Illus. by Catherine Stock. Houghton Mifflin, 1996.
A young Mexican girl eagerly awaits her absent father's return and hopes that he will bring enough money so that she can walk to school in new shoes.

1251. Torres, Leyla. LILIANA'S GRANDMOTHERS. *SEE 172.*

1252. Winter, Jeanette. JOSEFINA. Harcourt Brace, 1996.
A counting book, inspired by Mexican folk artist Josefina Aguilar, who makes painted clay figures.

1253. Yacowitz, Caryn. PUMPKIN FIESTA. Illus. by Joe Cepeda. Harper Collins, 1998.
Hoping to win a prize for the best pumpkin at the fiesta, Foolish Fernando, in a tale set in Mexico, tries to duplicate Old Juan's successful gardening techniques.

Geographical Settings – Latin America – Easy Readers

1254. Alphin, Elaine Marie. A BEAR FOR MIGUEL. Illus. by Joan Sandin. Trophy, 1997 (pap).
A young Salvadoran girl goes to the market with her father and helps her family obtain necessities by trading a precious item of her own.

1255. Lewis, Thomas P. HILL OF FIRE. Harper, 1971; Trophy, 1983 (pap).
An easy-to-read account of the birth of the Paribicutin volcano in the field of a poor Mexican farmer.

1256. Marzollo, Jean. SOCCER COUSINS. Illus. by Irene Trivas. Cartwheel, 1997 (pap).
When David visits his cousin in Mexico, he not only celebrates the Day of the Dead but he also plays a big part in Miguel's soccer tournament.

Geographical Settings – Latin America – Fiction

1257. Alexander, Lloyd. THE EL DORADO ADVENTURE. Yearling, 1990 (pap).
Vesper tries to stop a villain from building a canal which would destroy a Central American Indian tribe's homeland.

1258. Castaneda, Omar S. AMONG THE VOLCANOES. Yearling, 1993 (pap).
In the small Guatemalan village where she lives, Isabel Pacay must go against the traditions of her people in order to realize her dream of becoming a teacher.

1259. Chambers, Veronica. MARISOL AND MAGDALENA: THE SOUND OF OUR SISTERHOOD. Jump at the Sun, c1998.
Separated from her best friend in Brooklyn, thirteen-year-old Marisol spends a year with her grandmother in Panama where she secretly searches for her real father.

1260. Clark, Ann Nolan. SECRET OF THE ANDES. Viking, 1976 (pap).
An Indian boy who tends llamas in a hidden valley in Peru learns the traditions and secrets of his Inca ancestors.

1261. Griffin, Adele. RAINY SEASON. Houghton Mifflin, 1996.
While living on an army base on the Panama Canal Zone in 1977, twelve-year-old Lan tries to cope with the aftermath of a fatal car crash.

1262. Paulsen, Gary. THE CROSSING. Laureleaf, 1993 (pap).
A street kid fighting for survival in a Mexican border town develops a strange friendship with an emotionally disturbed American soldier.

1263. Temple, Frances. GRAB HANDS AND RUN. Orchard, 1993; Trophy, 1995 (pap).
After his father disappears, twelve-year-old Felipe, his mother, and his younger sister set out on a difficult and dangerous journey, trying to make their way from their home in El Salvador to Canada.

1264. Temple, Frances. TONIGHT, BY SEA. Orchard, 1995; Trophy, 1997 (pap).
A contemporary story, told through the eyes of a teenager, of the Haitian boat people.

Geographical Settings – Caribbean – Picture Books

1265. Belpre, Pura. FIREFLY SUMMER. Arte Publico, 1996.
At a plantation in rural Puerto Rico around the turn of the century, the foreman pursues the mystery surrounding his family.

1266. Dorros, Arthur. ISLA. Illus. by Elisa Kleven. Dutton, 1995; Puffin, 1999 (pap).
A young girl and her grandmother take an imaginary journey to the Caribbean island where her mother grew up, and where some of her family still lives.

1267. Garne, S.T. BY A BLAZING BLUE SEA. Harcourt Brace, c1999.
A rhyming description of the simple and colorful life of a Caribbean fisherman.

1268. Gershator, David. PALAMPAM DAY. Illus. by Enrique O. Sanchez. Marshall Cavendish, 1997.
One day in the West Indies when the coconuts, dogs, frogs, fish and bananas talk to him, Turo goes to ask wise old Papa Tata Wanga for advice.

1269. Gershator, Phillis. SWEET, SWEET FIG BANANA. Illus. by fritz Millvoix. Whitman, 1996.
Soto, a boy living in the Caribbean, takes some of the bananas he has grown to share with his friends at the Market Square where his mother works.

1270. Hanson, Regina. THE TANGERINE TREE. Illus. by Harvey Stevenson. Clarion, 1995.
Ida is heartbroken when Papa has to leave Jamaica to work in America, but she knows that he needs her to care for the tangerine tree in their yard, and he promises to return before it blooms again.

1271. Joseph, Lynn. AN ISLAND CHRISTMAS. *SEE 418.*

1272. Joseph, Lynn. JUMP UP TIME: A TRINIDAD CARNIVAL STORY. Illus. by Linda Saport. Clarion, 1998.
Although she is jealous of all the attention being paid to her older sister's Carnival costume, Lily helps her when she gets nervous before going on stage.

1273. Lauture, Denize. RUNNING THE ROAD TO ABC. Illus. by Reynold Ruffins. Simon & Schuster, 1996; Aladdin, 2000 (pap).
Long before the sun rises, Haitian children run to school where they learn the letters, sounds and words of their beautiful books.

1274. Lessac, Frane. MY LITTLE ISLAND. HarperCollins, 1985.
A young boy goes with his best friend to visit the little Caribbean island where he was born.

1275. London, Jonathan. HURRICANE. Illus. by Henri Sorenson. Lothrop Lee, 1998.
A Puerto Rican family packs up and heads for a shelter as a hurricane threatens.

1276. Mitchell, Rita Phillips. HUE BOY. *SEE 715.*

1277. Orr, Katherine Shelley. MY GRANDPA AND THE SEA. First Avenue, 1991 (pap).
When grandpa, a traditional fisherman in Saint Lucia, is forced from his livelihood because of the short supply of fish, he creates an ecologically sound solution.

1278. Rahaman, Vashanti. O CHRISTMAS TREE. Illus. by Frane Lessac. Boyds Mills, 1996.
A boy wants an evergreen tree for Christmas in this story set in the West Indies.

1279. Sisnett, Ana. GRANNIE JUS' COME. Illus. by Karen Lusebrink. Children's Book Press, 1997.
Anticipating her Grannie's weekly visit, a young girl is eager to make the beloved older woman feel right at home by inviting her to make herself comfortable, in a story accentuated by rhythmic Caribbean English dialect.

1280. Van Laan, Nancy. MAMA ROCKS, PAPA SINGS. Illus. by Roberta Smith. Knopf, 1995.
A little Haitian girl describes how her parents' house fills up with babies as relatives drop off their children on their way to work.

1281. Williams, Karen Lynn. PAINTED DREAMS. Illus. by Catherine Stock. Lothrop Lee, 1998.
Because her Haitian family is too poor to be able to buy paints for her, Ti Marie finds a way to create pictures that make the heart sing.

1282. Williams, Karen Lynn. TAP-TAP. Clarion, 1994.
After selling oranges in the market, a Haitian mother and daughter have enough money to ride the tap-tap, a truck that picks up passengers and lets them off when they bang on the side of the vehicle.

Geographical Settings – Caribbean – Easy Readers

1283. Pomerantz, Charlotte. THE OUTSIDE DOG. Illus. by Jennifer Plecas. HarperCollins, 1993; Trophy, 1995 (pap).
Marisol, a Puerto Rican Girl, wants a dog very much but her grandfather will not let her have one, until a skinny mutt wins him over.

Geographical Settings – Caribbean – Fiction

1284. Berry, James. A THIEF IN THE VILLAGE AND OTHER STORIES. Viking, 1990 (pap).
A collection of stories about life in contemporary Jamaica, such as a young boy's desire for special shoes for the cricket team, and a girl's adventures on a coconut plantation.

1285. Bontemps, Arna. POPO AND FIFINA. Oxford, 1993.
Popo and Fifina move to a village in Haiti where Papa Jean plans to earn a living as a fisherman.

1286. Hodge, Merle. FOR THE LIFE OF LAETITIA. Farrar Straus, 1994 (pap).
A twelve-year-old Caribbean girl is the first in her family to go to secondary school, and struggles with a variety of problems including a cruel teacher and a difficult home life.

1287. Mohr, Nicholasa. GOING HOME. Puffin, 1999 (pap).
Feeling like an outsider when she visits her relatives in Puerto Rico, eleven-year-old Felita tries to come to terms with the heritage she always took for granted.

1288. Pomerantz, Charlotte. THE CHALK DOLL. Trophy, 1993 (pap).
Rosy's mother remembers the pleasures of her childhood in Jamaica and the very special dolls she used to play with.

1289. Taylor, Theodore. THE CAY. *SEE 519.*

1290. Taylor, Theodore. TIMOTHY OF THE CAY. Flare, 1994 (pap)
Tells the life story of Timothy, a West Indian man, and the events that led up to the events in The Cay.

Geographical Settings – Canada – Picture Books

1291. Booth, David. THE DUST BOWL. Illus. by Karen Reczuch. Kids Can Press, 1997.
A grandfather on a Canadian farm reminisces about the hard times during the 1930's Dust Bowl.

1292. Jam, Teddy. THE YEAR OF FIRE. Illus. by Ian Wallace. Douglas & McIntyre, 1992.
While they boil down sap from their maple trees to make syrup, a Canadian grandfather tells his granddaughter of the worst fire he has ever known.

Geographical Settings – Canada – Fiction

1293. Burnford, Sheila. THE INCREDIBLE JOURNEY. Yearling, 1990 (pap).
A Siamese cat, an old bull terrier and a young Labrador retriever travel 250 miles together through the Canadian wilderness to find their human family.

1294. London, Jack. WHITE FANG. Viking, 1989; Scholastic, 1989 (pap).
The adventures of a dog who is part wolf in the northern Yukon wilderness, and how he comes to make his peace with men.

1295. Lottridge, Celia Barker. WINGS TO FLY. Groundwood Books, 1998.
Sequel to Ticket to Canada. Eleven-year-old Josie is well-settled into her life on the prairie and has begun to dream about her future, but she becomes even more content when the friend she has been longing for finally moves into the neighborhood.

1296. Montgomery, Lucy Maud. ANNE OF GREEN GABLES. Bantam, 1998; Yearling, 1999 (pap).
Anne, an eleven-year-old orphan, is sent by mistake to live with a lonely middle-aged brother and sister on a Prince Edward Island farm.

1297. Sterling, Shirley. MY NAME IS SEEPEETZA. Groundwood, 1992 (pap).
Seepeetza keeps a diary during the time she attends sixth grade in an Indian residential school in British Columbia during the 1950's.

1298. Van Stockum, Hilda. CANADIAN SUMMER. Bethlehem Books, 1996 (pap).
A family with six children moves to Canada where the only house they can find is in the woods, which are full of animals and adventures.

Geographical Settings – Arctic Regions and Antarctica – Picture Books

1299. Fowler, Susi L. CIRCLE OF THANKS. Scholastic, 1998.
An evocation of the beauty and power of the Alaskan tundra and the animals and people who live there.

1300. George, Jean Craighead. ARCTIC SON. Illus. by Wendell Minor. Hyperion, 1997.
A baby boy is given an Inupiat name to go with his English one, and grows up learning the traditional ways of the Eskimo people.

1301. Kusugak, Michael. ARCTIC STORIES. Illus. by Vladyana Krykorka. Annick Press, 1998 (pap).
Stories of the Arctic, Inuit Indians, and the Northwest territories.

1302. Scott, Ann Herbert. ON MOTHER'S LAP. Illus. by Glo Coalson. Clarion, 1992.
A small Eskimo boy discovers that mother's lap is a very special place with room for everyone.

Geographical Settings – Arctic Regions and Antarctica – Fiction

1303. Conrad, Pam. CALL ME AHNIGHITO. Illus. by Richard Egielski. HarperCollins, 1995.
A huge meteorite describes how it lay half-buried in Greenland for centuries until it is finally excavated by members of a Peary expedition and begins a new journey.

1304. Easley, Maryann. I AM THE ICE WORM. Boyds Mills, 1996; Yearling, 1998 (pap).
When the plane carrying her to visit her mother crashes above the Arctic Circle, fourteen-year-old Allison Atwood is rescued by an Inupiat man who takes her back to his village.

1305. George, Jean Craighead. JULIE OF THE WOLVES. *SEE 337.*

1306. George, Jean Craighead. JULIE. HarperCollins, 1994; Trophy, 1996 (pap).
When Julie returns to her father's Eskimo village, she struggles to find a way to save her beloved wolves in a changing Arctic world.

Historical Settings – Prehistoric Times – Picture Books

1307. Brett, Jan. THE FIRST DOG. Harcourt, 1988.
Kip the cave boy and Paleowolf each face hunger and danger on a journey in Paleolithic times. When they decide to join forces and help one another, Paleowolf becomes the first dog.

Historical Settings – Prehistoric Times – Easy Reader

1308. Hoff, Syd. STANLEY. Harper, 1962; Trophy, 1992 (pap).
Chased away by the other prehistoric people because he is different, Stanley finds a new and better way of living.

Historical Settings – Prehistoric Times - Fiction

1309. Cowley, Marjorie. ANOOKA'S ANSWER. Illus. by Bryn Barnard. Clarion, 1999.
While living in a river valley in Southern France during the Paleolithic era, thirteen-year-old Anooka rejects the ways of her clan.

1310. Cowley, Marjorie. DAR AND THE SPEAR-THROWER. Clarion, 1994.
A young Cro-Magnon boy is initiated into manhood by his clan and sets off on a journey to trade his valuable fire rocks for an ivory spear thrower.

1311. Craig, Ruth. MALU'S WOLF. *SEE 331.*

1312. Denzel, Justin F. BOY OF THE PAINTED CAVE. Philomel, 1988; Paper Star, 1996 (pap).
Forbidden to make pictures, Tao yearns to be a cave painter, recording the figures of the mammals, rhinos, bison and other animals of his prehistoric times.

Historical Settings – Ancient Times – Picture Books

1313. James, J. Allen. THE DRUMS OF NOTO HANTO. DK, 1999.
The people in a small village in ancient Japan manage to drive off the forces of a powerful warlord using only their ingenuity and the many different village drums.

1314. Sabuda, Robert. TUTANKHAMEN'S GIFT. Simon & Schuster, 1994
After his unpopular brother mysteriously dies, ten-year-old Tutankhamen becomes ruler of the ancient Egyptian people.

1315. Stolz, Mary. ZEKMET, THE STONE CARVER. Harcourt, 1997.
Chosen to design a magnificent monument for a vain Pharaoh, an Egyptian stone cutter conceives of and begins work on the Sphinx, which still stands in the Egyptian desert.

Historical Settings – Ancient Times – Fiction

1316. Barrett, Tracy. ANNA OF BYZANTIUM. Delacorte, 1999.
In the eleventh century the teenage princess Anna Comnenea fights for her birthright, the throne to the Byzantine Empire, which she fears will be taken from her by her younger brother John because he is a boy.

1317. Blacklock, Dyan. PANKRATION: THE ULTIMATE GAME. Whitman, 1999.
Having been kidnapped from a ship leaving plague-ridden Athens in 430 B.C., twelve-year-old Nic attempts to escape his captors and keep his promise to meet his friend at the Olympic games.

1318. Speare, Elizabeth. THE BRONZE BOW. Houghton Mifflin, 1961.
Daniel, a Jewish rebel, follows the teaching of Jesus and learns to love instead of hate. Set in the time of Jesus.

Historical Settings – Middle Ages - Fiction

1319. Cushman, Karen. CATHERINE, CALLED BIRDY. Clarion, 1994; Trophy, 1995 (pap).
The thirteen-year-old daughter of an English country knight, in the year 1290, keeps a journal in which she records the events of her life, particularly her efforts to avoid being married off by her father to a filthy, ill-mannered, but rich neighbor.

1320. Cushman, Karen. THE MIDWIFE'S APPRENTICE. Clarion, 1995; Trophy, 1996 (pap).
In medieval England, a homeless girl is taken in by a midwife and eventually gains the three things she most wants: a full belly, a contented heart, and a place in this world.

1321. Guarnieri, Paolo. A BOY NAMED GIOTTO. Farrrar Straus & Giroux, 1999.
Eight-year-old Giotto the shepherd boy confesses his dream of becoming an artist to the painter Cimabue, who teaches him how to make marvelous pigments from minerals, flowers, and eggs and takes him on as his pupil.

1322. Kelly, Eric Philbrook. THE TRUMPETER OF KRAKOW. Macmillan, 1929; Aladdin, 1992 (pap).
The people and character of medieval Poland are profiled in this tale of a fifteen-year-old boy and his family who are forced to hide a priceless jewel from the plundering Tartars.

1323. Morris, Gerald. THE SQUIRE, THE KNIGHT AND HIS LADY. Houghton Mifflin, 1999.
After several years at King Arthur's court, Terence, as Sir Gawain's squire and friend, accompanies him on a perilous quest that tests all their skills and whose successful completion could mean certain death for Gawain.

1324. Skurzynski, Gloria. THE MINSTREL IN THE TOWER. Random, 1988 (pap).
In the year 1195, eleven-year-old Roger and his eight-year-old sister Alice travel through the French countryside in search of their ailing mother's estranged brother, a wealthy baron.

Historical Settings – 15th and 16th Centuries – Picture Books

1325. Anno, Mitsumasa. ANNO'S USA. Paper Star, 1998 (pap).
In wordless panoramas, a lone traveler approaches the New World from the West in the present day, and journeys the width of the country backward through time, departing from the east coast as the Santa Maria appears over the horizon.

Historical Settings – 15th and 16th Centuries – Fiction

1326. Dorris, Michael. MORNING GIRL. Hyperion, 1992 (pap).
Morning Girl and her younger brother describe their life on an island in pre-Columbian America, and witness the arrival of the first Europeans.

1327. Dorris, Michael. SEES BEHIND TREES. *SEE 333.*

Historical Settings – 17th Century – Picture Books

1328. Harness, Cheryl. THREE YOUNG PILGRIMS. Simon & Schuster, 1992; Aladdin, 1995 (pap).
Mary, Remember, and Bartholomew are among the Pilgrims who survive the harsh early years in America and see New Plymouth grow into a prosperous colony.

Historical Settings – 17th Century – Fiction

1329. Bulla, Clyde R. A LION TO GUARD US. HarperCollins, 1981; Trophy, 1989 (pap).
Left on their own in seventeenth century London, three impoverished children try to make their way to the Virginia colony in search of their father.

1330. Hildick, E.W. HESTER BIDGOOD, INVESTIGATRIX OF EVILL DEEDES. Macmillan, 1995.
Thirteen-year-old Hester and her friend Rob investigate the stoning and branding of a kitten in a New England town, caught in the grip of witchcraft rumors during the year 1692.

1331. Kirkpatrick, Katherine. TROUBLE'S DAUGHTER; THE STORY OF SUSANNA HUTCHINSON, INDIAN CAPTIVE. Delacorte, 1998; Yearling, 2000 (pap).
When her family is massacred by Lenape Indians in 1643, nine-year-old Susanna, daughter of Anne Hutchinson, is captured and raised as a Lenape.

1332. Lenski, Lois. INDIAN CAPTIVE: THE STORY OF MARY JEMISON. HarperCollins, 1941; Trophy, 1995 (pap).
In 1758, Mary's family is captured by Indians, and Mary chooses not to return to the white settlements.

1333. O'Dell, Scott. THE SERPENT NEVER SLEEPS: A NOVEL OF JAMESTOWN AND POCAHONTAS. Houghton Mifflin, 1987; Juniper, 1990 (pap).
Serena travels to the New World and comes to know the hardships of colonial life and the extraordinary Princess Pocahontas.

1334. Petry, Ann. TITUBA OF SALEM VILLAGE. HarperCollins, 1991 (pap).
Tituba, a slave from Barbados, is one of the first three "witches" condemned at the Salem Witch Trials in 1692.

1335. Speare, Elizabeth George. THE WITCH OF BLACKBIRD POND. *SEE 356.*

Historical Settings – 18th Century – Picture Books

1336. Turner, Ann. KATIE'S TRUNK. Illus. by Ronald Himler. Simon & Schuster, 1992; Aladdin, 1997 (pap).
Katie, whose family is not sympathetic to the rebel soldiers during the American Revolution, hides under the clothes in her mother's trunk when they invade her home.

Historical Settings – 18th Century – Easy Readers

1337. Benchley, Nathaniel. SAM THE MINUTEMAN. Harper, 1969; Trophy, 1987 (pap).
Sam and his father fight as minutemen against the British in the battle of Lexington.

Historical Settings – 18th Century - Intermediate

1338. Berleth, Richard. SAMUEL'S CHOICE. Illus. by James Watling. Whitman, 1990.
A fourteen-year-old slave in Brooklyn in 1776 faces a difficult choice when the fighting between the British and the colonists reaches his doorstep.

1339. Bruchac, Joseph. THE ARROW OVER THE DOOR. Dial, c1998.
In the year 1777, a group of Quakers and a party of Indians have a memorable meeting.

1340. Gauch, Patricia L. THIS TIME, TEMPE WICK? Illus. by Margot Tomes. Coward, 1974.
Everyone knows Tempe Wick is a most surprising girl, but she exceeds even her own reputation when two mutinous Revolutionary War soldiers try to steal her beloved horse.

1341. Walker, Sally M. THE 18 PENNY GOOSE. Harpercollins, c1998; Trophy, 1999 (pap).
Eight-year-old Letty attempts to save her pet goose from marauding British soldiers in New Jersey during the Revolutionary War.

Historical Settings – 18th Century – Fiction

1342. Avi. THE FIGHTING GROUND. HarperCollins, 1984; Trophy, 1987 (pap).
Thirteen-year-old Jonathan goes off to fight in the Revolutionary War and discovers the real war is being fought within himself.

1343. Collier, James Lincoln. JUMP SHIP TO FREEDOM. Yearling, 1996 (pap).
In 1787, a fourteen-year-old slave escapes from his dishonest master and tries to buy freedom for himself and his mother by cashing in the soldiers' notes received by his father.

1344. Collier, James Lincoln. MY BROTHER SAM IS DEAD. Simon & Schuster, 1974; Scholastic, 1989 (pap).
Recounts the pain of the Meeker family during the Revolution when one son joins the rebel forces while the rest of the family tries to stay neutral in a Tory town.

1345. Collier, James Lincoln. WAR COMES TO WILLY FREEMAN. *SEE 330.*

1346. Edmonds, Walter. THE MATCHLOCK GUN. Illus. by Paul Lantz. Doubleday, 1941; Paper Star, 1998 (pap).
In 1756, during the French and Indian War, ten-year-old Edward decides to protect his family with a heavy Spanish gun.

1347. Field, Rachel. CALICO BUSH. Illus. by Allen Lewis. Simon & Schuster, 1932; Aladdin, 1998 (pap).
In 1742, thirteen-year-old Marguerite moves from France with her family to be a pioneer in Maine.

1348. Forbes, Esther. JOHNNY TREMAIN. *SEE 511.*

1349. Lawson, Robert. BEN AND ME. Little Brown, 1939.
A new and astonishing life of Benjamin Franklin as written by his mouse, Amos.

1350. Lawson, Robert. MR. REVERE AND I. Little, 1953.
An account of certain episodes in the career of Paul Revere as revealed by his horse, Scheherezade.

1351. Myers, Anna. THE KEEPING ROOM. Walker, 1997; Puffin, 1999 (pap).
Left in charge of the family by his father who joins the Revolutionary War effort, thirteen-year-old Joey undergoes such great changes that he fears he may be betraying his beloved parent.

1352. O'Dell, Scott. MY NAME IS NOT ANGELICA. Houghton Mifflin, 1989; Yearling, 1994 (pap).
The experiences of a young Senegalese girl, brought as a slave to the Caribbean island of St. John, as she participates in the slave revolt of 1733-1734.

1353. Paterson, Katherine. THE MASTER PUPPETEER. Trophy, 1989 (pap).
A thirteen-year-old boy describes the poverty and discontent of eighteenth-century Osaka and of the world of puppeteers in which he lives.

1354. Speare, Elizabeth. THE SIGN OF THE BEAVER. Houghton Mifflin, 1983; Yearling, 1997 (pap).
Left alone to guard the family's wilderness home in eighteenth-century Maine, a boy is hard-pressed to survive until local Indians teach him their skills.

Historical Settings – 19th Century – Picture Books

1355. Gerrard, Roy. WAGONS WEST. Farrar, 1996.
A rhyming story of a family's move by wagon train between Missouri and Oregon in the 1850's.

1356. Hall, Donald. THE OX-CART MAN. Illus. by Barbara Cooney. Viking, 1979.
A description of the day-to-day life throughout the changing seasons of an early nineteenth-century New England family.

1357. Joosse, Barbara M. LEWIS AND PAPA: ADVENTURE ON THE SANTA FE TRAIL. Chronicle, c1998.
While accompanying his father on the wagon train along the Santa Fe Trail, Lewis discovers what it is to be a man.

1358. Karim, Roberta. KINDLE ME A RIDDLE: A PIONEER STORY. Greenwillow, c1999.
The riddles that a pioneer family share explain the origin of such things in their lives as their log cabin, johnnycakes, the broom, a cloak, candles, and more.

1359. Kent, Peter. QUEST FOR THE WEST: IN SEARCH OF GOLD. Millbrook, 1997.
In 1849 the impoverished Hornik family decides to leave Bohemia and emigrate to California in search of gold.

1360. Levitin, Sonia. BOOM TOWN. Illus. by Cat Bowman Smith. Orchard, 1997.
After her family moves to California in the 1940's her father goes to work in the gold fields and Amanda decides to make her own fortune by baking pies.

1361. Polacco, Patricia. THE KEEPING QUILT. Simon & Schuster, 1988.
A homemade quilt ties together the lives of four generations of an immigrant Jewish family.

1362. Schroeder, Alan. MINTY: A STORY OF YOUNG HARRIET TUBMAN. Illus. by Jerry Pinkney. Dial, 1996.
Young Harriet Tubman, known as Minty, dreams of escaping slavery in the late 1820's.

1363. Turner, Ann W. DRUMMER BOY. Illus. by Mark Hess. HarperCollins, 1998.
A thirteen-year-old soldier, coming of age during the Civil War, beats his drums to raise everyone's spirits.

1364. Van Leeuwen, Jean. NOTHING HERE BUT TREES. Dial, c1998.
A close-knit pioneer family carves out a new home amidst the densely forested land of Ohio in the early nineteenth century.

1365. Van Leeuwen, Jean. GOING WEST. Illus. by Thomas B. Allen. Viking, 1977; Puffin, 1997 (pap).
Follows a family's emigration by prairie schooner from the East, across the plains to Kansas.

Historical Settings – 19th Century – Easy Readers

1366. Brenner, Barbara A. WAGON WHEELS. *SEE 148.*

1367. Brill, Marlene T. ALLEN JAY AND THE UNDERGROUND RAILROAD. *SEE 769.*

1368. Coerr, Eleanor. CHANG'S PAPER PONY. *SEE 867.*

1369. Greeson, Janet. AN AMERICAN ARMY OF TWO. Carolrhoda, 1992.
During the War of 1812, Rebecca and Abigail save their township from the British by playing on a drum and fife to simulate the approach of American troops.

1370. Kramer, Sydelle. WAGON TRAIN. Grosset, 1997 (pap).
Hundreds of pioneers suffer hardships while traveling through 2,000 miles of wilderness on a wagon trail to California in 1848.

1371. Monjo, F.N. THE DRINKING GOURD. *SEE 768.*

1372. Ross, Alice. THE COPPER LADY. Carolrhoda, 1997 First Avenue, 1996 (pap).
After helping Monsieur Bartholdi build the Statue of Liberty, a Parisian orphan stows away on the ship carrying the statue to America.

Historical Settings – 19th Century – Intermediate

1373. Banks, Sara H. ABRAHAM'S BATTLE: A NOVEL OF GETTYSBURG. Atheneum, c1999.
In 1863, as the Civil War approaches his home in Gettysburg and he realizes that a big battle is about to begin, a freed slave named Abraham decides to join the ambulance corps on the of the Union Army.

1374. Brill, Marlene Targ. DIARY OF A DRUMMER BOY. Illus. by Michael Garland. Millbrook, 1998.
The fictionalized diary of a twelve-year-old boy who joins the Union Army as a drummer, and ends up fighting in the Civil War.

1375. Chambers, Veronica. AMISTAD RISING: A STORY OF FREEDOM. Harcourt Brace, c1998.
A fictional account of the 1839 revolt of Africans aboard the slave ship Amistad and the subsequent legal case argued before the Supreme Court in 1841 by former president John Quincy Adams.

1376. Crist-Evans, Craig. MOON OVER TENNESSEE: A BOY'S CIVIL WAR JOURNAL. Houghton Mifflin, 1999.
A thirteen-year-old boy sets off with his father from their farm in Tennessee to join the Confederate forces on their way to fight at Gettysburg.

1377. Fleming, Candace. A BIG CHEESE FOR THE WHITE HOUSE: THE TRUE TALE OF A TREMENDOUS CHEDDAR. DK, 1999.
In 1801, in Chesire, Massachusetts, Elder John Leland organizes his fellow townspeople to make a big cheese for President Jefferson who up until that time had been forced to eat inferior cheeses.

1378. Kalman, Esther. TCHAIKOVSKY DISCOVERS AMERICA. Illus. by Laura Fernandez. Orchard, 1995.
A young girl recognizes the famous composer in a train's dining car, and they share their experiences.

1379. Krensky, Stephen. THE IRON DRAGON NEVER SLEEPS. Illus. by John Fulweiler. Delacorte, 1994; Yearling, 1995 (pap).
In 1867 California, ten-year-old Winnie meets a Chinese boy and discovers the role of the Chinese people in completing the transcontinental railroad.

1380. MacLachlan, Patricia. SARAH, PLAIN AND TALL. *SEE 150.*

1381. MacLachlan, Patricia. SKYLARK. Trophy, 1997 (pap).
When a drought tests Sarah's commitment to her new home on the prairie, her stepchildren hope they will be able to remain a family

1382. Minahan, John A. ABIGAIL'S DRUM. Pippin, 1995.
Abigail and Rebecca outwit the British sailors who have taken their lighthouse keeper father hostage and plan to burn the town. Based on an actual event.

1383. Polacco, Patricia. PINK AND SAY. Philomel, 1994.
A white youth from Ohio and a black youth from Georgia meet as young soldiers with the Union Army.

1384. Roop, Peter. GRACE'S LETTER TO LINCOLN. Illus. by Stacey Schuett. Hyperion, 1998.
Grace decides to write to Lincoln, suggesting he might win more votes if he grew a beard, and she becomes a celebrity when he decides to do so.

1385. Stevens, Carla. LILY AND MISS LIBERTY. Little Apple, 1993 (pap).
A little girl raises money by making crowns to help buy the pedestal needed for the Statue of Liberty.

1386. Turner, Ann. DAKOTA DUGOUT. Illus. by Ronald Himler. Aladdin, 1989 (pap).
A woman describes her experiences living with her husband in a sod house on the Dakota prairie.

1387. Welch, Catherine A. CLOUDS OF TERROR. Illus. by Laurie K. Johnson. Carolrhoda, 1994.
A brother and sister living on a farm in Minnesota during the 1870's try to help their family cope with plagues of locusts.

1388. Whelan, Gloria. THE INDIAN SCHOOL. Illus. by Gabriela Dellasso. HarperCollins, 1996; Trophy, 1997 (pap).
Newly-orphaned Mary goes to live with her missionary aunt and uncle who run a school for Indian children in Michigan, in 1839.

1389. Whelan, Gloria. NIGHT OF THE FULL MOON. Random, 1996 (pap).
When she sneaks away to visit her friend, a young girl is caught up in the forced evacuation of a group of Indians from their tribal lands in the Michigan of the 1840's.

Historical Settings – 19th Century - Fiction

1390. Brink, Carol Ryrie. CADDIE WOODLAWN. *SEE 328.*

1391. Calvert, Patricia. SOONER. Atheneum, c1998.
With the realization that his father may not return now that the Civil War is over, thirteen-year-old Tyler finds himself the man of their Missouri farm and the master of a new dog, the strikingly colored Sooner.

1392. Cushman, Karen. THE BALLAD OF LUCY WHIPPLE. Houghton Mifflin, 1996; HarperCollins, 1998 (pap).
A twelve-year-old is very unhappy when her mother moves the family from Massachusetts to a rough California mining town in 1849.

1393. DeFelice, Cynthia C. THE APPRENTICESHIP OF LUCAS WHITAKER. Farrar Straus, 1996; Camelot, 1998 (pap).
After his family dies of consumption in 1849, twelve-year-old Lucas becomes a doctor's apprentice.

1394. Doherty, Berlie. STREET CHILD. *SEE 35.*

1395. Duffy, James. RADICAL RED. *SEE 334.*

1396. Fleischman, Sid. BANDIT'S MOON. Greenwillow, c1998; Yearling, 2000 (pap).
Twelve-year-old Annyrose relates her adventures with Joaquin Murieta and his band of outlaws in the California gold-mining region during the mid-1800's.

1397. Fox, Paula. THE SLAVE DANCER. Simon & Schuster, 1973; Yearling, 1993.
Kidnapped by the crew of an Africa-bound ship, a thirteen-year-old finds himself on a slaver, and his job is to play music for the exercise period of the human cargo.

1398. Fritz, Jean. THE CABIN FACED WEST. Coward, 1958; Viking, 1987 (pap).
Ten-year-old Ann overcomes loneliness and learns to appreciate the importance of her role in settling the wilderness of western Pennsylvania.

1399. Holland, Isabelle. PAPERBOY. *SEE 951.*

1400. Houston, Gloria. BRIGHT FREEDOM'S SONG: A STORY OF THE UNDERGROUND RAILROAD. Harcourt Brace, c1998.
In the years before the Civil War, Bright discovers that her parents are providing a safehouse for the Underground Railroad and helps to save a runaway slave named Marcus.

1401. Howard, Ellen. THE GATE IN THE WALL. Atheneum, c1999.
In nineteenth-century England, ten-year-old Emma, accustomed to working long hours and the poverty and hunger of her sister's house, finds her life completely changed when she gets a job on a canal boat carrying cargoes between several northern towns.

1402. Hunt, Irene. ACROSS FIVE APRILS. Berkley, 1987 (pap).
Nine-year-old Jethro must run the family farm on his own during the Civil War.

1403. Keith, Harold. RIFLES FOR WATIE. HarperCollins, 1957; Trophy, 1987 (pap).
During the Civil War, Jeff, a farm boy, becomes a Union boy, then a scout.

1404. Love, D. Anne. THREE AGAINST THE TIDE. Holiday, 1998; Yearling, 2000 (pap).
After her father is called away from their plantation near Charleston, S.C. during the Civil War, twelve-year-old Susanna must lead her brothers on a difficult journey in hopes of being reunited with him.

1405. Lyons, Mary E. LETTERS FROM A SLAVE GIRL: THE STORY OF HARRIET JACOBS. Atheneum, 1992; Aladdin, 1996 (pap).
A fictionalized version of the life of Harriet Jacobs, told in the form of letters that she might have written during her slavery and as she prepared for escape in 1842.

1406. McKissack, Pat. RUN AWAY HOME. *SEE 1043.*

1407. O'Dell, Scott. SING DOWN THE MOON. Yearling, 1992 (pap).
A young Navajo girl recounts the events of 1864 when her tribe was forced to march to Fort Sumter as prisoners of white soldiers.

1408. Paterson, Katherine. JIP: HIS STORY. Lodestar, 1996; Puffin, 1998 (pap).
While living on a Vermont poor farm during 1855, Jip learns his identity and that of his mother.

1409. Paterson, Katherine. LYDDIE. Lodestar, 1991; Puffin, 1994 (pap).
An impoverished Vermont farm girl is determined to gain her independence by becoming a factory worker in Massachusetts in the 1840's.

1410. Paulsen, Gary. SARNY: A LIFE REMEMBERED. Delacorte, c1997; Bantam, 1999 (pap).
Continues the adventures of Sarny through the aftermath of the Civil War during which time she taught other African-Americans and lived until age ninety-four.

1411. Rawlings, Marjorie Kinnan. THE YEARLING. Atheneum, 1985; Aladdin, 1998 (pap).
A young boy living in the Florida backwoods is forced to decide the fate of a fawn he has lovingly raised as a pet.

1412. Reeder, Carolyn. CAPTAIN KATE. Avon, c1999.
Kate knows every mile of the waterway she must take to deliver her family's coal, but a solo journey during the Civil War is out of the question. Can Kate and her stepbrother make it together?

1413. Robinet, Harriette. THE TWINS, THE PIRATES, AND THE BATTLE OF NEW ORLEANS. Atheneum, c1997.
Twelve-year-old African-American twins attempt to escape in the face of pirates, an American army, and British forces during the Battle of New Orleans in 1815.

1414. Twain, Mark. THE ADVENTURES OF TOM SAWYER. Grosset, 1994; Puffin, 1995 (pap).
Relates the hilarious adventures and experiences of Tom and his friends in a nineteenth century Mississippi town.

1415. Van Leeuwen, Jean. BOUND FOR OREGON. Puffin, 1996 (pap).
A fictionalized account of the journey of a nine-year-old and her family from their home in Arkansas westward over the Oregon Trail in 1852.

Wilder, Laura Ingalls
1416. BY THE SHORES OF SILVER LAKE. HarperCollins, 1953; Trophy, 1973 (pap).
1417. FARMER BOY. HarperCollins, 1953; Trophy, 1953 (pap).
1418. THE FIRST FOUR YEARS. HarperCollins, 1971; Trophy, 1972 (pap).

1419. LITTLE HOUSE IN THE BIG WOODS. HarperCollins, 1953; Trophy, 1953 (pap).
1420. LITTLE HOUSE ON THE PRAIRIE. HarperCollins, 1953; Trophy, 1973 (pap).
1421. LITTLE TOWN ON THE PRAIRIE. HarperCollins, 1953; Trophy, 1973 (pap).
1422. THE LONG WINTER. HarperCollins, 1953; Trophy, 1953 (pap).
1423. ON THE BANKS OF PLUM CREEK. HarperCollins, 1953; Trophy, 1973 (pap).
1424. THESE HAPPY GOLDEN YEARS. HarperCollins, 1953; Trophy, 1953 (pap).
In this autobiographical series of novels, Laura Ingalls Wilder shares her hopes, dreams, and adventures growing up a pioneer with her family from when she is a young girl until she has a daughter of her own.

1425. Wisler, G. Clifton. THE DRUMMER BOY OF VICKSBURG. Lodestar, 1997; Puffin, 1999 (pap).
In this fact-based story, a fourteen-year-old drummer boy displays great bravery during a Civil War battle.

1426. Wisler, G. Clifton. RED CAP. Puffin, 1994 (pap).
A young Yankee drummer boy displays great courage when he's captured and sent to Andersonville Prison.

1427. Yep, Laurence. DRAGON'S GATE. HarperCollins, 1993; Trophy, 1995 (pap).
After he accidentally kills a Manchu, a fifteen-year-old Chinese boy is sent to America to join his father and uncle in the building of the transcontinental railroad.

Historical Settings – 20th Century – Picture Books

1428. Bartone, Elisa. PEPPE THE LAMPLIGHTER. *SEE 21.*

1429. Birchman, David Francis. A GREEN HORN BLOWING. Lothrop Lee & Shepard, c1997.
During the Depression, a farm hand teaches a young boy to play the horn on a special gourd known as the trombolia, and the lessons teach him about life as well as music.

1430. Booth, David. THE DUST BOWL. *SEE 1291.*

1431. Cech, John. MY GRANDMOTHER'S JOURNEY. Illus. by Sharon McGinley-Nally. Bradbury, 1991.
A grandmother tells the story of her eventful life in early twentieth-century Europe, and her arrival in the United States after World War II.

1432. Hall, Donald. LUCY'S SUMMER. Illus. by Michael McCurdy. Voyager, 1998 (pap).
For Lucy Wells, who lives on a farm in New Hampshire, the summer of 1910 is filled with helping her mother can fruits and vegetables and other activities.

1433. Harvey, Brett. IMMIGRANT GIRL: BECKY OF ELDRIDGE STREET. *SEE 920.*

1434. Hest, Amy. WHEN JESSIE CAME ACROSS THE SEA. *SEE 921.*

1436. McDonald, Megan. THE POTATO MAN. Illus. by Ted Lewin. Orchard, 1991.
Grandpa tells stories about the fruit and vegetable man in his childhood neighborhood.

1437. Provenson, Alice. THE GLORIOUS FLIGHT: ACROSS THE CHANNEL WITH LOUIS BLERIOT, JULY 25, 1909. Viking, 1983 (pap).
A story about the man whose fascination with flying machines produced the Bleriot XI, which crossed the English Channel in thirty-seven minutes in the early 1900's.

1438. Rand, Gloria. BABY IN A BASKET. Cobblehill, 1997; Puffin, 1999 (pap).
While Marie and her children are leaving Alaska by sleigh for the winter, in 1917, disaster strikes during a snowstorm.

1439. Say, Allen. GRANDFATHER'S JOURNEY. *SEE 860.*

1440. Stewart, Sarah. THE GARDENER. Illus. by David Small. Farrar Straus, 1997.
Lydia Grace goes to live with her Uncle Jim in the city when her father loses his job, but she takes her love for gardening with her.

1441. Tunnell, Michael O. MAILING MAY. Illus. by Ted Rand. Greenwillow, 1997.
In 1914, because her family cannot afford a train ticket to her grandmother's house, May rides the mail car on the train.

Historical Settings – 20th Century – Easy Readers

1442. Kilborne, Sarah S. LEAVING VIETNAM. *SEE 900.*

1443. Turner, Ann. DUST FOR DINNER. *SEE 28.*

20th Century – Intermediate

1444. Blos, Joan W. BROOKLYN DOESN'T RHYME. Illus. by Robert Birling. Atheneum, 1994.
At the request of her sixth grade teacher, Edwina Rose records events in the lives of her Polish immigrant family and their friends living in Brooklyn in the early 1900's.

1445. Ginsburg, Marvell. THE TATTOOED TORAH. Illus. by Jo Gersham. UAHC, 1994.
A small Torah stolen and desecrated by Nazi soldiers in Czechoslovakia is eventually rescued and restored to people who appreciate it.

1446. Hest, Amy. LOVE YOU, SOLDIER. Putnam, 1993 (pap).
Katie, a Jewish girl living in New York City during World War II, sees many dynamic changes as she grows from age seven to ten, waiting for her father to return from the war.

1447. Lasky, Karen. MARVEN OF THE NORTH WOODS. Harcourt Brace, c1997.
When his Jewish parents send him to a Minnesota logging camp to escape the influenza epidemic of 1918, ten-year-old Marven finds a special friend.

1448. Lewis, Zoe. KEISHA DISCOVERS HARLEM. *SEE 770.*

1449. Mayerson, Evelyn W. THE CAT WHO ESCAPED FROM STEERAGE. *SEE 937.*

1450. Mochizuki, Ken. BASEBALL SAVED US. *SEE 872.*

1451. Santiago, Chiori. HOME TO MEDICINE MOUNTAIN. Children's Book Press, c1998.
Two young Maidu Indian brothers sent to live at a government-run Indian residential school in California in the 1930's find a way to escape and return home for the summer.

1452. Taylor, Mildred D. THE GOLD CADILLAC. *SEE 771.*

1453. Taylor, Mildred D. MISSISSIPPI BRIDGE. *SEE 772.*

1454. Taylor, Mildred D. THE WELL: DAVID'S STORY. *SEE 773.*

Historical Settings – 20th Century – Fiction

1455. Adler, David A. THE BABE AND I. *SEE 20.*

1456. Antle, Nancy. LOST IN THE WAR. *SEE 545.*

1457. Bradley, Kimberly Brubaker. ONE-OF-A-KIND MALLIE. *SEE 251.*

1458. Buck, Pearl. THE BIG WAVE. Trophy, 1986 (pap).
After a tidal wave destroys their village, two Japanese boys learn about tragedy and the necessity of building a new life.

1459. Choi, Sook Nyul. YEAR OF IMPOSSIBLE GOODBYES. *SEE 1156.*

1460. Cochrane, Patricia A. PURELY ROSIE PEARL. *SEE 689.*

1461. Curtis, Christopher Paul. BUD, NOT BUDDY. *SEE 778.*

1462. Cutler, Jane. THE SONG OF THE MOLIMO. Farrar Straus & Giroux, 1998.
When twelve-year-old Harry comes from Kansas to visit the St. Louis World's Fair in 1904, he befriends an African pygmy who is part of an anthropology exhibit, works for the first female news photographer, and becomes involved in a burgeoning scientific controversy.

1463. English, Karen. FRANCIE. Farrar Straus & Giroux, 1999.
When the sixteen-year-old boy whom she tutors in reading is accused of attempting to murder a white man, Francie gets herself in serious trouble for her efforts at defending him.

1464. Greene, Bette. SUMMER OF MY GERMAN SOLDIER. *SEE 467.*

1465. Hautzig, Esther. THE ENDLESS STEPPE. *SEE 1226.*

1466. Hesse, Karen. LETTERS FROM RIFKA. *SEE 1210.*

1467. Hesse, Karen. OUT OF THE DUST. Scholastic, 1997; Little Apple, 1999 (pap).
Fifteen-year-old Billie Jo relates the hardships of living on her family's wheat farm in Oklahoma during the dust bowl years of the Depression.

1468. Kerr, Judith. WHEN HITLER STOLE PINK RABBIT. *SEE 1212.*

1469. Levitin, Sonia. JOURNEY TO AMERICA. *SEE 1214.*

1470. Lindquist, Susan Hart. SUMMER SOLDIERS. Delacorte, 1999; Yearling, 2000 (pap).
After his father goes off to war during the summer of 1918, eleven-year-old Joe, along with his friends, contends with the town bullies and tries to learn the meaning of courage.

1471. Nelson, Vaunda Micheaux. BEYOND MAYFIELD. Putnam, c1999.
In 1961 the children of Mayfield are mainly concerned with air-raid drills and fallout shelters, but the Civil Rights Movement becomes real when a neighbor joins the Freedom Riders.

1472. Salisbury, Graham. UNDER THE BLOOD-RED SUN. Yearling, 1995 (pap).
A boy's biggest concerns are baseball, homework, and a local bully until life with his Japanese family in Hawaii changes drastically after Pearl Harbor.

1473. Sawyer, Ruth. ROLLER SKATES. Peter Smith, 1990.
Liberated for a year from her parents' restrictions, ten-year-old Lucinda discovers true freedom in the care of her temporary guardians as she roller skates around the streets of turn-of-the-century New York.

1474. Taylor, Mildred. ROLL OF THUNDER, HEAR MY CRY. *SEE 175.*

1475. Taylor, Sydney. ALL-OF-A-KIND FAMILY. *SEE 451.*

1476. Uchida, Yoshiko. JAR OF DREAMS. *SEE 883.*

1477. Uchida, Yoshiko. JOURNEY HOME. Illus. by Charles Robinson. McElderry, 1978; Aladdin, 1992 (pap).
After their release from an internment camp, a Japanese American girl and her family try to reconstruct their lives amidst strong anti-Japanese feelings.

1478. Uchida, Yoshiko. JOURNEY TO TOPAZ. Creative Arts, 1988.
After the Pearl Harbor attack, an eleven-year-old Japanese-American girl and her family are forced to go to a camp for aliens in Utah.

1479. Yep, Laurence. DRAGONWINGS. Harper, 1975; Trophy, 1977 (pap).
During the early twentieth century, a young Chinese boy joins his father in San Francisco and helps him realize his dream of making a flying machine.

1480. Yep, Laurence. HIROSHIMA. Scholastic, 1995; Apple, 1996 (pap).
Describes the dropping of the atomic bomb on Hiroshima, particularly as it affects Sachi, who becomes one of the Hiroshima Maidens.

1481. Yep, Laurence. THE STAR FISHER. *SEE 891.*

1482. Yolen, Jane. THE DEVIL'S ARITHMETIC. *SEE 452.*

In addition to the above individual titles, there are also a number of series that have historical settings. They are:

1483. AMERICAN DIARIES – published by Aladdin Books.
1484. AMERICAN GIRLS – published by Pleasant Company
1485. CHILDREN OF AMERICA – published by Random House
1486. COURAGE OF THE STONE – published by Roberts Rinehart
1487. DAUGHTERS OF LIBERTY – published by Minstrel Books
1488. DEAR AMERICA – published by Scholastic
1489. GIRLHOOD JOURNEYS – published by Simon & Schuster and Aladdin Books
1490. HER STORY – published by Silver Burdett
1491. MAIN STREET – published by Avon
1492. ONCE UPON AMERICA – published by Viking
1493. ORPHAN TRAIN CHILDREN – published by Delacorte
1494. ORPHAN TRAIN ADVENTURES – published by Delacorte
1495. SURVIVAL! – published by Aladdin Books

City/Country – Picture Books

1496. Cohen, Miriam. DOWN IN THE SUBWAY. *SEE 1008.*

1497. Cooper, Elisha. COUNTRY FAIR. Greenwillow, c1997.
Describes the activities that go on at a county fair, from the animal exhibits, food tasting, and ox pulls to a woodchopping exhibition.

1498. DeSaix, Frank. HILARY AND THE LIONS. Illus. by Deborah Durland Desaix. Farrar Straus, 1996 (pap).
On her first visit to New York City, Hilary dreams that the lions in front of the New York Public Library on Forty-Second Street come to life, and take her on a magical adventure through Manhattan.

1499. Isadora, Rachel. CITY SEEN FROM A TO Z. Greenwillow, 1983; Mulberry, 1992 (pap).
Twenty-six black and white drawings of scenes of city life suggest words beginning with each letter of the alphabet.

1500. Johnson, Stephen T. ALPHABET CITY. Viking, 1995; Puffin, 1999 (pap).
Paintings of objects in an urban setting represent the letters of the alphabet.

1501. Karas, G. Brian. HOME ON THE BAYOU. Simon & Schuster, 1996.
Because he loves cowboys but can't imagine that a cowboy could live in a swamp, Ned hates the move which he and his mom make to live with Grandpa near a bayou.

1502. London, Jonathan. LIKE BUTTER ON PANCAKES. Illus. by G. Brian Karas. Puffin, 1998 (pap).
As the sun rises and sets, its rays highlight simple aspects and situations of farm life.

1503. Maestro, Betsy. TAXI: A BOOK OF CITY WORDS. Illus. by Giulio Maestro. Clarion, 1990 (pap).
The reader is introduced to such typical city words as theater, museum, and office building as a taxi travels through a hectic workday in and around the city.

1504. Miller, Jane. FARM ALPHABET BOOK. J. M. Dent and Sons, 1981; Scholastic, 1987 (pap).
The various letters of the alphabet are illustrated by descriptions of farm animals and discussions of life on a farm.

1505. Quattlebaum, Mary. UNDERGROUND TRAIN. Illus. by Cat Bowman Smith. Doubleday, c1997.
A ride on the subway with Mama provides many vivid and exciting sights and sounds.

1506. Shannon, George. CLIMBING KANSAS MOUNTAINS. Illus. by Thomas B. Allen. Aladdin, 1996 (pap).
Shimmering illustrations full of visual surprises record the journey of a father and his son, to the towering grain elevators that dot the Kansas landscape in the mid-day heat.

1507. Tarsky, Sue. BUSY BUILDING BOOK. Illus. by Alex Ayliffe. Putnam, 1998.
Shows what happens on the construction site for a new office building.

1508. Wellington, Monica with Andrew Kupfer. NIGHT CITY. Dutton, c1998.
An hour by hour look at some night workers in a city that never sleeps, including fire fighters, a museum night watchman, musicians, and newspaper pressmen.

City/Country – Easy Readers

1509. Anderson, C.W. BILLY AND BLAZE. Buccaneer, 1992; Aladdin, 1992 (pap).
Billy is given a pony, whom he names Blaze, and with whom he rides all over the countryside.

1510. Berends, Polly. THE CASE OF THE ELEVATOR DUCK. Illus. by Diane Allison. Random, 1989 (pap).
Recounts the adventures of an eleven-year-old detective after he finds a duck in the elevator of his apartment building.

1511. Godwin, Laura. FOREST. Illus. by Stacey Schuett. HarperCollins, 1998.
A young girl goes to investigate a noise in the forest, and finds a small fawn that seems to be all alone.

1512. Herman, Gail. THERE IS A TOWN. Random, 1995.
Illustrations and simple text draw the reader into a family celebration where a girl receives a dollhouse in which a birthday party is also taking place.

City/Country – Intermediate

1513. Rylant, Cynthia. THE BLUE HILL MEADOWS. Illus. by Ellen Beier. Harcourt Brace, c1997.
Tells the story of the Meadows family and the life they lead in the quiet country town of Blue Hill, Virginia.

City/Country - Fiction

1514. Byars, Betsy. THE MIDNIGHT FOX. *SEE 329.*

1515. Fitzhugh, Louise. HARRIET THE SPY. *SEE 242.*

1516. George, Jean Craighead. MY SIDE OF THE MOUNTAIN. Dutton, 1988; Scholastic, 1997 (pap).
A young boy spending a year living alone in the Catskill Mountains tells of his struggle for survival.

1517. George, Jean Craighead. ON THE FAR SIDE OF THE MOUNTAIN. Dutton, 1990; Puffin, 1991 (pap).
Sam's peaceful existence in his wilderness home is disrupted when his sister runs away and his pet falcon is confiscated by a conservation officer.

1518. Greene, Constance C. A GIRL CALLED AL. Puffin, 1994 (pap).
A seventh grade girl, her friend and the assistant superintendent of their apartment building form a mutually needed friendship.

1519. Holman, Felice. SLAKE'S LIMBO. Aladdin, 1996 (pap).
A homeless thirteen-year-old, hounded by fears and misfortunes, flees into the New York City subway tunnels.

1520. Kinsey-Warnock, Natalie. AS LONG AS THERE ARE MOUNTAINS. Cobblehill, c1997.
Thirteen-year-old Iris dreams of one day running the family farm in northern Vermont, but the summer of 1956 holds many shocking changes that threaten the life Iris loves.

1521. Konigsburg, E.L. FROM THE MIXED-UP-FILES OF MRS. BASIL E. FRANKWEILER. Atheneum 1967; Aladdin, 1987 (pap).
A twelve-year-old runs away with her young brother to live in the Metropolitan Museum of Art.

1522. Lenski, Lois. STRAWBERRY GIRL. Lippincott, 1945; Trophy, 1995 (pap).
A young girl dreams of becoming the best strawberry girl in the Florida backwoods.

1523. MacLachlan, Patricia. SARAH, PLAIN AND TALL. *SEE 1523.*

1524. Mead, Alice. JUNEBUG. Farrar Straus, 1995; Yearling, 1997 (pap).
A young boy who lives with his mother and sister in a rough housing project in New Haven approaches his tenth birthday worried about the possibility of being forced to join a gang against his wishes.

1525. Myers, Walter Dean. THE YOUNG LANDLORDS. Viking, 1979.
Five devoted friends become landlords and try to make their Harlem neighborhood a better place to live.

1526. Paulsen, Gary. THE WINTER ROOM. *SEE 955.*

1527. Peck, Richard. A LONG WAY FROM CHICAGO. Dial, c1998.
A boy recounts his annual summer trips to rural Illinois with his sister during the Great Depression to visit their larger-than-life grandmother.

1528. Ruckman, Ivy. IN CARE OF CASSIE TUCKER. Delacorte. c1998; Yearling, 2000 (pap).
When her teenage cousin moves in with her family on their Nebraska farm in 1899, eleven-year-old Cassie learns a lot, including the meaning of the words "heathen" and "bigot."

1529. Rylant, Cynthia. SILVER PACKAGES: AN APPALACHIAN CHRISTMAS STORY. Orchard, 1997.
Every Christmas a rich man rides a train through Appalachia and throws gifts to poor children in order to repay a debt he owes the people who live there.

1530. Selden, George. THE CRICKET IN TIMES SQUARE. Dell, 1960; Dell, 1989 (pap).
The adventures of a country cricket who unintentionally arrives in New York and is befriended by Tucker Mouse and Harry Cat.

1531. White, E.B. STUART LITTLE. Harper, 1945; Trophy, 1974 (pap).
A debonair mouse sets out into the wide world to seek out his dearest friend, a little bird who stayed a few days in his family's garden.

1532. White, E.B. CHARLOTTE'S WEB. Harper, 1952; Trophy, 1999 (pap).
Wilbur the pig is desolate when he discovers he is to be the farmer's Christmas dinner, until his friend Charlotte, the spider, decides to help him.

1533. Wiggin, Kate D. REBECCA OF SUNNYBROOK FARM. Buccaneer, 1984.
Talkative Rebecca goes to live with her two unmarried aunts, with whom she spends seven difficult but rewarding years growing up.

1534. Wilder, Laura Ingalls. LITTLE HOUSE ON THE PRAIRIE. *SEE 1420.*

City/Country - Nonfiction

1535. Bial, Raymond. MIST OVER THE MOUNTAIN: APPALACHIA AND ITS PEOPLE. Houghton Mifflin, 1997.
An overview of life past and present in the geographic region known as Appalachia.

1536. Bial, Raymond. PORTRAIT OF A FARM FAMILY. Houghton Mifflin, 1995.
Tells the story of Dennis and Jane Steidinger and their eight children, portraying the difficult but rewarding way of life for a farm family.

1537. Bouchard, Dave. IF YOU'RE NOT FROM THE PRAIRIE.... Illus. by Henry Ripplinger. Atheneum, 1998.
A boy provides a look at life on the prairies of North America and describes the effects of the climate on the people who grow up in the heartland of the continent.

1538. De Fina, Allan A. WHEN A CITY LEANS AGAINST THE SKY: POEMS. Illus. by Ken Condon. Boyds Mills, 1997.
A collection of poems about cities and the life that is lived in them, divided into such categories as "City Streets," "City Sights," "Above Ground," "Underground," "City People," and "City Skies."

1539. Dean, Julia. A YEAR ON MONHEGAN ISLAND. Ticknor & Fields, 1995.
A full-color photo essay captures life among members of the close-knit community on Monhegan Island, a small island off the coast of Maine, from the tranquil isolation of their winters to the huge influx of tourists during the summer season.

1540. Geisert, Bonnie. PRAIRIE TOWN. Illus. by Arthur Geisert. Walter Lorraine, 1998.
A description of a year in the life of a prairie town, including the effect of seasons and of economics on the ebb and flow of this agricultural community.

1541. Gravelle, Karen. GROWING UP IN A HOLLER IN THE MOUNTAINS: AN APPALACHIAN CHILDHOOD. Watts, 1997.
Tells of the home, activities, and contemporary life in the Appalachian region through the story of a ten-year-old and his family.

1542. Rylant, Cynthia. APPALACHIA: THE VOICES OF SLEEPING BIRDS. Illus. by Barr Moser. Harcourt 1991; Voyager, 1998 (pap).
Celebrates the Appalachian region and its people, looks at Appalachian homes, foods and surroundings, and gives their views of the outside world.

1543. Sandburg, Carl. GRASSROOTS: POEMS. Browndeer, 1998.
Fourteen poems with mid-western themes or settings.

1544. Warren, Scott. DESERT DWELLERS: NATIVE PEOPLE OF THE AMERICAN SOUTHWEST. Chronicle , 1997.
Examines the traditions, beliefs, customs, and histories of Native Americans of the southwestern United States, including the Hopi, Navajo, and Apache.

1545. Wolfman, Judy. LIFE ON A PIG FARM. Carolrhoda, c1998.
Describes the experiences of a young girl as she raises pigs as part of a 4-H project.

1546. Yolen, Jane. SKYSCRAPE/CITY SCAPE: POEMS OF CITY LIFE. Illus. by Ken Condon. Boyds Mills, 1996.
A collection of poetry on cities and city life.

Education and Learning – Picture Books

1547. Ahlberg, Janet. STARTING SCHOOL. Illus. by Allen Ahlberg. Puffin, 1988.
Introduces the serious and fun activities of students just starting school.

1548. Anholt, Laurence. BILLY AND THE BIG NEW SCHOOL. Whitman, 1999.
Billy is nervous about starting school, but as he cares for a sparrow that eventually learns to fly on its own, he realizes that he too can look after himself.

1549. Baer, Edith. THIS IS THE WAY WE GO TO SCHOOL. Illus. by Steve Bjorkman. Scholastic, 1992 (pap).
Describes, in text and illustrations, the many different modes of transportation used by children all over the world to go to school.

1550. Bemelmans, Ludwig. MADELINE. *SEE 1188.*

1551. Cohen, Miriam. STARRING FIRST GRADE. Illus. by Lillian Hoban. Morrow, 1985; Doubleday, 1996 (pap).
The production of the first graders' version of "The Three Billy Goats Gruff" becomes a lesson in cooperation when Jim learns to overcome his dissatisfaction with his assigned part and helps his friend deal with stage fright.

1552. Cohen, Miriam. WHEN WILL I READ? Illus. by Lillian Hoban. Morrow, 1977.
Impatient to read, a first-grader doesn't realize there is more to reading than books.

1553. Cohen, Miriam. WILL I HAVE A FRIEND? Illus. by Lillian Hoban. Simon & Schuster, 1967.
Jim's anxieties on his first day of school are happily forgotten when he makes a new friend.

1554. Finchler, Judy. MISS MALARKEY DOESN'T LIVE IN ROOM 10. Illus. by Kevin O'Malley. Walker, 1995.
A student is absolutely, positively sure his teacher and all the other teachers live in the school.

1555. Giff, Patricia Reilly. TODAY WAS A TERRIBLE DAY. *SEE 563.*

1556. Havill, Juanita. JAMAICA AND THE SUBSTITUTE TEACHER. Houghton Mifflin, 1999.
Jamaica copies from a friend during a spelling test because she wants a perfect paper, but her substitute teacher Mrs. Duval helps her understand that she does not have to be perfect to be special.

1557. Johnson, Dolores. WHAT WILL MOMMY DO WHEN I'M AT SCHOOL? Aladdin, 1998 (pap).
A child worries how her mother will cope at home while she is at school.

1558. Johnston, Tony. SPARKY AND EDDIE: THE FIRST DAY OF SCHOOL. Scholastic, c1997.
Even though they are not in the same class, two young friends are glad that they decided to give school a try.

1559. Langreuter, Jutta. LITTLE BEAR GOES TO KINDERGARTEN. Illus. by Vera Sobat. Millbrook, 1977.
Little Bear likes the teacher, other children, and activities on his first day in kindergarten, but he does not want his mother to leave.

1560. Lauture, Denize. RUNNING THE ROAD TO ABC. *SEE 1273.*

1561. McGeorge, Constance W. BOOMER GOES TO SCHOOL. Illus. by Mary Whyte. Chronicle, 1996.
Boomer, the golden retriever, accompanies his owner to school for show and tell.

1562. McMillan, Bruce. MOUSE VIEWS: WHAT THE CLASS PET SAW. Holiday, 1993.
Photographic puzzles follow an escaped pet mouse through a school, and readers are challenged to recognize the objects as seen from the mouse's point of view.

1563. Martin, Linda. WHEN DINOSAURS GO TO SCHOOL. Chronicle, c1999.
Dinosaurs spend a day at school with reading, writing, arithmetic, music, fingerpaints, exercise and pizza.

1564. Rogers, Jacqueline. TIPTOE INTO KINDERGARTEN. Scholastic, c1999.
A young preschooler accompanies her big brother to kindergarten and discovers a fun atmosphere, full of blocks and books, paints and puzzles.

1565. Yashima, Taro. CROW BOY. Puffin, 1955.
A Japanese boy hides under the schoolhouse on the first day of school.

Education and Learning - Intermediate

1566. Adler, Susan. SAMANTHA LEARNS A LESSON. Pleasant Publications, 1986.
Samantha is determined to help nine-year-old Nellie, who is attending school for the first time, and learns a great deal about what is it like to be a poor child and work in a factory.

1567. Caudill, Rebecca. DID YOU CARRY THE FLAG TODAY, CHARLEY? Dell, 1988 (pap).
Charley Cornett, a newcomer to the Little School in the Appalachian Mountains, is a dreamer and a curious soul who has his classmates wondering if he will ever be responsible enough to earn the honor of carrying the flag.

1568. Cleary, Beverly. MUGGIE MAGGIE. Camelot, 1991 (pap).
Maggie discovers that knowing how to read and write cursive promises to open up an entirely new world of knowledge for her.

1569. Estes, Eleanor. THE HUNDRED DRESSES. Illus. by Louis Slobodkin. Harcourt, 1972.
In winning a medal she is no longer there to receive, a tight-lipped little Polish girl teaches her classmates a lesson.

1570. Giff, Patricia Reilly. THE BEAST IN MS. ROONEY'S ROOM. *SEE 562.*

1571. Giff, Patricia Reilly. PURPLE CLIMBING DAYS. Yearling, 1991 (pap).
Terrified to climb up the rope in gym, Richard "Beast" Best attempts to hide his fears from his friends, but Mrs. Miller, the meanest substitute teacher in the school, discovers his secret.

1572. Lorbiecki, Marybeth. SISTER ANNE'S HANDS. Illus. by Wendy Popp. Dial, 1998.
A seven-year-old has her first encounter with racism when an African American nun comes to teach at her parochial school.

1573. Park, Barbara. JUNIE B. JONES AND THE STUPID SMELLY BUS. Illus. by Denise Brunkus. Dial, 1998; Random, 1992 (pap).
A young girl describes her feelings about starting kindergarten, and what happens when she decides not to ride the bus home.

1574. Porter, Connie. ADDY LEARNS A LESSON. Pleasant Publications, 1993.
Addy, a courageous girl determined to be free in the midst of the Civil War, attends a segregated school.

1575. Shaw, Janet. KIRSTEN LEARNS A LESSON. *SEE 944.*

1576. Surat, Michele Maria. ANGEL CHILD, DRAGON CHILD. *SEE 686.*

1577. Tripp, Valerie. JOSEFINA LEARNS A LESSON. Pleasant Publications, 1997.
Josefina and her sisters distrust learning to read and write, as well as other changes their Tia Dolores is bringing into the household, because they fear they will lose memories of their mother.

1578. Tripp, Valerie. MOLLY LEARNS A LESSON. Pleasant Publications, 1986.
During World War II, nine-year-old Molly goes to school and with her friends tries to aid the war effort.

Schools and Education – Fiction

1579. Alcott, Louisa May. JO'S BOYS. Little Brown, 1994 (pap).
A sequel to Little Men. Jo and Professor Bhaer arrange a reunion for the March family and the original twelve boys of Plumfield.

1580. Alcott, Louisa May. LITTLE MEN. Apple, 1992 (pap).
The adventures of Jo March of Little Women and her husband as they try to make their school for boys a happy, comfortable, and stimulating place.

1581. Bartlett, Susan. SEAL ISLAND SCHOOL. Viking, 1999.
On Seal Island off the coast of Maine, a place swarming with pets of all kinds, nine-year-old Pru plans to keep her teacher from leaving by finding her a dog.

1582. Bunting, Eve. CHEYENNE AGAIN. Illus. by Toddy Irving. Clarion, 1995.
In the late 1880's a Cheyenne boy is taken to a boarding school to learn the white man's ways.

1583. Burnett, Frances Hodgson. A LITTLE PRINCESS (a.k.a. SARA CREWE). *SEE 1203.*

1584. Carbone, Elisa Lynn. STARTING SCHOOL WITH AN ENEMY. *SEE 59.*

1585. Creech, Sharon. BLOOMABILITY. HarperCollins, 1998; Trophy, 1999 (pap).
When her aunt and uncle take her from New Mexico to Lugano, Switzerland to attend an international school, a thirteen-year-old discovers an expanding world and her place within it.

1586. Dahl, Roald. MATILDA. Illus. by Quentin Blake. *SEE 332.*

1587. DeClements, Barthe. SIXTH GRADE CAN REALLY KILL YOU. *SEE 572.*

1588. Hurwitz, Johanna. CLASS CLOWN. Morrow, 1987; Scholastic, 1995 (pap).
Lucas, the most obstreperous boy in the third grade, finds it very hard to turn over a new leaf when he decides to become the perfect student.

1589. Nordstrom, Ursula. THE SECRET LANGUAGE. Illus. by Mary Chalmers. Harper, 1998 (pap).
An eight-year-old is miserable in the boarding school she is sent to until she gets to know another girl who has a secret language.

1590. Santiago, Chiori. HOME TO MEDICINE MOUNTAIN. *SEE 1451.*

1591. Schenker, Dona. THE SECRET CIRCLE. Knopf, 1998.
Sixth-grader Jamie enters a new school and must decide if membership in an exclusive clique, the Secret Circle, is worth the price of betraying a friend.

1592. Shreve, Susan Richards. THE FLUNKING OF JOSHUA T. BATES. *SEE 565.*

1593. Shreve, Susan Richards. JOSHUA T. BATES IN TROUBLE AGAIN. Knopf, 1997.
After finally being promoted to fourth grade, Joshua is so worried about the bully who rules the boys that he makes some unwise decisions.

1594. Shreve, Susan Richards. JOSHUA T. BATES TAKES CHARGE. Random, 1997 (pap).
Joshua is worried about fitting in at school and feels awkward when the new student he is supposed to be helping becomes the target of the fifth grade's class bully.

1595. Spinelli, Jerry. FOURTH GRADE RATS. Apple, 1996 (pap).
Fourth grader Suds learns that a fear of spiders or a babyish lunchbox will never get him into the coveted Fourth Grade Rats. Nevertheless he finds out that you don't have to be tough to be grown-up.

1596. Webster, Jean. DADDY LONG-LEGS. Everyman's Library, 1993; Puffin, 1995 (pap).
An orphaned boarding school student yearns to meet the wealthy guardian with whom she has corresponded for years, but has never met.

1597. Wilder, Laura Ingalls. THESE HAPPY GOLDEN YEARS. *SEE 1424.*

1598. Winslow, Vicki. FOLLOW THE LEADER. *SEE 789.*

Schools and Education – Nonfiction

1599. Bridges, Ruby. THROUGH MY EYES. *SEE 794.*

1600. Coles, Robert. THE STORY OF RUBY BRIDGES. *SEE 824.*

1601. Dakos, Kalli. THE GOOF WHO INVENTED HOMEWORK, AND OTHER SCHOOL POEMS. Illus. by Denise Brunkus. Dial, 1996.
A collection of poems that reflect the varied, sometimes serious, sometimes funny activities and emotions of the school year.

1602. Dakos, Kalli. IF YOU'RE NOT HERE, PLEASE RAISE YOUR HAND: POEMS ABOUT SCHOOL. Simon & Schuster, 1995; Aladdin, 1995 (pap).
Thirty-eight poems capture the trials and tribulations, joys and sorrows, and ups and downs of elementary school life.

1603. Flanagan, Alice K. LEARNING IS FUN WITH MRS. PEREZ. Childrens Press, 1998.
Text and photographs follow a Cuban-American kindergarten teacher through her activities as she helps the children in her class to learn.

1604. Harrison, David L. SOMEBODY CATCH MY HOMEWORK: POEMS. Illus. by Betsy Lewin. Boyd Mills, 1995 (pap).
A collection of humorous poems about school pays tribute to the agony of tests, homework, cursive writing, and cafeteria food.

1605. Hill, Lee Sullivan. SCHOOLS HELP US LEARN. Carolrhoda, 1988.
An introduction to the various kinds of schools, size, location, and the kinds of learning provided by each.

1606. Howlett, Bud. I'M NEW HERE. *SEE 994.*

1607. McKissack, Pat. MARY MCLEOD BETHUNE. *SEE 507.*

1608. Powers, Mary Ellen. OUR TEACHER'S IN A WHEELCHAIR. Whitman, 1986.
Text and photographs depict the activities of Brian Hanson, who is able to lead an active existence as a nursery school teacher despite partial paralysis requiring the use of a wheelchair.

1609. Pringle, Laurence P. ONE ROOM SCHOOL. Illus. by Barbara Garrison. Boyds Mills Press, 1998.
A look back at events and the changing of the season at a one-room school in rural New York during the last year of the Second World War.

1610. Shields, Carol Diggory. LUNCH MONEY AND OTHER POEMS ABOUT SCHOOL. Illus. by Paul Meisel. Puffin, 1998 (pap).
Provides young readers with a colorful and amusing collection of twenty-four poems about school and school-time events.

1611. Voetberg, Julie. I AM A HOME SCHOOLER. Illus. by Tasha Owens. Whitman, 1995.
Describes the experiences of a nine-year-old girl who is taught by her mother on their farm in Washington State.

Settings – Series

1612. COLORS OF THE WORLD. Carolrhoda.
Uses colors to focus on history, physical features and culture in various regions of the world.

1613. COUNTRIES OF THE WORLD. Bridgestone Books.
Discusses the history, landscape, people and country of each featured country.

1614. CHILDREN JUST LIKE ME. DK.
Brilliant captioned photographs demonstrate the appearance and customs of children from different countries.

1615. CITIES OF THE WORLD. Children's Press.
A look at the history, culture, daily life, and points of interest in major world cities.

1616. COUNTRY STUDIES. Heinemann Library.
Profiles the history, geography, population, ecosystems and natural resources of various countries.

1617. ENCHANTMENT OF THE WORLD, SECOND SERIES. Children's Press.
A thorough introduction to the geography, history, culture and people of countries around the world.

1618. EXPLORING CULTURES OF THE WORLD. Benchmark Books.
Discusses the geography, history, people, and culture of countries in this series.

1619. FAMILIES AROUND THE WORLD. Raintree Steck-Vaughn.
Each title follows a family during a typical day, providing brief information about everyday routines and customs.

1620. GAMES PEOPLE PLAY. Children's Press.
Discusses the ways that children around the world have amused themselves from ancient times to the present with games, toys, and sports.

1621. GLOBE TROTTERS CLUB. Carolrhoda.
Overviews of countries emphasizing cultural aspects.

1622. ILLUSTRATED LIVING HISTORY SERIES. Chelsea House.
Advanced series gives detailed description of life during earlier times throughout history.

1623. LONG AGO AND TODAY. Heinemann Library.
Text, photographs and illustrations identify and trace patterns of continuity and change in cities, farms, schools or homes in the United States.

1624. MAJOR WORLD NATIONS. Chelsea House.
Examines the geography, history, government, society, economy, and transportation of various countries.

1625. PASSPORT SERIES. Franklin Watts.
Text and photographs highlight typical sights and activities, including information on history, people, culture and popular pastimes.

1626. PLACES AND PEOPLES OF THE WORLD. Chelsea.
Surveys history, topography, people and culture with an emphasis on each country's current economy, and place in the political world.

1627. SEE THROUGH HISTORY. Viking.
The customs and typical daily lives of ancient peoples are revealed in see-through cutaways.

1628. TICKET TO —. Carolrhoda.
Provides an overview of the geography, people, language, customs, religion, lifestyle, and culture of each country featured in the series.

1629. WAY PEOPLE LIVED. Lucent.
Describes the lifestyles of Vikings and other such groups in history.

1630. WELCOME TO MY COUNTRY. Gareth Stevens.
Overviews of countries that include information on geography, history, government, economy, people, and lifestyles.

1631. WORLD CELEBRATIONS AND CEREMONIES. Blackbirch Press.
Titles discuss coming-of-age, birth, harvest and New Year traditions in different countries.

1632. WORLD GUIDES. Davidson.
Each book features a country's landmarks, interesting facts, and cultures and customs of the people who live there.

1633. WORLD HISTORY SERIES. Lucent.
Describes politics, culture, religion and society in various regions and historical periods.

1634. THE WORLD'S CHILDREN. Carolrhoda.
Describes social life and customs of people who live in various countries around the world.

Languages

Language: Sign Language, Braille, and Bilingual Materials

Sign Language Materials

1635. Ancona, George. HANDTALK ZOO. Aladdin, 1996 (pap).
Words and sign language depict children at the zoo discovering how to sign the names of various animals and how to tell time.

1636. Baker, Pamela J. MY FIRST BOOK OF SIGN. Kendall Green, 1986.
Pictures of children demonstrate the forming in sign language of 150 basic alphabetically arranged words, accompanied by illustrations of the words themselves.

1637. Bornstein, Harry. LITTLE RED RIDING HOOD; TOLD IN SIGNED ENGLISH. Kendall Green, 1991.
The well-known fairy tale, accompanied by diagrams showing how to form the signs for each word of the text.

1638. Bornstein, Harry. NURSERY RHYMES FROM MOTHER GOOSE; TOLD IN SIGNED ENGLISH. Kendall Green, 1992.
Presents well-known Mother Goose rhymes accompanied by diagrams showing how to form the signs for each word in the poems.

1639. Fain, Kathleen. HANDSIGNS: A SIGN LANGUAGE ALPHABET. Chronicle, 1995 (pap).
Presents an animal for each letter of the alphabet, accompanied by the corresponding sign for that letter in American Sign Language.

1640. Moore, Clement. THE NIGHT BEFORE CHRISTMAS: TOLD IN SIGNED ENGLISH. Gallaudet, 1994.
This well-known poem about an important Christmas Eve visitor is told in signed English.

1641. Rankin, Laura. THE HANDMADE COUNTING BOOK. Dial, c1998.
Shows how to count from one to twenty and twenty-five, fifty, seventy-five and one hundred using American Sign Language.

1642. Wojcio, Michael David. MUSIC IN MOTION: 22 SONGS IN SIGNING EXACT ENGLISH FOR CHILDREN. Modern Sign Press, 1982 (pap).
A book of children's songs which includes lyrics in standard English print and sign language pictures.

The following companies also produce materials available in sign language:

Garlic Press
100 Hillview Lane #2
Eugene, OR 97401

Gallaudet University Press
800 Florida Avenue NE
Washington, D.C. 20002-3695

Language – Braille Materials

A list of Braille materials for children is available from the following company:

Seedlings
P.O. Box 51924
Livonia, MI 48151-5924
e-mail: seedlink@aol.com

This company produces Print-Braille and Picture books, which are meant to introduce Braille to children who are blind, and also provide a way for blind adults to read to sighted children. They also have Print-and-Braille books, which are double-spaced easy readers with the print words typed just above each Braille letter. Blind and sighted readers can enjoy these together.

Bilingual Materials:

Listed on the next pages are some of the bilingual children's books that are currently owned by agencies of Queens Borough Public Library. The text is in both English and another language, as indicated.

Distributors for bilingual materials are:
Multicultural Books and Videos
28880 Southfield Road – Suite 183
Lathrup Village, MI 48076
Handles many publishers, such as Mantra, Milet and Pan-Asian which produce in Indian Subcontinent and East Asian langauges.

Asia for Kids
4480 Lake Forest Dr. Suite 302
Cincinnati, OH 45242-3726
website: www.asiaforkids.com

Russian House
253 Fifth Avenue
New York, NY 10016

Bilingual Materials – Bengali/English

1643. Carle, Eric. THE VERY HUNGRY CATERPILLAR. Mantra, 1992.
A very hungry caterpillar pops out of its egg, eats a different food on each day of the week, builds a cocoon for itself and emerges as a beautiful butterfly.

1644. Hamanaka, Sheila. PTRTHIBUEIRA SABA KAGYARTI RAGNGA = ALL THE COLOURS OF THE EARTH. Mantra, 1996.
Children come in all the colors of the earth, in every shade of you and me. A celebration of the dazzling diversity of children.

1645. Lindbergh, Reeve. NOBODY OWNS THE SKY. Mantra, 1996.
The inspiring story of Bessie Coleman, who grew up in a time when it was very difficult for any woman to become a pilot, but for a black woman it seemed impossible.

1646. McCrory, Moy. DEADEIRA GALPA = GRANDMOTHER'S TALE. Magi Hayes, 1989.
As they do each week, Grandmother takes Nazan to the market. As they are waiting in line, Grandmother starts to relate a tale to Nazan about her childhood in Turkey.

1647. Martinez I Vendrell, Maria. SILIYEARA EKA BHEAI = A BROTHER FOR CELIA. Magi, 1989.
A new baby is born in Celia's house.

Bilingual Materials – Chinese/English

1648. Carle, Eric. FEI CH'ANG CHI E TI MAO MAO CH'UNG: THE VERY HUNGRY CATERPILLAR. Mantra, 1992. *SEE 1643*.

1649. Goldstein, Peggy. L'ONG IS A DRAGON: CHINESE WRITING FOR CHILDREN. China Books, 1991.
Explains how Chinese writing developed, and demonstrates how to write seventy-five Chinese characters, using detailed instructions and examples.

1650. Lee, Huy Voun. IN THE PARK. Holt, 1998.
On the first day of spring, a mother and her son go to the park where they draw Chinese characters that represent words relating to the season.

1651. MacDonald, Amy. LITTLE BEAVER AND THE ECHO = HSIAO HO LI YHU HUI SHENG. Magi, 1990.
Unaware that the voice from across the pond telling him he's lonely is his echo, a little beaver sets out to make friends with that voice.

Bilingual Materials – French/English

1652. Bishop, Dorothy. LE LION ET LA SOURIS: LEONARD THE LION AND RAYMOND THE MOUSE. National Textbook Co., 1988.
Recounts the tale of the tiny mouse that helped the mighty lion when he became ensnared by hunters.

Bilingual Materials – Gujarati/English

1653. Carle, Eric. KHUBAJA BHUKHYO KERTARAPILARA = THE VERY HUNGRY CATERPILLAR. Mantra, 1992. *SEE1643*

1654. Desai, Niru. THE RAJA'S BIG EARS = REAJEA NEA MOTEA KEANA. Jennie Ingham, 1989.
The royal barber can't keep a secret, so he whispers it to a tree thinking it will be safe.

1655. Hamanaka, Sheila. EAPNEI DHARATEINERM NAVEINABHARYEA RAGNGA = ALL THE COLOURS OF THE EARTH. Mantra, 1996. *SEE 1644*.

1656. Hill, Eric. SPOT'S BIRTHDAY PARTY = SPORTANEA JANMA DIVASANEI PEARTEI. Baker, 1987.
A game of hide and seek at the party as readers lift flaps to see who's hiding.

1657. Lindbergh, Reeve. EAKEABSANO KOEI MEALIKE NATHEI = NOBODY OWNS THE SKY. Mantra, 1996. *SEE 1645*.

1658. McCrory, Moy. DEADEMEANEI VEARTEA = GRANDMOTHER'S TALE. Magi, 1989. *SEE 1646.*

1659. Stone, Susheila. MITTHU THE PARROT = MEIRTHU POPARTAL. Jennie Ingham, 1989.
A rich merchant unwittingly teaches his parrot a trick which enables it to escape.

Bilingual Materials – Haitian-Creole/English

1660. Heurtelou, Maude. PITIT LYON = LION CUB. Educa Vision, 1996.
Roger, Chantal, Simone and John visit a zoo in the city of Les Cayes and are very excited to be able to see a lion cub for the first time.

Bilingual Materials – Hebrew/English

1661. Edwards, Michelle. BLESSED ARE YOU: TRADITIONAL EVERYDAY HEBREW PRAYERS. Lothrop Lee, 1993.
A collection of thirteen traditional prayers for children: prayers of thanksgiving and wonder, peace and comfort, getting up in the morning and going to sleep at night.

Bilingual Materials – Hindi/English

1662. Aggrey, James. UKEABA JO URRATEA NAHEIM THEA = THE EAGLE THAT WOULD NOT FLY. Magi, 1988.
A well-known story about an eagle who thinks it is a chicken. An allegory to describe the fate of the African people as seen by the teller.

1663. James, Christopher. BUMPA PEARKA MERM = BUMP IN THE PARK. Magi, 1988.
Bump is a lovable but clumsy little elephant. Along with his small friend, Birdie, he has many adventures.

1664. McCrory, Moy. DEADEI MEARM KEI KAHEANEI = GRADMOTHER'S TALE. Magi, 1989. *SEE 1646.*

1665. Martinez i Vendrell, Maria. SEILIYEA KE LIYE EKA BHEAEI = A BROTHER FOR CELIA. Magi, 1989. *SEE 1647.*

Bilingual Materials – Japanese/English

1666. Takeshita, Fumiko. THE PARK BENCH. Kane Miller, 1988.
All through the sunny day the white bench in the park provides pleasure for the many people who come by, from the old man taking a walk to the children playing in the park.

Bilingual Materials – Korean/English

1667. Chang, Monica. THE MOUSE BRIDE: A CHINESE FOLKTALE. Yuan-Liou, 1994.
A mouse goes to the sun, cloud, wind and wall in search of the strongest husband for his daughter.

1668. Han, Suzanne Crowder. THE RABBIT'S ESCAPE = KUSA ILSAENGHAN TOOKKI. Holt, 1995.
A clever rabbit uses his wits to escape the underwater Kingdom where the Dragon king wants his liver.

1669. Han, Suzanne Crowder. THE RABBIT'S JUDGMENT. Holt, 1994.
Tricked into freeing a hungry tiger from a trap, a man refuses to let the tiger eat him until they get another opinion on the situation from a disinterested party.

1670. Paek, Min. AEKYUNG'S DREAM. Childrens, 1988.
A young Korean immigrant learns to adjust to her new life in America by heeding the words of an ancient Korean king.

Bilingual Materials – Punjabi/English

1671. Desai, Niru. THE RAJA'S BIG EARS = REAJE DE WHARDE-WHARDE KANNAL. *SEE 1654.*

1672. Hill, Eric. SPOT'S BIRTHDAY PARTY = SPAURTA DEI BARTHADRE PERRTEI. *SEE 1656.*

1673. Teague, Kati. GELA DEI BARATHARDE PEARARTEI = GAIL'S BIRTHDAY PARTY. Magi, 1991.
Gail's mom, dad and little brother Jack all prepare for Gail's special day.

Bilingual Materials – Spanish/English - Fiction

1674. Anzald'ua, Gloria. AMIGOS DEL OTRO LADO = FRIENDS FROM THE OTHER SIDE. Illus. by Consuelo Menendez. Childrens Book Press, 1993.
Having crossed the Rio Grande into Texas with his mother in search of a new life, Joaquin receives help and friendship from a young Mexican American girl.

1675. Anzald'ua, Gloria. PRIETITA Y LA LLORONA = PRIETITA AND THE GHOST WOMAN. Illus. by Christina Gonzalez. Childrens Book Press, 1995.
A young Mexican American girl becomes lost during her search for an herb to cure her mother, and is aided by the legendary ghost woman.

1676. Argueta, Manilo. LOS PERROS MAGICOS DE LOS VOLCANES = MAGIC DOGS OF THE VOLCANOES. Illus. by Elly Simmons. Childrens Book Press, 1990.
When the magic dogs who live on the volcanoes of El Salvador and protect the villagers are pursued by wicked soldiers made of lead, they are aided by two ancient volcanoes.

1677. Blanco, Alberto. ANGEL'S KITE = LA ESTRELLA DE ANGEL. Illus. by Rodolfo Morales. Childrens Book Press, 1994.
A young boy makes a kite that mysteriously restores a long-missing bell to the town church.

1678. Blanco, Alberto. LA SIRENA DEL DESIERTO = THE DESERT MERMAID. Illus. by Patricia Revah. Childrens Book Press, 1992.
A desert mermaid living in an oasis seeks to save her people by rediscovering the forgotten songs of their ancestors.

1679. Cisneros, Sandra. HAIRS = PELITOS. Illus. by Terry Ybanez. Dragonfly, 1997 (pap).
A child describes how each person in the family has hair that is different: Papa's hair is like a broom, Kiki's like fur, and Mama's has the smell of warm bread.

1680. Colon-Vila, Lillian. SALSA. Illus. by Roberta Collier-Morales. Arte Publico, 1998.
A young girl living in New York's El Barrio describes the Afro-Caribbean dance music, salsa, and imagines being a salsa director.

1681. Covault, Ruth M. PABLO Y PIMIENTE = PABLO AND PIMIENTE. Illus. by Francisco Mora. Northland Pub., 1999 (pap).
A ten-year-old falls out of his father's old truck on the way to pick melons in Arizona, but with the help of a coyote pup, he makes it across the border.

1682. Delgado, Maria Isabel. CHAVES MEMORIES = LOS RECUERDOS DE CHAVE. Pinata, c1996.
A woman recalls childhood visits to her grandparents' ranch in Mexico, where she and her brother played with their cousins and listened to the stories of an old ranch hand.

1683. Dorros, Arthur. RADIO MAN = DON RADIO: A STORY IN ENGLISH AND SPANISH. Illus. by Sandra Marulanda Dorros. Trophy, 1997 (pap).
As he travels with his family of migrant farm workers, Diego relies on his radio to provide him with companionship.

1684. Herrmann, Marjorie E. EL PAJARO CU = THE CU BIRD. National Textbook, 1987 (pap).
When the Cu bird, who has been naked since creation, is dressed with one feather from each of the other birds, he decides he is too handsome to remain with the others.

1685. Jimenez, Juan R. PLATERO Y YO = PLATERO AND I. *SEE 1211*.

1686. Keister, Douglas. FERNANDO'S GIFT = EL REGALO DE FERNANDO. Sierra Club for Children, 1995.
Fernando, who lives in the rain forest of Costa Rica, goes with his friend to look for her favorite climbing tree, only to find it has been cut down.

1687. Lomas Garza, Carmen. FAMILY PICTURES = CUADROS DE FAMILIA. Childrens Book Press, 1998 (pap).
The author describes, in bilingual text and in illustrations, her experiences growing up in a Hispanic community in Texas.

1688. Lopez de Mariscal, Blanca. THE HARVEST BIRDS = LOS PAJAROS DE LA COSECHA. Illus. by Enrique Flores. Childrens Book Press, 1995.
When his older brothers inherit his late father's land, Juan Zanate gives up his dream of becoming a Mexican farmer, until his friends, the harvest birds, help him realize his hopes.

1689. Luenn, Nancy. A GIFT FOR ABUELITA: CELEBRATING THE DAY OF THE DEAD = UN REGALO PARA ABUELITA. Illus. by Robert Chapman. Rising Moon, 1998.
After her beloved grandmother dies, Rosita hopes to be reunited with her as she prepares a gift to give her when her family celebrates the Day of the Dead.

1690. Maury, Inez. MY MOTHER THE MAIL CARRIER = MI MAMA LA CARTERA. Illus. by Lady McCrady. Feminist Press, 1976 (pap).
A five-year-old describes the loving and close relationship she has with her mother, a mail carrier, and also relates some aspects of her mother's job.

1691. Mora, Pat. THE DESERT IS MY MOTHER = EL DESIERTO ES MI MADRE. Illus. by Daniel Lechon. Arte Publico, 1994.
A poetic description of the desert as the provider of comfort, food, spirit and life.

1692. Mora, Pat. LISTEN TO THE DESERT = OYE AL DESIERTO. Illus. by Francisco Mora. Clarion, 1994.
A bilingual poem which describes some of the sounds of nature in a desert.

1693. Reiser, Lynn. TORTILLAS AND LULLABIES = TORTILLAS Y CANCIONCITAS. Illus. by Corazones Valientes. Greenwillow, 1998.
A young girl describes activities that her great-grandmother, grandmother, and mother all did with their daughters, and that she does with her doll.

1694. Seuss, Dr. EL GATO ENSOMBRERADO = THE CAT IN THE HAT. Random, 1967.
Two children sitting at home on a rainy day are visited by the Cat in the Hat who shows them some tricks and games.

Bilingual Materials – Spanish/English – Nonfiction

1695. Ada, Alma Flor. THE LIZARD AND THE SUN = LA LAGARTIJA Y EL SOL; A FOLKTALE IN ENGLISH AND SPANISH. Illus. by Felipe Davalos. Bantam, 1997; Yearling, 1999 (pap).
A traditional Mexican folktale in which a faithful lizard finds the sun, and thus brings light and warmth back to the world.

1696. Alarcon, Francisco. JITOMATES RISUEDNOS Y OTROS POEMAS DE PRIMAVERA: POEMAS = LAUGHING TOMATOES AND OTHER SPRING POEMS. Illus. by Maya Christina Gonzalez. Childrens Book Press, 1997.
A bilingual collection of humorous and serious poems about family, nature and celebrations by a renowned Mexican-American poet.

1697. Ancona, George. THE PIÑATA MAKER = EL PIÑATERO. Harcourt Brace, 1994.
A description of how a craftsman from southern Mexico makes piñatas for all the village birthday parties and other fiestas.

1698. Bishop, Dorothy Sword. LEONARDO EL LEON Y RAMON EL RATON = LEONARD THE LION AND RAYMOND THE MOUSE. *SEE 1652.*

1699. Chang, Monica. LA NOVIA RATON: CUENTO POPULAR CHINO = THE MOUSE BRIDE: A CHINESE FOLKTALE. *SEE 1667.*

1700. Ehlert, Lois. CUCKOO: A MEXICAN FOLKTALE = CUCU: UN CUENTE FOLKLORICO MEXICANO. Harcourt, 1997.
A traditional Mayan tale which reveals how the cuckoo lost her beautiful feathers.

1701. Ehlert, Lois. MOON ROPE: A PERUVIAN FOLKTALE = UNO LAZO A LA LUNA: UNA LEYENDA PERUANA. Harcourt Brace, 1992.
An adaptation of the Peruvian folktale in which Fox and Mole try to climb to the moon on a rope woven of grass.

1702. Gonzalez, Lucia M. THE BOSSY GALLITO = EL GALLO DE BODAS: A TRADITIONAL CUBAN FOLKTALE. Illus. by Lulu Delacre. Scholastic, 1994.
A bossy rooster dirties his beak when he eats a kernel of corn and must clean it before his parrot uncle's wedding.

1703. Johnston, Tony. MY MEXICO = MEXICO MIO. Philomel, 1996; Paper Star, 1999 (pap).
A bilingual collection of poems reflecting the author's memories and experiences in Mexico.

1704. Perl, Lila. PIÑATAS AND PAPER FLOWERS: HOLIDAYS OF THE AMERICAS IN ENGLISH AND SPANISH. Houghton Mifflin, 1983 (pap).
Brief descriptions of several Hispanic holidays as they are celebrated in North, Central, and South America.

1705. Rohmer, Harriet. ATARIBA AND NIGUAYONA: A STORY FROM THE TAINO PEOPLE OF PUERTO RICO. Childrens Book Press, 1992.
A Taino Indian legend about a young boy and his search for the healing caimoni tree.

1706. Rohmer, Harriet. COMO VINIMOS AL QUINTO MUNDO = HOW WE CAME TO THE FIFTH WORLD: A CREATION STORY FROM ANCIENT MEXICO. Illus., by Joe Sam. Childrens Book Press, 1993 (pap).
A bilingual Aztec creation myth which tells how the Fifth World of peace and happiness came into existence after four futile attempts.

1707. Rohmer, Harriet. THE INVISIBLE HUNTERS: A LEGEND FROM THE MISKITO INDIANS OF NICARAGUA = LOS CAZADORES INVISIBLES. Childrens Book Press, 1990.
This Miskito Indian legend set in seventeenth-century Nicaragua illustrates the impact of the first European traders on traditional life.

1708. Simon, Norma. WHAT DO I DO? Illus. by Joe Lasker. Whitman, 1969.
A little Puerto Rican girl tells what she does in various work and play situations throughout one day.

1709. SOL A SOL: BILINGUAL POEMS. Illus. by Emily Lisker. Holt, 1998.
A collection of poems by various Hispanic American writers that celebrate a full day of family activities.

1710. THE TREE IS OLDER THAN YOU ARE: A BILINGUAL GATHERING OF POEMS AND STORIES FROM MEXICO. Simon & Schuster, 1995; Aladdin, 1998 (pap).
Stories, poems and artwork by Mexican writers and artists.

Bilingual Materials – Swahili/English

1711. Bozylinsky, Hannah Heritage. LALA SALAMA. Philomel, 1993.
An African lullaby in Swahili and English in which a little boy says good night to all the animals and ends with his mother.

Bilingual Materials – Turkish/English

1712. Hamanaka, Sheila. YERYHUZHUNHUN THUM RENKLERI = ALL THE COLOURS OF THE EARTH. *SEE 1644.*

1713. Lindbergh, Reeve. GHOKYHUZHU KIMSENIN DEFGILDIR = NOBODY OWNS THE SKY. *SEE 1645.*

1714. Teague, Kati. GAIL.IN DOFGUM GHUNHU PARTISI = GAIL'S BIRTHDAY PARTY. Magi, 1991. *SEE 1673.*

1715. Teague, Kati. GIMRAN.8N KLINIFGI = IMRAN'S CLINIC. Magi, 1991.
Imran's baby brother needs to get his injections. After visiting a real doctor, Imran decides to start his own clinic in Anna's bedroom.

Bilingual Materials – Urdu/English

1716. ANVITEA AUR JEADEUGAR = ANITA AND THE MAGICIAN. *SEE 1715*

1717. Carle, Eric. BAHUT HEI BHEUKEA KUMLEA = THE VERY HUNGRY CATERPILLAR. *SEE 1643.*

1718. Hamanaka, Sheila. ZAMEIN KE SEARE RANG = ALL THE COLOURS OF THE EARTH. *SEE 1644.*

1719. Lindbergh, Reeve. EASMEAN KISVI MILKVIYAT NAHVIVN HAI = NOBODY OWNS THE SKY. *SEE 1645.*

1720. Stone, Susheila. MITTHU THE PARROT = MEIYEAVN MIRTRTHEU. *SEE 1659.*

1721. Teague, Kati. Gail kei sealgirah kei pearrti = Gail's birthday party. *SEE 1673.*

1722. Teague, Kati. OIMREAN KEI KLEINIK = IMRAN'S CLINIC. *SEE 1715.*

Bilingual Materials – Vietnamese/English

1723. Nguyen, Thi Nhuan. TAM CAM: THE VIETNAMESE CINDERELLA STORY: A BILINGUAL VIETNAMESE CLASSIC TALE. Th'e Gi'oi.
This bilingual Vietnamese version of the Cinderella story features Tam, who was given a beautiful shoe by a magic fish. After she loses the shoe and it is found by a prince, she shows the prince that she has the mate and they live happily ever after.

Author Index

Armstrong	Drew and the Homeboy Question	775
Armstrong	Patrick Doyle is Full of Blarney	932
Asbjornsen	Man Who Kept House, The	361
Asch	Goodbye House	48
Aseltine	I'm Deaf and It's OK	476
Ashabranner	Our Beckoning Borders: Illegal Immigration to America	737
Ashley	Cleversticks	835
Auch	Out of Step	262
Avi	Abigail Takes the Wheel	313
Avi	Fighting Ground, The	1342
Avi	Man from the Sky	567
Avi	True Confessions of Charlotte Doyle	326
Axworthy	Anni's India Diary	1153
Bacon	Finn	629
Badt	Good Morning, Let's Eat	1098
Badt	Hair There and Everywhere	1099
Badt	Let's Go!	1100
Badt	On Your Feet!	1101
Badt	Pass the Bread!	1102
Baer	This is the Way We Go to School	1549
Bahr	Memory Box, The	594
Baker	My First Book of Sign	1636
Balgassi	Peacebound Trains	1154
Balgassi	Tae's Sonata	873
Ballard	When I Am a Sister	256
Banfield	Joan of Arc	371
Banks	Abraham's Battle: a Novel of Gettysburg	1373
Banks	Egg-Drop Blues	568
Banks	Farthest-Away Mountain	327
Banks	New One, The	250
Bantle	Diving for the Moon	586
Barrett	Anna of Byzantium	1316
Barrie	Adam Zigzag	569
Barron	Where is Grandpa?	618
Bartlett	Seal Island School	1581
Bartoletti	Dancing with Dziadziu	916
Bartone	Peppe the Lamplighter	21, 142, 917
Bauer	On my Honor	630
Beck	Elliot Bakes a Cake	292
Behrens	Gung Hay Fat Choy	893
Belpre	Firefly Summer	1265
Bemelmans	Madeline	1188, 1550
Bemelmans	Madeline in London	1189
Benchley	Sam the Minuteman	1337
Benjamin	Duck So Small, A	711
Bennett	Zink	607
Benson	Little Penguin, The	712
Berends	Case of the Elevator Duck, The	1510
Berleth	Samuel's Choice	1338
Bernardo	Fitting In	1013
Bernhard	Happy New Year!	1103
Bernstein	Family that Fights, A	16
Bernstein	My Brother, the Pest	116
Berry	Thief in the Village and other Stories, A	1284
Betancourt	My Name is ~~Brain~~ Brian	570

Brown	Arthur Babysits	293
Brown	Arthur's Eyes	693
Brown	Arthur's Nose	708
Brown	Chinese New Year	894
Brown	Dead Bird, The	619
Brown	Dinosaurs Divorce	90
Brown	When Dinosaurs Die	650
Brown	You're Dead, David Borelli	189
Bruchac	Arrow Over the Door, The	1339
Bruchac	Eagle Song	1030
Bruchac	Heart of Chief: a Novel, The	1035
Bruchac	Thirteen Moons on Turtle's Back	1046
Buchanan	Falcon's Wing, The	538
Buchanan	Gratefully Yours	202, 632
Buck	Big Wave, The	1458
Buckley	Grandfather and I	168
Buckley	Grandmother and I	169
Buettner	Sovietrek: a Journey by Bicycle Across Russia	1225
Bulla	Lion to Guard Us, A	1329
Bulla	Poppy Seeds, The	1234
Bulla	Shoeshine Girl	314
Bunting	Cheyenne Again	1582
Bunting	Day Before Christmas	154
Bunting	Fly Away Home	32, 144
Bunting	Going Home	982
Bunting	Market Day	1192
Bunting	Road to Somewhere	200
Bunting	So Far From the Sea	868
Bunting	Some Frog!	78
Bunting	Spying on Miss Muller	1202
Burnett	Little Princess, A	1203, 1583
Burnett	Secret Garden, The	203
Burnford	Incredible Journey, The	1293
Burns	Black Stars in Orbit: NASA's African American Astronauts	817
Byars	Good-bye Chicken Little	633
Byars	Midnight Fox, The	329, 1514
Byars	Night Swimmers, The	239
Byars	Pinballs, The	190
Byars	Summer of the Swans, The	550
Byers	Jaime Escalante: Sensational Teacher	1001
Cadnum	Lost and Found House, The	49
Caines	Abby	176
Calvert	Glennis Before and After	95
Calvert	Sooner	1391
Cameron	Most Beautiful Place in the World, The	1235
Candana	Anita and the Magician	1716
Cannon	Bat in the Boot, The	155
Caple	Biggest Nose, The	709
Carbone	Starting School with an Enemy	59, 1584
Carle	Very Hungry Caterpillar, The	1643, 1648, 1653, 1717
Carlson	Arnie and the New Kid	477
Carlson	Family Under the Bridge, The	34, 1204
Carlson	Harriet and Walt	117
Carlson	Louanne Pig in Making the Team	294

Parton	Coat of Many Colors, The	682
Patel	Magic Glasses	695
Paterson	Bridge to Terabithia	643
Paterson	Flip-Flop Girl	112, 692
Paterson	Great Gilly Hopkins, The	196
Paterson	Jacob Have I Loved	130, 252
Paterson	Jip: His Story	1408
Paterson	King's Equal, The	321
Paterson	Lyddie	1409
Paterson	Master Puppeteer	1353
Paterson	Park's Quest	152, 879
Paton-Walsh	Gaffer Sampson's Luck	72
Paulsen	Christmas Sonata, A	644
Paulsen	Crossing, The	1262
Paulsen	Hatchet	87
Paulsen	Monument, The	516
Paulsen	Sarny: a Life Remembered	1410
Paulsen	Winter Room, The	955, 1526
Peacock	Cerebral Palsy	615
Peacock	Diabetes	660
Peacock	Leukemia	614
Peacock	Sugar Was My Best Food: Diabetes and Me	659
Pearl	Elijah's Tears: Stories for the Jewish Holidays	450
Pearson	Awake and Dreaming	674
Peck	Long Way from Chicago, A	1527
Peck	Strays Like Us	221
Pellegrini	Families are Different	181, 856
Perl	Piñatas and Paper Flowers	1704
Peters	Revenge of the Snob Squad	730
Petersen	Some Days, Other Days	165
Peterson	I Have a Sister - My Sister is Deaf	506
Petry	Tituba of Salem Village	1334
Pfister	Rainbow Fish, The	683
Phelps	Tatterhood and Other Tales	366
Philip	Earth Always Endures: Native American Poems	1057
Pinkney	Alvin Ailey	384, 832
Pinkney	Duke Ellington: the Piano Prince and his Orchestra	833
Pirner	Even Little Kids Get Diabetes	661
Pitkanen	Grandchildren of the Vikings, The	1231
Polacco	Boat Ride with Lillian Two-Blossom	1025
Polacco	Just Plain Fancy	419
Polacco	Keeping Quilt	1361
Polacco	Mrs. Katz and Tush	462
Polacco	Pink and Say	1383
Polacco	Trees of the Dancing Goats	926
Pomeranc	American Wei, The	857
Pomerantz	Chalk Doll, The	1288
Pomerantz	Outside Dog, The	1283
Porte	Leave that Cricket Be, Alan Lee	858
Porte	Something Terrible Happened	588
Porter	Addy Learns a Lesson	1574
Powell	Daisy	11
Powers	Our Teacher's in a Wheelchair	507, 1608
Poynter	Marie Curie: Discoverer of Radium	385
Pringle	One Room School	1609

Title Index

Billy and the Big New School	Anholt	1548
Birchbark House, The	Erdich	1037
Birth	Spirn	1114
Birthday Basket for Tia, A	Mora	977
Blabber Mouth	Gleitzman	1183
Black Frontiers	Schlissel	809
Black Indians	Katz	291
Black is Brown is Tan	Adoff	290, 723
Black Like Kyra, White Like Me	Vigna	764
Black Snowman, The	Mendez	757
Black Stars in Orbit: NASA's African American Astronauts	Burns	817
Black Women of the Old West	Katz	799
Black, Blue and Gray	Haskins	796
Black, White, Just Right	Davol	278
Blessed are You: Traditional Everyday Hebrew Prayers	Edwards	1661
Bloomability	Creech	1585
Blubber	Blume	727
Blue Hill Meadows	Rylant	1513
Blue Sword, The	McKinley	349
Blue Willow	Gates	243
Blue-Eyed Daisy, A	Rylant	8, 544
Boat Ride with Lillian Two-Blossom	Polacco	1025
Boggart, The	Cooper	1205
Boom Town	Levitin	1360
Boomer Goes to School	McGeorge	1561
Boomer's Big Day	McGeorge	54
Bosnian Family, A	Silverman	1232
Bossy Gallito	Gonzalez	1702
Bottles Break	Tabor	2
Bound for Oregon	Van Leeuwen	1415
Boundless Grace	Hoffman	260
Boy Named Giotto, A	Guarneiri	1321
Boy of the Painted Cave	Denzel	1312
Boy on a Black Horse	Springer	959
Bracelet, The	Uchida	864
Brave as a Mountain Lion	Scott	1029
Bridge to Terabithia	Paterson	643
Bright Freedom's Song	Houston	1400
Brigid, Beware!	Leverich	690
Bronze Bow, The	Speare	1318
Brooklyn Doesn't Rhyme	Blos	1444
Brother for Celia, A	Martinez I Vendrell	1647, 1665
Brown Angels	Myers	814
Bud, Not Buddy	Curtis	778, 1461
Buddha Stories	Demi	412
Buddy the First Seeing Eye Dog	Moore	495
Buffalo Soldiers	Reef	807
Bump in the Park	James	1663
Burnt Stick, The	Hill	1184
Busy Building Book, The	Tarsky	1507
By a Blazing Blue Sea	Garne	1267
By the Dawn's Early Light	Ackerman	19
By the Shores of Silver Lake	Wilder	1416

Latchkey Kids	Terris	881
Laughing Tomatoes and Other Spring Poems	Alarcon	1696
Learning by Heart	Young	792
Learning is Fun with Mrs. Perez	Flanagan	1603
Leave that Cricket Be, Alan Lee	Porte	858
Leaves in October	Ackerman	33
Leaving for America	Bresnick-Perry	1191
Leaving Morning, The	Johnson	53
Leaving Vietnam	Kilborne	900, 1442
Left-Handed Shortstop	Giff	706
Legend of the Poinsettia, The	De Paola	428
Lei for Tutu, A	Fellows	1020
Leo the Late Bloomer	Kraus	560
Leo, Zack and Emmie	Ehrlich	297
Leonard the Lion and Raymond the Mouse	Bishop	1652, 1698
Leslie's Story	McNey, Martha	556
Let's Go!	Badt	1100
Let's Talk about Going to a Funeral	Johnston	652
Let's Talk About It*		734
Let's Talk About It: Adoption	Rogers	186
Let's Talk Library*		735
Letters from a Slave Girl: the Story of Harriet Jacobs	Lyons	1405
Letters from Rifka	Hesse	1210, 1466
Leukemia	Peacock	614
Lewis and Papa: Adventure on the Santa Fe Trail	Joosse	1357
Librarian Who Measured the Earth	Lasky	375
Library of African American History*		1068
Lichee Tree	Russell	1165
Life on a Pig Farm	Wolfman	1545
Lights for Gita	Gilmore	843
Like Butter on Pancakes	London	1502
Like Jake and Me	Jukes	261, 318
Liliana's Grandmothers	Torres	172, 1251
Lily and Miss Liberty	Strevens	1385
Lily and the Wooden Bowl	Schroeder	668
Lily Cupboard, The	Oppenheim	1198
Lily's Crossing	Giff	950
Linda Ronstadt	Amdur	1000
Lion Cub	Heurtelou	1660
Lion Dancer: Ernie Wan's Chinese New Year	Waters	904
Lion to Guard Us, A	Bulla	1329
Lion Who Had Asthma, The	London	599
Listen for the Bus: David's Story	McMahon	503
Listen to the Desert	Mora	1692
Listening for Leroy	Hearne	783
Little Bear Goes to Kindergarten	Langreuter	1559
Little Beaver and the Echo	MacDonald	1651
Little Fishes	Haugaard	40
Little House in the Big Woods	Wilder	1419
Little House on the Prairie	Wilder	1420, 1534
Little Men	Alcott	1580
Little Penguin, The	Benson	712

Appendix

Queens Borough Public Library Mission and Vision Statements

Mission Statement

The mission of the Queens Borough Public Library is to provide quality services, resources, and lifelong learning opportunities through books and a variety of other formats to meet the informational, educational, cultural, and recreational needs and interests of its diverse and changing population.

The Library is a forum for all points of view and adheres to the principles of intellectual freedom as expressed in the Library Bill of Rights formulated by the American Library Association. Adopted January 1991

Vision Statement

The Queens Borough Public Library represents a fundamental public good in our democracy. It assures the right, the privilege and the ability of individuals to choose and pursue any direction of thought, study or action they wish.

The Library provides the capital necessary for us to understand the past and plan for the future. It is also our collective memory, since history and human experience are best preserved in writing.
As Queens Library enters its second century, it will be universally recognized as the most dynamic public library in the nation. This recognition will arise from: the Library's dedication to the needs of its diverse communities; its advocacy and support of appropriate technology; the excellence of its collections; the commitment of its staff to its customers and the very highest ideals of library service.

We at Queens Library believe deeply in equity and that libraries are fundamental in empowering people to take charge of their lives, their governments and their communities. In this way, Queens Library has an essential role to play in the new millennium. The collections we build, the access we provide and the technologies we embrace will carry the people of Queens into a productive and creative future. Please join the Library in this quest.